METALLICA
AND
PHILOSOPHY

"The most elucidative dissertation on Metallica ever written. And a
kick-ass read to boot!!!"

Scott Ian, guitarist for Anthrax

"Like philosophy itself, Metallica's music can scare the uninitiated,
who fear their brains will hurt. This book makes both philosophy
and Metallica accessible to the curious while deepening the experience of those already in the know."

Theodore Gracyk, author of *Rhythm and Noise*
and Listening to Popular Music

"*Metallica and Philosophy* is, at long last, the book which finally
gives everyone's favorite headbangers due credit for being intelligent,
questioning, and even cerebral."

Joel McIver, author of *Justice For All:*
The Truth About Metallica

"Not just heavy metal, not just rock n' roll, not just angst or anger or
conceptual analysis, but a monster in a category of its own that shows
us something dangerous about ourselves and our post-industrial
culture."

Dale Jacquette, Pennsylvania State University

The Blackwell Philosophy and PopCulture Series
Series editor William Irwin

A spoonful of sugar helps the medicine go down, and a healthy helping of popular culture clears the cobwebs from Kant. Philosophy has
had a public relations problem for a few centuries now. This series
aims to change that, showing that philosophy is relevant to your
life—and not just for answering the big questions like "To be or not
to be?" but for answering the little questions: "To watch or not to
watch *South Park*?" Thinking deeply about TV, movies, and music
doesn't make you a "complete idiot." In fact it might make you a
philosopher, someone who believes the unexamined life is not worth
living and the unexamined cartoon is not worth watching.

South Park and Philosophy
Edited by Robert Arp

Metallica and Philosophy
Edited by William Irwin

Forthcoming

Family Guy and Philosophy
Edited by J. Jeremy Wisnewski

The Daily Show and Philosophy
Edited by Jason Holt

Lost and Philosophy
Edited by Sharon Kaye

24 and Philosophy
Edited by Richard Davis, Jennifer Hart Weed, and Ronald Weed

The Office and Philosophy
Edited by J. Jeremy Wisnewski

METALLICA AND PHILOSOPHY

A CRASH COURSE IN BRAIN SURGERY

EDITED BY WILLIAM IRWIN

Blackwell
Publishing

© 2007 by Blackwell Publishing Ltd

BLACKWELL PUBLISHING
350 Main Street, Malden, MA 02148-5020, USA
9600 Garsington Road, Oxford OX4 2DQ, UK
550 Swanston Street, Carlton, Victoria 3053, Australia

The right of William Irwin to be identified as the Author of the Editorial
Material in this Work has been asserted in accordance with the UK
Copyright, Designs, and Patents Act 1988.

First published 2007 by Blackwell Publishing Ltd

1   2007

Library of Congress Cataloging-in-Publication Data

Metallica and philosophy : a crash course in brain surgery / edited by William
Irwin.
     p. cm. — (The Blackwell philosophy and PopCulture series)
     Includes bibliographical references and index.
     ISBN-13: 978–1–4051–6348–4 (pbk. : alk. paper)   1. Metallica (Musical
group)—Criticism and interpretation.   2. Heavy metal (Music)—United
States—History and criticism.   I. Irwin, William, 1970–

     ML421.M48M47 2007
     782.42166092′2—dc22
                                                                2006033448

A catalogue record for this title is available from the British Library.

Set in 10.5/13pt Sabon
by Graphicraft Ltd, Hong Kong
Printed and bound in Singapore by Markono Print Media Pte Ltd

The publisher's policy is to use permanent paper from mills that operate
a sustainable forestry policy, and which has been manufactured from
pulp processed using acid-free and elementary chlorine-free practices.
Furthermore, the publisher ensures that the text paper and cover board
used have met acceptable environmental accreditation standards.

For further information on
Blackwell Publishing, visit our website:
www.blackwellpublishing.com

CONTENTS

Contents

HEROES OF THE DAY: ACKNOWLEDGMENTS

This book was a labor of love, literally. I loved working on it. Never before have I had a chance to combine two things I felt so passionately about, Metallica *and* philosophy. It was, of course, a team effort. So first of all Mega-Metalli-Thanks to all the contributing authors. It may be a crude way to express gratitude, but metal up your ass!

Like the road crew who make the concert possible, many people labored tirelessly behind the scenes of this book. Joanna Corwin, in addition to contributing her own fine chapter, offered detailed commentaries on each chapter that immeasurably helped the various authors and me improve the final product. Joanna is also the Phantom Lord who created the index. Joie Hyman read every chapter and checked the lyrics and the Metalli-facts for accuracy. She saved us from hitting plenty of duff notes. Anything that remains out of tune is my bad. Eileen Sweeney, my Metalli-colleague from the King's College English Department, read every chapter and drew on both her years as a fan and her years as a composition teacher to help improve the book. My friend and former student Candice Alaimo read every chapter, double-checked lyrics, and offered unwavering support. Shai Biderman, Kimberly Blessing, Jason Eberl, Jaime McAndrew, Jack McSherry, and Alex Schroeder all helped with feedback, research, and inspiration.

Jeff Dean, Danielle Descoteaux, Jamie Harlan, and all the great folks at Blackwell have been a delight to work with. I'm fortunate to have found such a first-rate publisher. Many thanks to my students and colleagues at King's College, especially my friend and Chair, Greg

Bassham, and the Academic VP, Nick Holodick, for their wonderful support and encouragement.

Thanks to my lovely wife, Megan, and our two head-banging children, Daniel and Kate, who have cheerfully endured strange music and even stranger conversations. Thanks to my parents. When I got metal up the ass they didn't make me take it out.

A big shout out to all my buddies from back in the day who listened to me babble on about philosophy while we were drinking beer and listening to Metallica. Here's to you (in alphabetical order): Pete Campbell, Eugene Chiuli, Anthony Ciopa, Mr. D, Sissy Dugan, The Great Guldna, Jack Laughlin, J.R. Lombardo, Uncle Larry Lovallo, T. Roy Rex Marzziotti, Ken Murphy, Big Al Rappa, Ronzo, Chris Saunda, Joe Schmidt, Steve the Wise, and Joey the X-Man Ximenez. Rage on! And finally, of course, thanks to Metallica for making such inspiring, thought-provoking music!

HIT THE LIGHTS

I "discovered" Metallica in 1984—they had been around for two years. I "discovered" philosophy in 1985—it had been around for 2,500 years. Since then, for me, the two have been inextricably tied together. Metallica changed my life—hell, they saved my life. Listening to "Fade to Black" while the rain fell on hopeless high school nights, I felt I wasn't alone, that someone else knew my pain. If Metallica didn't change your life then this book is not for you. Put it back on the shelf and put on your favorite Poison album. I can only feel sorry for you.

Too often dismissed early on as mindless noise, Metallica came to be known as the "thinking man's" metal band and the headbanger's CNN. Let's set the record straight: Hetfield's lyrics are rock poetry rivaling Dylan and the Doors and more philosophically significant than the Beatles and U2. Of course, not all the words of all the songs are direct expressions of Hetfield's own point of view. The narrator is sometimes a kind of character or persona, not necessarily the same as the man behind the microphone, though we may suspect that even these songs sometimes reveal the soul of the singer. As James says, "Writing is therapy for me."[1]

Echoing the "I Don't Know" of Ozzy and Socrates, in "My World" Hetfield sings: "Not only do I not know the answer / I don't even know what the question is." James and the boys are not philosophers, nor would they necessarily know the connections to philosophy this book

---

[1] *All Metallica.com*, www.allmetallica.com/info/interviews/guitar98.php (2006).

makes. Still, our goal here is to apply Metallica's intentions faithfully to philosophy, to demonstrate the band's philosophical significance.[2]

And then there's the music. Twenty-five years into their career most bands lucky enough to still be around are touring nostalgia shows, pale imitations of their former selves. But Metallica is still making very credible music—even if not all the old fans like it. It would not be without controversy, but I would say without hesitation, Metallica is the greatest American rock band of all time.

This book includes essays by both kinds of Metallica fans, the kind that think the band hasn't made a good album in quite a while and the kind who continue to appreciate Metallica's music to this day. I place myself in the second group. Though I've found some of Metallica's more recent albums disappointing, there are songs I connect deeply with on each and every album. A bad Metallica album beats a good album by anyone else any day. Well, that's a bit overstated, but you get the point.

Think of this book as like a box set. Twenty essays are divided among five "discs." There's a reason the essays are in the order they're in; they flow better and make more sense that way. But feel free to hit the "random" button and skip around. Who am I to tell a Metallica fan to conform?

This is not a biography of the band and its members, though we occasionally draw on the lives of the Metallicans. Some of the contributing authors are amateur musicians, but as professional philosophers we're better versed at analyzing words than notes. So we focus on the lyrics rather than the music. This is not a fan club publication or a complete love-fest; some of the chapters are pretty critical. You won't like everything written in this book; you won't agree with all the views and opinions expressed.

Metallica constantly challenges us to think, and this book can serve as a guide for thinking through the soundtrack of your life. So start your CD player, fire up your iPod, or, better yet, break out some of the old vinyl. We're goin' for a ride with the four horsemen and a few philosophers, too.

---

[2] For a discussion of intention and the interpretation of rock lyrics, see Theodore Gracyk, *I Wanna Be Me: Rock Music and the Politics of Identity* (Philadelphia: Temple University Press, 2001), pp. 33–50.

DISC 1
ON THROUGH THE NEVER

CHAPTER 1

WHISPER THINGS INTO MY BRAIN
Metallica, Emotion, and Morality

ROBERT FUDGE

The experience is unmistakable—"just a freight train coming your way." As Metallica starts playing through your speakers, adrenaline starts pumping through your veins. Your heart rate, blood pressure, metabolism, and energy levels all rise.[1] You don't just *listen* to Metallica's music—you *experience* it, and the music's sheer power can simultaneously stimulate and drain you. These physical effects are often accompanied by strong emotional responses that match the emotions expressed by the music. Listening to "Enter Sandman"— "Dreams of war, dreams of liars / Dreams of dragon's fire / And of things that will bite"—hardly has a calming effect that helps one drift "Off to never-never land." Indeed, the result is quite often the opposite.

But it's precisely because of these kinds of physical and emotional responses that philosophers have long worried about the potentially corrosive effects of certain styles of music on the listener's moral character. If listening to, say, angry Metallica songs makes us angry, and if feeling angry makes us act in less than desirable ways, then it follows that angry Metallica songs have a negative effect on our morals. To counter this, one might argue that listening to Metallica in certain

---

[1]   On the physical effects of listening to music, see Julius Portnoy, *Music in the Life of Man* (Westport, CT: Greenwood Press, 1973).

contexts often elicits positive emotional responses and is thus not morally corrupting. Further, fans of Metallica don't listen to the music simply because of the visceral experience it produces, but also because of its content, and this is where the music has some potentially redeeming moral qualities. Metallica not only performs songs that deal with important personal and social issues—the dangers of substance abuse, nuclear holocaust, the horrors of war, hypocritical religious leaders— but they also do it in a way that is arguably morally instructive.

And I Want My Anger To Be Healthy: Morality and the Emotions

The philosophical debate over the moral effects of the arts is hardly new; we can trace it back at least as far as the writings of Plato (ca.428– ca.348 BCE) and his most famous student, Aristotle (384–322 BCE). Plato argues that we should be suspicious of the so-called "imitative arts,"[2] because they arouse our passions—"Frantic tick tick tick tick tick tock"—and thereby corrupt our moral character. Unless artists like Metallica can demonstrate the moral benefits of their art, Plato suggested that they should be banished from the state.[3] Against his teacher, Aristotle argued that the imitative arts (especially tragedies) can have a healthy effect on the soul, by purging the individual of destructive emotions—"And I need to set my anger free." A state devoid of artists like Metallica would be an unhealthy state, indeed! The important point to note is that both philosophers agree that art's ability to stir our emotions has moral implications; the question we need to resolve is whether these effects are on balance good or bad.

[2] To understand what Plato means by the imitative arts, consider the difference between "For Whom the Bell Tolls" and "The Call of Ktulu." The former imitates the sounds of war (gunshots, helicopters, and falling bombs), as well as the experience of fighting a battle. The latter song, while nominally "about" something, does not attempt to imitate anything.
[3] Plato's attitude towards the arts is arguably more complex than I suggest. In some dialogues, especially in the *Symposium*, he is more accommodating of them. For an extended discussion of this issue, see Elizabeth Asmis, "Plato on Poetic Creativity," in *The Cambridge Companion to Plato*, ed. Richard Kraut (Cambridge: Cambridge University Press, 1992), pp. 338–64.

One of Plato's key psychological insights concerns the struggle we all face between reason on the one hand, and the appetites and desires on the other. A person in the grips of an addiction has lost this battle entirely: "Master of puppets, I'm pulling your strings / Twisting your mind and smashing your dreams / Blinded by me, you can't see a thing / Just call my name, 'cause I'll hear you scream." While the addict often knows how she should act (and perhaps even wishes that she could act otherwise), she finds herself incapable of overcoming her desires. The ease with which people relapse into their addictions demonstrates the grip our desires can have on us. But we need not have ever suffered from an addiction to know how difficult it can sometimes be to keep our desires in check. All of us are susceptible to weakness of will, in which our desires lead us to act in regrettable ways.

The problem with highly emotional art, Plato argued, is that it stirs the passions, thereby undermining some of the control our reason has over our nonrational desires. This is especially problematic when the passions aroused by art are negative. There are at least two ways this can happen. First, artworks can be about certain topics that elicit strong emotional responses. To consider just a few examples, the title song of . . . *And Justice for All* concerns corruption in the legal system. Reflecting on such corruption can arouse strong feelings of indignation and impotent rage: "Justice is lost / Justice is raped / Justice is gone / Pulling your strings / Justice is done / Seeking no truth / Winning is all / Find it so grim, so true, so real." Prosecutors and defense attorneys often seem less interested in seeking the truth than in winning debates. Further, as many high-profile cases have suggested, and as illustrated by the album's cover art, money too often determines the quality of legal representation one gets and, ultimately, strongly influences the likelihood that the accused will be acquitted. Focusing too much on these injustices, especially when the focus is emotionally charged, can cause us to overlook the merits of our justice system. Despite its problems, our system works very well.

The same general point can be made about "Unforgiven," which expresses strong feelings of resentment over a life ruled by the imposed values of others: "They dedicate their lives / To running all of his / He tries to please them all / This bitter man he is / Throughout his life the same / He's battled constantly / This fight he cannot win / A tired man they see no longer cares / The old man then prepares / To die regretfully / That old man here is me." Most all of us, at some time in our lives, feel compelled to conform to others' expectations, whether in our schooling, our jobs, or our relationships. At times, this feeling can be overwhelming, to the point of leading to an existential crisis. At the extreme, these rules can crush the individual's spirit and lead to bitterness and the feeling that we have wasted our lives. But again, while this might in some cases be a valid complaint, it doesn't tell the whole story. At their best, social norms can provide the structure necessary for human flourishing, and when people reject them entirely they generally end up feeling alienated from society, which leads to its own form of bitterness. The point is, a primarily emotion-based attitude towards social norms and influences, promoted by songs like "Unforgiven," can blind us to a more tempered, reason-based perspective.

Music can also stir our passions more directly. Consider in more detail the sorts of physical responses we might have when a song like "Enter Sandman" starts playing on the radio. In addition to the more "internal" bodily responses like adrenaline flow, there are also more "external" responses. Perhaps our brows furrow into a scowl, our teeth clench, and our feet start tapping to the beat. We certainly don't sink back into our chairs and enter a state of serenity. The significance of these responses is that our felt emotions are strongly tied to our bodily states. Psychologists and philosophers disagree about whether emotions cause our bodily states or vice versa (or perhaps both), but no one denies that there is a link between them. Think about going through a meditative exercise in which you relax your forehead, your eyes, your jaw, your shoulders, your hands, your stomach, and finally your legs. Then imagine feeling rage while in this state. You can't. The emotion is entirely incompatible with your physical state. Conversely, listening to Metallica may cause adrenaline to pump and brows to furrow, putting us in more intense moods and making us more prone to feel anger, resentment, and so on.

Given that Metallica has the power to elicit strong (negative) emotions, we can still rightly ask why this is a problem morally. Plato reasoned that the emotions produced by experiencing certain kinds of art can spill over into our private lives. In short, listening to music full of anger and resentment makes us angry and resentful—"Then the unnamed feeling / It comes alive / Then the unnamed feeling / Takes me away." While we might value the music for the way it makes us feel, Plato warns that we are causing ourselves harm in listening to it, since angry and resentful feelings are harmful not only to the person experiencing them, but also to those who have to deal with behaviors borne of anger and resentment—"Blood follows blood and we make sure / Life ain't for you and we're the cure."

In short, music that arouses negative emotions can harm our moral character.

At this point, many Metallica fans are probably scratching their heads, thinking, "Other than some lingering resentment over *Load* and *ReLoad*, I haven't suffered any emotional or moral harm from listening to Metallica. If anything, listening to Metallica has benefited me by purging me of negative emotions." This insight is at the core of Aristotle's argument. Like Plato, Aristotle believed that our psychologies have both rational and non-rational elements. Also, like Plato, Aristotle argued that the human good is promoted in part by reason controlling our non-rational passions and appetites. Consider, for example, the emotion of anger. If we allow ourselves to be consumed by anger, we suffer in a variety of ways. Not only do we damage our relationships with others, but we also damage our health. Recognizing this, we might be tempted to suppress our anger altogether, as the ancient stoics would have advised. But too little anger is also unhealthy. Bottling up anger can cause just as many health problems (physical and psychological) as can expressing anger too freely. Thus, Aristotle advised, we must seek a midpoint between the extremes of feeling too little and too much anger, for it is at this midpoint that we find moral virtue; it is at this midpoint that our anger becomes healthy.[4]

Because the arts arouse many different kinds of emotions, they can play a central role in the development of moral virtue. Aristotle believed tragic theater was especially useful in this regard, because of its ability to arouse the emotions of pity and fear. Neither of these emotions is healthy, especially when experienced over an extended period. But, in getting us to experience pity and fear in an artificial setting, tragedies have the effect of purging the emotions and making

---

[4] Aristotle defines moral virtue as "a state that decides, consisting in a mean, the mean relative to us, which is defined by reference to reason, that is to say, to the reason by reference to which the prudent person would define it. It is a mean between two vices, one of excess and one of deficiency." See his *Nicomachean Ethics*, 2nd edn., trans. Terence Irwin (Indianapolis: Hackett Publishing, 1999), 1107a.

us less likely to experience them in real life. While Metallica's songs are not strictly speaking tragedies, they can arouse many of the same feelings. The clearest example of this is "One," which deals with the horrific aftermath of war: "Darkness imprisoning me / All that I see / Absolute horror / I cannot live / I cannot die / Trapped in myself / Body my holding cell / Landmine has taken my sight / Taken my speech / Taken my hearing / Taken my arms / Taken my legs / Taken my soul / Left me with life in hell." The "absolute horror" of being in this situation is almost too much to contemplate. We cannot help but feel pity for the person suffering this fate, as well as fear at the thought of someday being in a similar position (whether because of an accident, a crippling disease, or some other cause). But it is through facing this possibility that we can deal with our pity and fear and face up to the tragic realities that we all inevitably confront. Against Plato, then, who worried that the arousal of strong emotions by art is corrupting, Aristotle argued that such arousal is healthy, because it has the effect of purging us of negative emotions.

In the *Politics*, Aristotle widens his analysis of potentially beneficial art to include "wild and restless music."[5] Aristotle recognized that many forms of music produce a strong physical reaction. This, in turn, provides a strong emotional response that allows the hearer to be "calmed and restored as if they had undergone a medical or purgative treatment."[6] I would venture that nearly all of us have had this experience, especially when dealing with difficult periods in our lives. For example, when dealing with breakups, we often turn to a favorite song or album to help us work through the emotional aftermath: "And my ties are severed clean / The less I have, the more I gain / Off the beaten path I reign / Rover, wanderer / Nomad, vagabond / Call me what you will." We are instinctively drawn to such music, because of the emotions it elicits. By arousing our anger, our anguish, or our resentment, music helps us deal with our emotions and get over them sooner. The purpose of this exercise is not to beat us into insensibility, but to return us to a more balanced and healthy emotional state. The

[5] S.H. Butcher, *Aristotle's Theory of Poetry and Fine Art*, 4th edn. (London: Macmillan, 1907), p. 248. In this work, Butcher carefully compares Aristotle's treatment of catharsis as it appears in both the *Poetics* and the *Politics*.

[6] Aristotle, *Politics*, ed. & trans. Ernest Barker (Oxford: Oxford University Press, 1946), 1342a10.

process is like recovering from a physical ailment, as when we wake up feeling healthy after a long bout with the flu. We don't feel drained, but even more robust and fully alive than usual.

The cathartic effect of experiencing strong emotions has not only physical, but also moral benefits. In Aristotle's terms, art can help us become more virtuous. Consider James Hetfield's thoughts on the value of writing "St. Anger" while going through alcohol rehabilitation. In a variety of interviews, Hetfield suggested that his struggles with unresolved anger contributed to his addiction. By writing "St. Anger" he was able to express these emotions and purge himself of them, thus allowing him to achieve a healthier emotional state. In effect, art can become a powerful ally of reason in controlling certain of our desires and passions; in other words, it helps us develop moral virtue.

As with most philosophical debates, what makes the one we have been considering so difficult to resolve is that both sides seem to have some intuitive backing. On the one hand, listening to hard rock does seem to have the potential to encourage destructive behavior. Not surprisingly, researchers have found a correlation between listening to rock music and certain adolescent behavioral problems, including a greater likelihood to do drugs, have sex, and perform poorly in school.[7] Correlation, however, is not causation. While listening to hard rock might contribute to behavioral problems, it could also be that at-risk adolescents are drawn to this music precisely because (*à la* Aristotle) it helps them deal with their preexisting issues. In short, the emotional effects of listening to rock music are complex, and the overall moral consequences of experiencing these emotions have yet to be fully demonstrated.

Do You Feel What I Feel?
Metallica, Empathy, and Morality

Consider for a moment what it's like to attend a Metallica concert. The audience gets whipped into a frenzy and soon starts feeding off

---

[7]   Kevin J. Took and David S. Weiss, "The Relationship between Heavy Metal and Rap Music and Adolescent Turmoil: Real or Artifact?" *Adolescence* 29 (1994): 613–21.

its own energy; fans sing in unison with their favorite songs and chant raucously between them. In sum, the emotions of the audience are contagious, to an almost irresistible degree. The performers can also get caught up in the emotion of the performance. In the liner notes to *S&M*, it's reported that members of the San Francisco Symphony regretted not bringing a change of clothes for intermission. This capacity to "catch" the emotions of others (that is, to empathize with them) is a necessary component of morality, and it plays an especially useful role in our moral development. In light of this, many philosophers have argued that art has the ability to help us grow morally, precisely when it helps us refine our empathic abilities. This line of reasoning can be extended to at least some of Metallica's music.

The economist and moral philosopher Adam Smith (1723–90) developed what is arguably the most subtle and sophisticated empathy-based moral theory in the western canon. One aspect of his theory that is particularly instructive is the recognition that empathy can arise in a variety of ways. At the most basic cognitive level, we can "catch" the emotions of others directly and effortlessly. So again, consider the experience of attending a Metallica concert. You are surrounded by people who are excited, pumped, and full of energy. While it's not impossible to resist feeling these things yourself, it is difficult. (By way of comparison, imagine being the only person in an auditorium, with Metallica playing on stage. While you'd almost certainly enjoy the performance, you would not get nearly as riled up as if the auditorium were full of like-minded fans.)

A more cognitively complex form of empathy involves imaginatively placing ourselves in others' situations. As discussed, "One" details the plight of someone seriously injured by a landmine, with nothing left to experience but his own thoughts: "Now the world is gone, I'm just one / Oh God, help me hold my breath as I wish for death / Oh please God, help me." It's not merely the lyrics that arouse our passions, but the imaginative exercise of placing ourselves in his situation and considering what such an existence would be like. Similarly, "Master of Puppets" vividly illustrates the helpless feeling of being caught in an addiction: "I will occupy / I will help you die / I will run through you / Now I rule you, too." By placing ourselves in the position of the addict, we can't help but feel his pain, fear, and sense of helplessness.

Granting that at least some Metallica songs lead us to place ourselves imaginatively in others' situations, the next question is why
this is morally significant. After all, some moral traditions treat acting
morally as simply following a set of fixed rules. The great German
philosopher Immanuel Kant (1724–1804), for example, argued that
we are bound by a set of inviolable duties, including the duty never
to commit suicide. While the commitment to preserve our own lives
certainly counts among our most central values, we can nevertheless
question whether we are always bound by it. This is where a song like
"One" becomes instructive. Where, we might ask, is the value of a
life when the body becomes a "holding cell"? Perhaps it is not life
as such that we value, but a life in which certain kinds of experiences
are possible (having meaningful relationships, engaging in significant
projects, and so on). The narrator of "One" has been utterly and permanently deprived of such experiences. We cannot help but contemplate what it might be like to live in such a state for, say, decades. I
leave it to the reader to decide which of these competing values—life
itself or quality of life—should be given priority in our moral delibera-
tions.[8] The point is that our capacity to empathize with others is what
allows us to perceive such a conflict in the first place, for again, few if
any of us will ever find ourselves in a situation as dire as the soldier in
"One." It takes an act of imaginative empathy to know what such a
situation would be like and, from there, to weigh our values against
one another.

Art can also be morally instructive when deliberating about more
abstract issues, like war. Western culture has a very powerful mythology
glorifying war, a mythology that artists continually try to counter.
Several of Metallica's songs take up this issue. "For Whom the Bell
Tolls" illustrates how the conditions under which soldiers must fight
are often intolerable: "Make his fight on the hill in the early day /
Constant chill deep inside." The purpose of war is often vague at best
and seemingly trivial at worst: "For a hill, men would kill. Why?
They do not know." And the sacrifice of war is ultimate: "Take a
look to the sky just before you die / It's the last time he will." This last
point is made even more powerfully in "Disposable Heroes," which
opens with the observation that being a soldier is not a game: "Bodies

---

[8]   See Jason Eberl's essay, "Living and Dying as One: Suffering and the Ethics of
Euthanasia," chapter 12 in this volume.

fill the fields I see, hungry heroes end / No one to play soldier now, no one to pretend / Running blind through killing fields, bred to kill them all / Victim of what said should be, a servant 'til I fall." Of course, the same points can be made in dry, academic prose, but they wouldn't have the same effect as when they're presented through the medium of art. Our moral reasoning is facilitated when we have vivid examples to contemplate, through the exercise of imaginative empathy.

One of the central worries here is that emotionally charged art might actually blind us to the inviolable nature of certain moral principles. Following Kant, one might argue that suicide is always wrong and that artists like Metallica undermine the validity of this principle, thus leading some people to commit seriously immoral actions. This argument works only if moral principles have universal validity, independent of our empathic capacities. Adam Smith challenges this idea, arguing instead that moral principles are mere generalizations that we form, to express what we learn through empathizing with others:

> [The general rules of morality] are ultimately founded upon experience of what, in particular instances, our moral faculties, our natural sense of merit and propriety, approve, or disapprove of. We do not originally approve or condemn particular actions; because, upon examination, they appear to be agreeable or inconsistent with a certain general rule. The general rule, on the contrary, is formed, by finding from experience, that all actions of a certain kind, or circumstanced in a certain manner, are approved or disapproved of.[9]

In other words, we form the principle that suicide is wrong, by generalizing from tragic cases of suicide (as when teenagers commit suicide because their problems seem overwhelming). The mistake we make is treating this principle as if it admits of no exceptions. The artist, through pieces like "One," leads us back to the particular case and asks us to consider whether our principles have the universal validity that we originally assumed. Of course, after much deliberation, we might conclude that the principle does in fact have universal validity, but this is not something that we determine independent of

[9] Adam Smith, *The Theory of Moral Sentiments*, ed. D.D. Raphael and A.L. Macfie (Indianapolis: Liberty Classics, 1976), p. 159.

a close examination of particular cases. It is precisely these cases that the artist can present to us so vividly.

What, then, can we conclude about the moral value of Metallica's music? In light of our discussion, it is decidedly mixed. Insofar as it has the potential to arouse negative emotions that lead to destructive behavior, it is morally damaging. Insofar as it helps purge us of destructive emotions, it is morally beneficial. And, insofar as it engages our imaginative empathy and gets us to think more clearly and deeply about controversial issues, it is morally edifying. So, while Metallica is unquestionably a monster of a rock band, it is far from obvious that they are some kind of monster.

CHAPTER 2

THIS SEARCH GOES ON
Christian, Warrior, Buddhist

WILLIAM IRWIN

Because they are restless seekers, not content to think and sound the same, Metallica has changed, James Hetfield has changed, not just musically but personally. As the lead singer, chief riff writer, and main lyricist, Hetfield is the band member fans most readily identify with. His struggle is our struggle, his virtues and vices our own.

Virtues are character traits that make a person a good person. We typically think of patience, self-control, and honesty as virtues, but power, well-placed aggression, and even manipulation can be virtues, according to some accounts.[1] Hetfield's lyrics and biography suggest that he has journeyed through three different sets of virtues.[2] The journey—the search—begins in Hetfield's youth with the rejection of

---

[1] In the history of western philosophy, the concept of virtue can be traced back to Plato and Aristotle. See Plato, *The Republic of Plato*, trans. by Allan Bloom (New York: Basic Books, 1991); Aristotle, *Nicomachean Ethics*, trans. by Terence Irwin (Indianapolis: Hackett Publishing, 1999). For a more recent account of the importance of the virtuous life, see Alasdair MacIntyre, *After Virtue* (Notre Dame, IN: Notre Dame Press, 1981). Plato, Aristotle, and MacIntyre view virtue in the more traditional "goody two-shoes" way; however, as we will see, there are alternate accounts of the virtuous life given by thinkers such as Friedrich Nietzsche, Thomas Hobbes, and Niccolò Machiavelli.

[2] I recognize that the narrators of Hetfield's songs cannot always be identified with their lyricist, but still they often provide a glimpse of his psyche. Also, let's note that these different sets of virtues overlap to some extent. For our purposes, though, we'll focus on their differences.

16

Christian virtues enforced by family. In their place come warrior virtues adopted in adolescence and adulthood, which—fueled by alcohol—finally failed. The result is, perhaps unwittingly, the acceptance of Buddhist virtues.

The God That Failed: Rejecting Christian Virtues

Pride, envy, gluttony, lust, anger, greed, and sloth are the Seven Deadly Sins. To get a sense of Christian virtues, consider the opposites of the Seven Deadly Sins: humility, benevolence, temperance, chastity, kindness, generosity, and diligence. Also, think of Jesus' Sermon on the Mount (Matthew 5:1–7:28), which highlights such Christian virtues as meekness, mercy, love of enemies, peacemaking, acceptance of persecution, refusal to judge, and forgiveness ("turn the other cheek").[3]

Christian virtues constitute part of what the German philosopher Friedrich Nietzsche (1844–1900) called the *slave morality*—a world-denying morality for those too timid to grab life by the balls. Not meant to liberate a person from earthly suffering, Christian virtues merely help a person endure it. Such virtues thus appeal to the downtrodden, to people who lack worldly power, who are willing to inject what Karl Marx (1818–83) called the *opium of the masses* (aka religion).

In rejecting the slave morality, Nietzsche famously proclaimed that "God is dead." Not so much a statement of atheism as a diagnosis of disease, this declaration means that belief in the God of Christianity has become worn out, practically impossible, dead—like a party with only three frat boys and some stale beer. Christian virtues have no transcendental home (they're not written in stone in some heavenly realm because there is *no such thing* as a heavenly realm), and they

---

[3] Christianity, specifically Catholicism, espouses Four Cardinal Virtues (wisdom, fortitude, temperance, and justice), Three Theological Virtues (faith, hope, and charity), and Five Intellectual Virtues (wisdom, science, understanding, prudence, and art). While these are certainly all important Christian virtues, a better sense of the set of Christian virtues can be gleaned from considering the Sermon on the Mount and the opposites of the Seven Deadly Sins.

benefit only the weak. Though it will be difficult and painful, we are better off burying "the God that Failed" and moving on.

Of course, the young James Hetfield could identify with this sentiment even if he never read Nietzsche or Marx. Hetfield was raised in the tradition of the Church of Christ, Scientist (also known as the Christian Science church), which, in addition to preaching traditional Christian virtues, forbids the practice of medicine. Bizarrely, in Christian Science medicine is forbidden because it wouldn't do any good in healing the body anyway. According to this church's doctrines, the body is really an illusory cage for the soul and, if someone is sick, all one can do is pray that God will heal the sick person. Whether a person lives or dies—sick or not—is totally in the hands of God. Add to this the idea that what is most important is your soul and what will happen to it in the life to come, and we can see why the Church of Christ, Scientist would seem dogmatic and world-denying. It's no wonder that Hetfield rejected the religion of his upbringing and, with it, many of the virtues it held dear.[4]

"So gather 'round young warriors now . . ."

But where do you turn once you've rejected the Christian virtues of your upbringing? One possibility is to adopt warrior virtues. Historically, warrior virtues arise out of warrior castes and classes and are most often associated with ancient civilizations and nomadic tribes.[5] Before Christianity, the Greeks and Romans looked upon their warriors with great admiration for their display of virtues such as courage, strength, and honor. Think of Achilles from Homer's *Iliad*,

---

[4] For an explanation of the theology and philosophy behind Christian Science, complete with criticisms, see Linda Kramer, *The Religion That Kills: Christian Science: Abuse, Neglect, and Mind Control* (Louisville, KY: Huntington House Publishers, 2000).

[5] A very different set of warrior virtues is espoused in the *Bhagavad Gita*, chapter 2. In this Hindu sacred text, obedience and conformity to duty are seen as virtues of the warrior. See *Bhagavad Gita*, trans. by Stephen Mitchell (New York: Three Rivers Press, 2000). Another prominent warrior code in the East is that of the Samurai. The Samurai are closer to the western ideal of the warrior than is the ideal offered in the *Bhagavad Gita*. See, for example, Yamamoto Tsunetomo, *Hagakure: The Book of the Samurai*, trans. by William Scott Wilson (Tokyo: Kodansha International, 2002).

played by Brad Pitt in *Troy*. Think of Schwarzenegger's Conan the Barbarian, who offers us a glimpse at a life governed by unrefined warrior virtues. Asked what is best in life, Conan responds: "To crush your enemies, to see them driven before you, and to hear the lamentation of their women." Here Conan echoes a quote attributed to the great conqueror Genghis Khan (ca. 1162–1227): "The greatest pleasure is to vanquish your enemies and chase them before you, to rob them of their wealth and see those dear to them bathed in tears, to ride their horses and clasp to your bosom their wives and daughters."

Although the word *virtue* can have a rather feminine connotation these days, as it is readily associated with such Christian virtues as meekness and chastity, the English word *virtue* is rooted in the warrior, coming from the Latin word *virtus*, meaning "manliness" (from the root word *vir*, man, as in "virile").[6] Surely this fits Hetfield, who hunts with Ted Nugent, watches old Western movies, and gets greasy with classic cars and custom bikes. He's indisputably a man's man, a warrior—not some pretty boy, politically correct rock star.

The warrior virtues get plenty of play in Metallica's music. Consider these: *courage* ("bloody, but never cry submission"), *hardness of heart* ("No remorse is the one command"), *self-sufficiency* ("by myself but not alone / I ask no one"), *proper pride* ("I have stripped of all but pride / so in her I do confide / and she keeps me satisfied / gives me all I need"), *aggressiveness* ("pounding out aggression"), *physical strength and health* ("move swift all senses clean"), *individuality* ("following our instinct, not a trend / go against the grain until the end"), *perseverance and endurance* ("We will never stop / we will never quit / 'cause we are Metallica"), *honor* ("dying on your feet for honesty"), *loyalty* ("We are as one as we all are the same / fighting for one cause"), and *emotional control* ("I adapt to the unknown"). But it's not just the lyrics; the music itself reinforces the warrior virtues, particularly aggressiveness and individuality.

---

[6] Consider the manly warrior kinds of virtues associated with the Brothers Grimm fairy tale entitled "Iron John." See Robert Bly, *Iron John: A Book About Men* (New York: Vintage Books, 1992). On the topic of manliness, see also Harvey Mansfield, *Manliness* (New Haven, CT: Yale University Press, 2006) and Judith Grant, "Bring the Noise: Hypermasculinity in Heavy Metal and Rap," *Journal of Social Philosophy* 27 (1996), pp. 5–30.

With songs including "Metal Militia," "Phantom Lord," "No Remorse," "Seek and Destroy," and "The Four Horsemen," *Kill 'Em All* is a pure celebration of warrior virtues. Using the imagery of the warrior to represent adolescent, existential crisis and rebellion, the message is clear: life is war, "war without end." Life is a struggle with no God or guardian angel looking out for you ("I know I'm my best friend"). Only the strong survive. For Metallica, like-minded individuals can choose—not be forced—to join together in a "metal militia." And they can un-choose that membership as well. There are no uniforms, just "your leathers and your spikes." The causes are not noble, just doing a little senseless destruction in the kill-or-be-killed world in which life, as Thomas Hobbes (1588–1679) said, is "solitary, poor, nasty, brutish, and short."[7]

The struggle is not to be taken literally of course. *Kill 'Em All* was unparalleled in its appeal to angry, alienated, suburban, white teenage males (like myself) for whom life was a struggle despite having no real war to fight and dwelling in seemingly comfortable circumstances. Rather than simply accept that life sucks and fade to black, we took up the fight against whoever, whatever. As we saw it, war is hell, and life itself is war.

The kill 'em all lifestyle calls to mind Nietzsche's "transvaluation of all values." Declaring that "God is dead" and finding the virtues of Christianity poisonous, Nietzsche advocated a new morality. Our new resolution and commandment, as Nietzsche's Zarathustra puts it, is "Stay true to the earth."[8] For Nietzsche, an action is good if it is done out of strength and bad if it is done out of weakness. So "scanning the scene in the city tonight / looking for you to start up the fight" is good if it is done out of strength, a feeling of power. "Remorse for the helpless one" is bad because it arises out of weakness. The warrior must be emotionally tough, immune to feelings of pity and remorse.

---

[7] See Hobbes' account of the state of nature in *Leviathan*, ed. by C.B. MacPherson (New York: Penguin, 1982). Hobbes' conception of virtue is similar to Nietzsche's in many ways, as both thinkers view deception, craftiness, and power as qualities a person must cultivate so as to survive and flourish in this world.

[8] Friedrich Nietzsche, *Thus Spoke Zarathustra* (New York: Penguin, 1966), p. 13. Here I have altered Walter Kaufmann's translation. Interestingly, in *Zarathustra* Nietzsche details three stages of life—not unlike the three sets of virtues we are discussing—the camel, the lion, and the child.

Life, as Nietzsche sees it, is governed by the "will to power," the innate drive to gain and express power. Getting shit-faced and causing some senseless destruction is one, unrefined, way to exercise the will power, but ultimately a more fulfilling way might be to rule a country, make billions like Bill Gates, become a movie star, or even make music that unites musicians and listeners. The aggressive thrash of *Kill 'Em All* is nothing if not an expression of power, a creative act to be shared with an audience, "when our fans start screaming / it's right."[9]

But while one's own power is to be expressed and celebrated, the power of others is to be watched and suspected. And so beginning with *Ride the Lightning* and *Master of Puppets* the lyrics become at times critical of literal war, reflecting on the abuse of the individual warrior by those in power. "For Whom the Bell Tolls" and "Disposable Heroes" portray individuals who are pawns in the games played by powerful war pigs. In a war he did not choose to fight the warrior kills for reasons he is not privy to. "Shouting gun, on they run through the endless gray / On the fight, for they are right, yes, but who's to say? / For a hill men would kill, why? They do not know." The warrior obeys the commands of those who care not for him—"Back to the front / you will do what I say, when I say / Back to the front / you will die when I say, you must die"—and to whom his death matters not—"Soldier boy, made of clay / now an empty shell / twenty-one, only son / but he served us well." Still worse, "One" from the *Justice* album, shows the unfortunate results of a soldier not lucky enough to die in battle, whose catastrophic injuries and disabilities leave him as nothing but "a wartime novelty."

Metallica's warrior virtues have a kinship with Stallone's Rambo, who justifies his actions by the principle of "first blood." The other side drew first blood and so retaliation is justified: "never begins it, never, but once engaged . . . / never surrenders, showing the fangs of rage." (If two wrongs don't make a right, what does?) Rambo was misused as a soldier. After fighting an unjust war in Vietnam he returned to be mistreated as a veteran. Rambo remains a warrior in his virtues, though opposed to unjust wars and suspicious of the government. Similarly, Metallica consistently espouse warrior virtues

---

[9] See Rachael Sotos, "Metallica's Existential Freedom: From We to I and Back Again," chapter 8 in this volume.

even while being highly critical of the loss of life and liberty due to the abuse of military and governmental power.

Still, Metallica are not whiney rock stars, wearing their convictions on their sleeves and shouting them from the stage.[10] And most of their anti-war songs are not overtly political. "Fight Fire with Fire," for example, features no holier-than-thou criticism of those making the decisions that lead to tragedy. Rather, the sad outcome simply seems the inevitable result of the warrior virtue of revenge in an absurd world. "Do unto others as they have done unto you / But what the hell is this world coming to? / Blow the universe into nothingness / Nuclear warfare shall lay us to rest."

"Blackened" is most often interpreted as a song about environmental abuse, but certain lines—"winter it will send"; "millions of our years in minutes disappear"—suggest themes of nuclear fear, echoing "Fight Fire with Fire." Indeed, "Fire to begin whipping dance of the dead" readily suggests helpless hordes fleeing the fallout of a nuclear winter. While conveying horror and disapproval, Metallica nonetheless makes something tragic sound cool. The only condemnation is of "the outcome of hypocrisy," a fault for sure, but one we are all guilty of to varying degrees. The nuclear "fire" is perhaps just the inevitable result of the warrior virtues, which Metallica, after all, share with the warlords.

Despite discussion of literal war, Metallica's emphasis has remained on the metaphorical battle, the struggle within. It's better to choose your own war—to be a vigilante member of the metal militia or Damage, Inc.—than to be the victim of someone else's. We need to be on guard and ready to fight in the defense of personal liberty. As "Don't Tread on Me" instructs, "To secure peace is to prepare for war."[11]

---

[10] Unlike many rock stars and celebrities, Hetfield wisely has avoided public declarations on particular wars, and on social issues in general. Although he has said it was sad and absurd to subject Iraqi prisoners of war to listen to Metallica, during a radio interview with NPR's Terry Gross of *Fresh Air*, Hetfield managed to joke about it, saying: "We've been punishing our parents, our wives, our loved ones with this music forever . . . Why should the Iraqis be any different?" See the newspaper article written by Lane DeGregory, "Iraq 'n Roll," *St. Petersburg Times*, November 21, 2004.

[11] "Don't Tread on Me" is not a pro-war anthem, and its writing preceded and was in no way related to the first Gulf War. Rather, the song celebrates the warrior virtues of honor, courage, freedom, and perseverance symbolized by the flag of the Minutemen of Culpepper County, Virginia.

Still, we shouldn't too quickly conclude that Metallica accepts and embodies *all* of the warrior virtues. "Man should be educated for war, and woman for the recreation of the warrior; all else is folly" (*Zarathustra*, p. 66). Thus speaks Nietzsche's character, Zarathustra. Indeed, sexual potency is often classed among the warrior virtues, but, because it is a rock and roll cliché, it gets little play by Metallica. Only the Nick Cave cover-song "Loverman" expresses it. While James and Lars have been known to frequent strip clubs, Metallica's lyrics are completely without the usual bullshit about fast women and fast cars (except "Fuel"). Metallica is noteworthy among metal bands for their lack of sleaziness and misogyny, recognizing that in life's war, as in Plato's *Republic*, men and women alike must wield the blade. Neither Plato nor Metallica are overt feminists, but both recognize that women too can "kick some ass tonight."

And kicking ass means facing the enemy head on. Craftiness—the trickery and deceit of one's enemies that Nicolò Machiavelli (1469–1527) advocated—is often classed among the warrior virtues.[12] Think of the Trojan horse trick by which the Greeks finally penetrated the walls of Troy. But craftiness is not a virtue Metallica endorses. Instead, they stand for a kind of death before dishonor, "dying on your feet for honesty." For Metallica at least, honesty is a warrior virtue. Indeed, "Honesty is my only excuse" and "When a man lies he murders / some part of the world."[13]

Metallica also lacks a further warrior virtue (particularly prior to *St. Anger*): emotional control. In western culture this virtue is most associated with stoicism, the philosophy that counsels self-control, detachment, and acceptance of one's fate. Clearly, there's not much stoicism in Metallica.[14] Instead, there's a lot of acting out of emotion; the warrior pounds out his aggression. But with *Load/Re-Load* Hetfield's lyrics become introspective and critical of an inability to

---

[12] Machiavelli's most famous work is a kind of rulebook for craftiness, *The Prince*, trans. by William Connell (New York: Bedford/St. Martin's Press, 2004).

[13] Apropos of our warrior theme, this line is actually lifted from the movie *Excalibur* in which Merlin says it to King Arthur.

[14] Stoicism in western philosophy can be traced back to Zeno of Citium in Cyprus (344–262 BCE). For discussions of the philosophy of Stoicism, see Brad Inwood (ed.), *The Cambridge Companion to the Stoics* (Cambridge: Cambridge University Press, 2003). Metallica has fleeting moments of stoicism in songs like "Escape" and "Wherever I May Roam."

manage emotions.[15] Consider "King Nothing's" self-destructive desire for control and the pointlessness of feeling bad for "Poor Old Twisted Me." Consider too the dawning realization of the futility of warrior virtues expressed by the sentiment "won't waste my hate on you."

Warrior virtues can only succeed with a healthy dose of stoicism, and stoicism itself will fail without a deep trust in fate. Yet stoicism and trust in fate are precisely what Metallica lack. Hetfield and company are driven by engaged emotions, not detached reason and spiritual acceptance. Without stoicism the life of the warrior virtues leads to nihilism—a belief in nothing anchored nowhere—and the inability to relieve one's own suffering or the suffering of others.[16] Looking outward for a fight is just a distraction. The warrior virtues don't relieve the suffering within. The lyrics on *St. Anger* reflect this defeat, this inability to overcome suffering. Consider these lines from "Frantic": "I've worn out always being afraid / An endless stream of fear that I've made / Treading water full of worry / This frantic tick tick talk of hurry." And these lines from "The Unnamed Feeling": "I just wanna get the fuck away from me / I rage, I glaze, I hurt, I hate / I wanna hate it all away."

The warrior lives by the code of an eye for an eye, which eventually leaves everyone blind. Just consider the outcome of "Fight Fire with Fire." Warrior virtues are adopted to fill the void, the emptiness inside, but warriors who don't die young eventually find the void swallows them whole. "My lifestyle determines my deathstyle." With time, the mental and emotional pain that comes from "dealing out the agony within" is too much to bear. The warrior virtues lead to self-destruction in the forms of addiction, madness, and despair. Sad but true.

[15] The "life is war" metaphor largely drops out for the loads. But "Where the Wild Things Are" with its "toy soldiers off to war" wonders whether the fate of a child will be "life is war," whether this earth will "keep you clean or stained through." Its military drum beat and cry of "never surrender" add to the martial mood.
[16] I leave it an open question whether the life of the warrior virtues can succeed if it is supplemented with stoicism. For further consideration, see Nancy Sherman, *Stoic Warriors: The Ancient Philosophy Behind the Military Mind* (New York: Oxford University Press, 2005).

Karmas Burning

If you're Hetfield what do you do at this point? You've taken two extreme paths. The life of the warrior virtues has taken its toll on you, and you can't go home again to Christian virtues. Christianity had you on your knees, and St. Anger choked you. Where to go? The good news is that the Buddha can remove the thorn within. Buddhism counsels taking the "middle way" with all things. And the middle way in this case is the mean between the extremes of the Christian and warrior virtues. Buddhist virtues include wisdom, kindness, compassion, and freedom from suffering.[17]

Although Kirk Hammett meditates and reads eastern philosophy, I'm not suggesting that Metallica have become Buddhists, no more than I'm suggesting that in the past they were actual warriors or devoted readers of Nietzsche.[18] Buddhism shares much in common with stoicism and its disciplining of the emotions. But as Hetfield's lyrics have gradually moved with maturity from the raging *reaction* of the warrior to the introspective *reflection* of the Buddhist, the search for emotional control is now paired better with Buddhist virtues than with the stoicism of warrior virtues.

There have been some surface-level Metalli-Buddha connections from early on. Consider a too-little-known fact: Buddha denied the existence of the gods and the soul. In opposition to the Hinduism of his day, which believed in many gods and taught that enlightenment could be achieved only after several lifetimes through reincarnation, Buddha instead offered a teaching for achieving enlightenment, nirvana, in this life. Similarly, Metallica has looked to this life and stayed true to the earth. For some of their peers—notably Venom, Slayer, and Exodus—rejection of Christian virtues took the form of a cartoonish advocacy of Satanic virtues. Metallica, though, despite one campy invitation to jump in the fire, stayed true to the earth while avoiding the silly satanic spirituality of the occult.

Believe it or not, Buddhists are instructed, "if you see the Buddha on the road, kill the Buddha." The message is simple. The historical

---

[17] Traditionally, the four primary Buddhist virtues are love, compassion, sympathetic joy, and impartiality.

[18] See The Metallica Interview in *Playboy*, April 2001, pp. 67–80, 164–5.

Buddha was not a god, just an example of what we all can be. So the place to look for the Buddha is not outside, not "on the road" or at some shrine. The Buddha is within.[19] You too can achieve nirvana. Similarly, early on at least, Metallica were not gods, not rock stars. They were heavy metal fans playing in a heavy metal band. The punk mantra "fuck your heroes" comes pretty close to suiting them.[20] On stage and off, Metallica wore the same clothes as their fans: jeans, concert t-shirts, denim and leather jackets. They refused to make videos for MTV; their music was a gift to fans they considered family. They were not to be worshipped. In other words, if you see the rock star on the stage, kill the rock star.[21]

The first noble truth of Buddhism is that "all life is suffering," something Metallica has been painfully aware of from its earliest days. "Life in the fast lane is just how it seems / hard and it is heavy / dirty and mean." The second noble truth, that desire (or craving) is the cause of suffering, is something Metallica were dimly—but not fully—aware of early on.[22] Certainly, there was the anti-materialist mentality of doing things on their own terms. They would not bow to MTV or commercial radio to make a buck. They stood against "halls of justice painted green / money talking." But sadly they did eventually become rock stars with fast cars, Lear jets, and expensive houses and divorces. Although Hetfield had once sung "Do you want what I want? / Desire not a thing," desire had in fact become the master of puppets. On *Load* the connection between suffering and desire began to dawn, and it became an issue of real concern on *St. Anger*, where there is more recognition of the need to detach from the self and from desire.

---

[19] See the chapter on Buddhism in Robert Ellwood and Barbara McGraw, *Many People, Many Faiths: Women and Men in the World's Religions* (Upper Saddle River, NJ: Prentice-Hall, 2004).

[20] David F. Smydra, Jr., "Zen and the Art of Slam Dancing: Buddhist Punks Find Enlightenment in the Pit," *Boston Globe*, September 19, 2004, www.boston.com/news/globe/ideas/articles/2004/09/19/zen_and_the_art_of_slam_dancing?

[21] Again, not literally, of course. May Dimebag Darrell rest in peace.

[22] There are four noble truths. The third noble truth is that we can be liberated from suffering. The fourth noble truth is that liberation requires following the eightfold path: 1. right views 2. right thoughts 3. right speech 4. right action 5. right livelihood 6. right effort 7. right mindfulness and 8. right concentration.

Compassion, ego deflation, and acceptance can potentially bring freedom from suffering. These Buddhist virtues are also the virtues of recovery, as Hetfield has learned. Ego deflation and acceptance begin to manifest in the lyrics of *St. Anger*. Consider the "Frantic" mention of "karmas burning" and the realization that "My lifestyle determines my deathstyle." This wisdom was gained through painful experience. Hetfield is aware of his unhealthy tendency to play the tripartite role of judge, jury, and executioner (too) in "Dirty Window," a song that also displays an awareness of suffering from a false self-image—surely an occupational hazard. "All Within My Hands" presents a self-mocking look at Hetfield's need to control people and situations: "Love is control / I'll die if I let go . . . All within my hands / Squeeze it in, crush it down / All within my hands / Hold it dear, hold it suffocate." "I will only let you breathe / My air that you receive / Then we'll see if I let you love me." If he is wise and fortunate, the warrior turned Buddhist learns that life is not a war (not even metaphorically) and paradoxically you must surrender to win. You can't swim against the current of the universe without being pulled under.

We've seen wisdom and freedom from suffering develop on *St. Anger*, but compassion and kindness are clearly undeveloped. Such virtues involve more than just renouncing the "no remorse" approach to life. They involve actively reaching out to alleviate the suffering of others. In his personal life since *St. Anger* Hetfield shows signs of developing in compassion and kindness, moving towards the Buddhist ideal, the Bodhisattva, who, having eliminated his own suffering, seeks to ease and eliminate the suffering of others. While Hetfield, like all of us, is far from perfect and surely no Mother Teresa, his work with other recovering alcoholics and addicts displays admirable compassion. On May 12, 2006 Hetfield received the Stevie Ray Vaughn Award for his "dedication and support of the MusiCares MAP Fund and his devotion to helping other addicts with recovery process." It's tough to imagine the warrior Hetfield of *Kill 'Em All* being honored for his service to others. But the Hetfield of today has moved from causing the suffering of others—most clearly his family—to alleviating the suffering of others.

So *St. Anger* begins to display some of the Buddhist virtues, and if Hetfield sticks with his recovery, future albums will likely display other Buddhist virtues as well. In "St. Anger" Hetfield sings "I want my anger to be healthy . . ." Of course, it would be better to have no anger at all, but handling anger in a constructive way is at least a step in the right direction. The warrior is not yet dead, as the "shoot me again" mentality demonstrates, but Buddhism, like recovery, is a matter of progress not perfection.

Practicing warrior virtues does not necessarily make one a warrior, of course, no more than practicing Christian virtues necessarily makes one a Christian. And so adopting Buddhist virtues does not necessarily make Hetfield a Buddhist. Though Kirk becomes one with the wave while surfing, reads Buddhist philosophy, and practices meditation, we shouldn't hold our breath waiting for Hetfield to start contemplating his navel and chanting OM. As much as we identify with him, Hetfield is no saint and surely he faces future challenges. Still, for many of us, his journey is our journey. His life and lyrics speak for our experience.

A Common Search?

While the journey from Christian, to warrior, to Buddhist makes sense, there is nothing inevitable about it. One set of virtues does not necessarily lead to the next, and I don't mean to suggest that Hetfield fits neatly into the categories. But this progression is one way of interpreting his journey, and Metallica's, and one that is common to many of us. Ultimately, I confess, Christian-Warrior-Buddhist is my story too, a life-cycle I've lived and am living, a search that goes on.[23]

[23] Metalli-thanks to Candice Alaimo, Rob Arp, Joanna Corwin, Jeff Dean, Robert Delfino, Jason Eberl, Bart Engelen, Peter Fosl, Rebecca Housel, Kyle Johnson, Megan Lloyd, J.R. Lombardo, Thomas Nys, Rachael Sotos, Eileen Sweeney, and Mark White.

CHAPTER 3

ALCOHOLICA
When Sweet Amber Becomes
the Master of Puppets

BART ENGELEN

No words can tell of the loneliness and despair I found in that bitter morass of self-pity. Quicksand stretched around me in all directions. I had met my match. I had been overwhelmed. Alcohol was my *master*.

> *Alcoholics Anonymous*, p. 8[1]

"Obey your master!" "Master!" Every true Metallica fan knows the chilling feeling of joining thousands in slavishly responding to James Hetfield's roaring call in concert. But what master is there to obey? Who or what is pulling our strings? The song "Master of Puppets" does not refer to a tyrannical or war-mongering government—as the *Master of Puppets* album cover might suggest—but rather to the enslaving effects of drugs, the heroin with which we "needlework the way" and the cocaine that makes you "chop your breakfast on a mirror."[2]

---

[1] *Alcoholics Anonymous: The Story of How Many Thousands of Men and Women Have Recovered From Alcoholism*, 3rd edn. (New York: Alcoholics Anonymous World Services, 1976). Further references to this book are given parenthetically in the body of the chapter as references to *AA* with page numbers.
[2] In fact, the word "addiction" is derived from the Latin word *addicere*, which originally means "enslavement." This is still clear in some languages, for example in Dutch where "addiction" (*verslaving*) literally means "to turn into a slave."

Alcoholica

But Hetfield didn't have a problem with—and perhaps never even used—heroin and cocaine. As he says, "It's pretty interesting, because I'd be writing about stuff I'd never tried—heroin or cocaine . . . But the stuff I was dealing with I wasn't writing about."[3] So let's focus on the effects of alcohol, "Sweet Amber," a drug as addictive as smack and crack and much better known to Hetfield and co. "She deals in habits, deals in pain / I run away but I'm back again."

Metallica has always been associated with alcohol, whether it be the "sweet amber" of Samuel Adams and Jack Daniels or their transparent cousins Smirnoff and Carnaby. Kirk Hammett explains: "Alcohol was never an issue. We always had it around us and we always had it around us in large amounts. When I first met these guys they were drinking vodka like it was water . . . It became part of our legend" (*mtvICON*). Metallica quickly gained a fitting nickname among fans and journalists: Alcoholica. Lars Ulrich, no stranger to the bottle himself, concedes Hetfield was the biggest drinker in the band: "If me and James started drinking at the same time, six hours of hard liquor later, I would be passed out. For quite a while, he was embracing alcohol at a different level from the rest of us" (*Playboy*).

"Master of Puppets," though written about drug addiction, can shed some light on alcoholism. The lyrics clearly suggest addiction's pernicious effects on the ways otherwise rational individuals come to act, believe, and desire. So let's consider how booze can turn a rational person into a submissive puppet.

Alcoholism

"Master of Puppets" describes the gradual process in which an addiction arises, grows, and dominates a person's life. In the first verse, Hetfield illustrates how the decision to take drugs ("taste me you will

---

[3] See The mtvICON Interviews, May 2003, available online at www.mtv.com/onair/icon/metallica/. Ulrich and Hammett have repeatedly stated they were into cocaine as well, adding that "James is the only one who never really engaged in any kind of drug abuse." See The Metallica Interview, *Playboy*, April 2001, pp. 67–80, 164–5.

see") can induce a craving that gradually builds up ("more is all you need"), becomes the dominating motivation within the addict ("you're dedicated to"), and ultimately leads to a life in ruins ("how I'm killing you"). This process closely reflects the phases of alcoholism: initiation, acceleration, maintenance, and relapse.[4]

Alcoholism, like other addictions, isn't easy to define. There are, however, a number of typical characteristics.[5] A first characteristic is the experience of pleasure. There's no doubt that the boys in Metallica have had lots of good times drinking. Hetfield claims he would often "have a bottle of Vodka just for fun" (*Playboy*). A second characteristic is the phenomenon of tolerance: as time passes the alcoholic needs more booze to get the same effect: "more is all you need." The third and perhaps most important characteristic of alcoholism is a sense of craving: a strong, visceral desire to achieve the pleasant and avoid the unpleasant effects. But the unpleasant effects are inevitable.

Typically, an alcohol addiction builds up gradually. Initially, most people simply seek the immediate pleasure of getting drunk and having a good time. After a while, however, this leads to a progressive deterioration. As the lyrics for "Harvester of Sorrow" suggest, booze can also induce aggression: "Drink up / Shoot in / Let the beatings begin / Distributor of pain / Your loss becomes my gain." Hetfield himself admits that his behavior while drinking caused a lot of suffering: "It was ripping my family apart" (*mtvICON*). The alcoholic gets caught in a vicious circle. As his problems pile up, he grabs the bottle in an attempt to escape from his misery. Sigmund Freud (1856–1939), father of psychoanalysis, thought drugs are often used to evade the real world and its hardships. So the alcoholic prescribes his own cure

---

[4] Jon Elster, *Strong Feelings: Emotion, Addiction and Human Behavior* (Cambridge, MA: MIT Press, 1999), p. 115. While relapse doesn't immediately correlate with the life in ruins mentioned above, the addict's difficulties with overcoming his addiction do illustrate the devastating effects of an advanced addiction.

[5] These characteristics come to the front in both the philosophical and clinical attempts to define addiction. See Jon Elster and Ole-Jorgen Skog (eds.), *Getting Hooked: Rationality and Addiction* (Cambridge: Cambridge University Press, 1999), pp. 8–14. In the *Fourth Edition of the Diagnostic and Statistical Manual of Mental Disorders* (DSM-IV), the term "addiction" is replaced by "substance abuse" and "substance dependence," of which the latter comes very close to what one ordinarily labels addiction. See Sharon C. Ekleberry (2000), *Dual Diagnosis: Axis II Personality Disorders and Addiction*, available online at www.toad.net/~arcturus/dd/pdsa.htm.

and self-medicates. Consider the lyrics for "Cure": "He thinks the answer is cold and in his hand / He takes his medicine / The man takes another bullet / He's been fooled again." If we take the bullets in "Cure" to be "Silver Bullets" (cans of Coors Lite, a beer Hetfield was known to drink), Hetfield seems to describe this insidious cycle. The cure is no better than the disease. In fact it is part of the disease of alcoholism.

Negative withdrawal effects are a fourth characteristic of alcoholism. Some alcoholics even get "the shakes," trembling after a period of abstinence. Consider the lyrics for "The House That Jack Built" in which Hetfield seems to refer to Jack Daniels. "And I shake as I take it in / Let the show begin / The higher you are, the farther you fall / The longer you walk, the farther you crawl / My body, my temple / This temple it tilts / Yes, this is the house that Jack built." Indeed, alcoholism had disastrous effects on Hetfield's physical condition. While his drinking may have been a good thing in some instances—if it wasn't for the booze, "Master of Puppets" would probably have never been written—it often held him back as well. As Hetfield says: "The first time I played sober was because I just forgot to drink. 'Damn,' I thought, 'I'm playing better'" (*Playboy*).

A final characteristic of alcoholism is difficulty in quitting. The craving for alcohol is often so powerful that the alcoholic would be unable to resist it if he wanted to. "This is the baffling feature of alcoholism as we know it—this utter inability to leave it alone, no matter how great the necessity or the wish" (*AA*, 34). As Hetfield says, "I got really sick of being hurt the next day. I got really tired of wasting days and feeling like shit" (*Playboy*). Despite managing to stay dry for over a year at the time he made that statement, Hetfield eventually returned to the bottle.

The Irrationality of Alcoholism

Experts continue to debate the extent to which the craving for alcohol and other drugs can be literally irresistible.[6] What counts, however,

6 See Justin Gosling, *Weakness of the Will* (London: Routledge, 1990), p. 142; William Charlton, *Weakness of Will: A Philosophical Introduction* (Oxford: Blackwell, 1988), pp. 155–61.

isn't whether the addict's need for drugs *is* completely overpowering, but whether he himself *believes* this to be the case. Often, repeatedly failing to quit leads an addict to become convinced that he is hopelessly lost. This destructive logic poses an enormous threat to an individual's rationality: drugs can overwhelm his rational considerations or even undermine his capacity to make rational decisions. To understand the impact of addiction on the rationality and autonomy of persons, let's consider its impact on actions, beliefs, and preferences.[7]

First, let's focus on actions. I have already hinted at the paradox that underlies the behavior of most addicts: even though they are initially capable of making rational decisions, addicts increasingly lose control over their own actions. Often, they suffer from weakness of the will, which means that they are more and more inclined to act against their well-considered judgment on what to do.[8] Even though they judge it best to quit, they can't overcome the craving. As Alcoholics Anonymous says, "The fact is that for reasons yet obscure, we have lost the power of choice in drink. Our so-called will power becomes practically nonexistent. We are unable, at certain times, to bring into our consciousness with sufficient force the memory of the suffering and humiliation of even a week or a month ago. We are without defense against the first drink" (*AA*, 24).

In western philosophy, this problem of weakness of the will or *akrasia* first appears in Plato's (ca.428–ca.348 BCE) *Protagoras*, where Socrates (470–399 BCE) argues that "it is absurd . . . to say that a man often does bad things though he knows they are bad and could refrain from doing them, because he is driven and overwhelmed by pleasures."[9] According to Socrates, it is simply incoherent that a rational person deliberately does what he judges wrong. Among philosophers, this has become known as the "Socratic paradox." If an alcoholic decides to take a drink rather than abstain, he must believe,

---

[7] In what follows, I focus almost exclusively on some of the most prominent authors within analytical philosophy of mind and action, like Donald Davidson and Jon Elster. My main reason for doing so is that their theories are central in contemporary thinking about human rationality.

[8] Donald Davidson, *How is Weakness of the Will Possible?*, in Donald Davidson, *Essays on Actions and Events* (Oxford: Clarendon Press, 1980), pp. 21–2.

[9] Plato, *Protagoras*, trans. by C.C.W. Taylor (Oxford: Oxford University Press, 2002), 355a.

there and then, that such indulgence is the best thing to do. Believing that the pleasure of having a drink is good, the alcoholic rationalizes his choice.

In his *Republic*, Plato resolves the paradox by dividing the soul into a rational part and an irrational (or desiring) part.[10] When these conflict with one another, the first is often able to keep the latter in check: "Can't we say there is something in their soul telling them to drink and also something stopping them? Something different from, and stronger than, the thing telling them they should drink?" (Book IV, 439c). In the case of the alcoholic, the rational part loses the battle against the irrational part.

According to Plato's student Aristotle (384–322 BCE), people who act out of weakness of will fail to reason out what is truly good for them. In Aristotle's view, the weak-willed person "tends to be carried away contrary to correct reason because of the ways he is affected. They overcome him to the extent that he does not act in accordance with correct reason, but not so that he becomes the sort to be convinced that he ought to pursue such pleasures unrestrainedly."[11] So according to Aristotle, someone who is weak-willed still knows what is good, but fails to act accordingly.

Addicts are often plagued by a loss of self-control and a terrible sense of ambivalence. Weakness of the will occurs only when the rational part of the addict loses "the struggle within" and the alienating craving comes out on top. Only after Hetfield realized in 2001 that he didn't want to be the kind of person he had become—an addicted puppet ruled by master booze—did he become an "unwilling addict," one who experiences a strong desire to take drugs (alcohol in his case) but doesn't want to act on this desire. He no longer endorsed this desire and simply didn't want to be an addict at all. Previously, Hetfield was a "willing addict," fully approving his desire to drink.[12] Fans will

[10] Plato, *The Republic*, trans. by T. Griffith, ed. by G.R.F. Ferrari (Cambridge: Cambridge University Press, 2000), Book IV, 439d. For reasons that are of no particular concern here, Plato also distinguishes a third, spirited part of the soul.
[11] Aristotle, *Nicomachean Ethics*, trans. by R. Crisp (Cambridge: Cambridge University Press, 2000), Book VII, 1151a.
[12] This terminology comes from Harry Frankfurt, whose views are analyzed more fully below. See Harry Frankfurt, *The Importance of What We Care About* (Cambridge: Cambridge University Press, 1988), pp. 17–25.

remember the sticker on Hetfield's guitar during the *And Justice for All* tour, proudly proclaiming he was always in for "more beer!" Still blind to his problem, Hetfield could nonetheless be considered rational, since he simply did what he deemed best.[13]

In contrast to Hetfield, the willing addict on the *Justice* tour, unwilling addicts acknowledge they have good reasons to quit, but nevertheless fail to translate these into action.[14] Since rational actions are based upon one's well-considered reasons, weak-willed behavior is often considered to be a paradigmatic form of irrationality. Following Socrates, the philosopher Donald Davidson (1917–2003) deems it completely incomprehensible how one can choose to do something contrary to what one "believes it would be better, all things considered, to do" (Davidson, 42). Davidson argues that the causal force of visceral urges (to drink) turn out to be stronger than the force of the reasonably deliberated intention (not to drink). The latter, which provides a good reason for acting, is bypassed by the former, which doesn't count as a reason itself.[15] The resulting action (drinking) is irrational, because it runs counter to what the addict himself believes to be best (not drinking).

The weak-willed person thus loses control: "when someone acts against his own better judgment, reason isn't in control of his actions. Another way of putting the point is to say that he is not in control of them" (Pears, 15). Upon taking the first drink alcoholics typically lose control over their further consumption, resulting in a binge. While a binge can be rationally chosen and pursued (as in the case of a person who simply wants to have a wild night out), it can also arise outside a person's volitional control (as in the case of an addict who puts aside his resolution to temper his alcohol use). As the title

[13] This doesn't imply that the whole phenomenon of addiction is rational, as has been argued. See Gary S. Becker & Kevin M. Murphy (1988), "A Theory of Rational Addiction," *Journal of Political Economy*, 96, pp. 675–700. This view can't explain the ambivalence that is typical of unwilling addicts.
[14] David Pears, *Motivated Irrationality* (Oxford: Clarendon Press, 1984), pp. 241–2.
[15] The addict's urge to drink is often characterized as purely physical. However, while drug dependence has physical aspects, I don't want to reduce it to something completely physiological. Instead of analyzing the unwilling addict's ambiguity in a dualistic way—his sober mind is fighting against his addicted body—I argue that physical forces influence his mental states, causing these to conflict.

of their live CD (and DVD) *Live Shit: Binge and Purge* suggests, Metallica has some experience with binging. Ulrich speaks of "the binge mentality; I'd go every night for three days, then I wouldn't touch a drop for the next four" (*Playboy*).

Believer Deceiver

Let's consider how addiction affects beliefs. In a narrow sense, beliefs are irrational if they are inconsistent. For example, alcoholics often believe both that booze is bad for them but that one more drink won't do anybody any harm. In a broader sense, "beliefs are irrational when they are shaped by distorting influences of various kinds" (Elster, 144). One source of irrational belief formation is wishful thinking in which one believes that something is true, simply because one wants it to be true. Alcoholics often regard their drinking as unproblematic. As Hetfield puts it in "Master of Puppets," the drugs are capable of "twisting your mind." They can cloud your clear vision: "Blinded by me, you can't see a thing." Excessive drinking can also cause blackouts, as Hetfield no doubt knows. In fact, fellow Metallican Kirk Hammett explains he "can't really recall most of the *Kill 'Em All* tour" (*mtvICON*).

Another source of irrational belief formation is self-deception in which one believes something because one wants to—like wishful thinking—but realizes that one has no reason for doing so. Alcoholics will, for example, trick themselves into believing that they can quit as soon as they want to. In these cases, the visceral urge to drink has an influence in forming this belief. A related kind of irrational belief formation is rationalization: after alcoholics understand they are addicted, they tend to "seek extra justification for their continued behavior" (Elster, 130).

Another familiar characteristic of addiction is denial. Addicts "deny that they have a problem or, if they admit it, deny that they can do anything about it" (Elster, 73). Denial forms the central theme of "Dirty Window": "I see my reflection in the window / This window clean inside, dirty on the out / I'm looking different than me / This house is clean, baby / This house is clean." Hetfield suggests that booze can help sustain the illusion that nothing is wrong: "I drink from the cup of denial." While people in his environment already see the problem, the addict maintains that everything is okay. Hetfield himself admits that he didn't "realize what a problem it was" (*mtvICON*) until his wife Francesca repeatedly threatened to throw him out of the house.

Now, let's turn our attention to how addiction affects desires. Here too, irrationality in a narrow sense means inconsistency. Unwilling addicts want mutually incompatible things: even though they want to stop drinking, they still long for booze. Desires are irrational in a broader sense if they aren't formed properly. Addicts often regard the urge to take drugs as an alienating force that overwhelms their reasons for acting. It enslaves them, since they don't identify with it and don't want to be moved by it. The desire for booze guides the alcoholic, not because he believes he has good reasons for it, but because he is physically and psychologically dependent on alcohol. It comes about almost by itself, without being subject to the person's rational scrutiny.

The Problem of Alcoholism

One might ask what all the fuss is about: so what if an addiction induces irrational acts, beliefs, and desires? Well, the problem is that human beings want to be rational and autonomous creatures. They want to be in control of their own acts, beliefs, and desires. But alcoholism thwarts these desires and turns people into puppets, "subjects of King Alcohol, shivering denizens of his mad realm" (*AA*, 151).

To be clear, the problem is alcohol addiction, *not* consumption. Often, people without an addictive past decide to get drunk for whatever reason, which isn't necessarily irrational. The point isn't that the desire for alcohol is irrational in itself. Rather, the problem arises when the craving for booze is in charge of the person, when it becomes the master of the enslaved addict: "I will run through you / now I rule you too."

To clarify the problem of alcoholism, let's consider the contemporary philosopher Harry Frankfurt's distinction between first-order desires and second-order desires. Frankfurt argues that people are continuously moved by first-order desires. These are natural inclinations, basic motivations that pull one towards what is pleasant and push one away from what is unpleasant. Sometimes, these contradict each other: I want a drink, but I also want to avoid a hangover and "the hideous Four Horsemen—Terror, Bewilderment, Frustration, Despair" (*AA*, 151). People, however, can distinguish between desires they want to have and desires they would rather be rid of. They are able to take sides in the inner struggle between first-order desires. People thus have a reflective and rational capacity to form second-order desires. A person may have a second-order desire not to be moved by the desire to drink or a second-order desire to be moved by the desire to drink. Second-order desires partly constitute a person's identity and are crucial in determining whether a person is rational or not. Furthermore, a person can identify with a certain desire, thus wanting it to constitute his will.

What is most important isn't simply the desire for alcohol, but whether one endorses it. The willing addict subscribes to his desire for booze, while the unwilling addict does not. Since willing addicts are at peace with themselves and their situation, they proceed in a completely rational way when having a drink. As long as Hetfield's first-order preferences (to drink and get drunk) were in accordance with his second-order preferences, he had complete volitional control. It was only after he formed a second-order preference (he made the desire to stop drinking his own) that his continued use of alcohol became a sign of irrationality. Unwilling addicts thus act irrationally when taking a drink, because they no longer identify with the desire to drink.[16]

You don't have to be an alcoholic to understand the alienating effects of liquor. Anyone who has ever been drunk probably knows what it feels like to do, believe, and desire things that one would normally refrain from. If someone gets overly mellow or aggressive after a few drinks, we often say that the booze is talking. As Kirk Hammett says: "Alcohol brought out everything that we needed to

---

[16] Next to the willing and unwilling addict, Frankfurt mentions the wanton addict, who "has no identity apart from his first-order desires" (Frankfurt, p. 18). Simply following his immediate first-order inclinations, such an addict doesn't identify with either the desire to drink or to stop. Lacking any higher-order volitions, such an addict can't even be considered a person.

say to each other that we couldn't say to each other when we were sober" (*mtvICON*).

The Solution to Alcoholism

The craving for booze tends to crowd out all other things from the addict's life. In the end, it may even lead to his complete self-destruction. Sweet Amber "holds the pen that spells the end / she traces me and draws me in." Luckily for Hetfield, Metallica, and their fans, things don't always turn out that way. In 2001 Hetfield faced his addiction and entered rehab. He had finally identified with his desire to quit, and was motivated to find a solution to his problem.

There's nothing about recovery from alcoholism on *Master of Puppets* (1986), but it is well documented in the rockumentary *Some Kind of Monster* (2004) and some of the lyrics on *St. Anger* (2003). "Frantic," for example, can be interpreted as describing the difficulty of staying sober: "Do I have the strength / to know how I'll go? / Can I find it inside / to deal with what I shouldn't know?" Though most addicts initially try to quit by pure strength of will, more than sheer will power is often needed to overcome an addiction. Even though the *Load* song "Until It Sleeps" is inspired by the death of Hetfield's father from cancer, the lyrics nicely illustrate the persistence of alcoholism: "Where do I take this pain of mine? / I run but it stays right by my side / So tear me open, pour me out / The things inside that scream and shout." The lyrics also illustrate the "sleeping tiger" of addiction. Though the addiction may be dormant due to abstinence, a single drink can turn the sleeping tiger into a beast on the prowl: "Just like a curse, just like a stray / You feed it once and now it stays." So the recovering alcoholic must always be on guard against the temptation of Sweet Amber: "Once an alcoholic, always an alcoholic" (*AA*, 44). This doesn't mean that the alcoholic is doomed, but it does mean he can never drink safely.

So unwilling addicts often resort to indirect strategies to maintain their sobriety and restore their rationality, strategies that help them to act upon their second-order desire to quit and stay quit. Trust in God or some other higher power is a key part of abstinence and recovery for many alcoholics. But because we're dealing with philosophy and not theology, let's focus on more earthly strategies. One way of restoring self-control is to make the drug in question less available. This strategy is based on "belief dependence": the simple belief that booze is available increases the alcoholic's longing for it. So recovering alcoholics typically resist the temptation by avoiding people, places, and things associated with drinking. They essentially "bind" or "pre-commit" themselves to increase the chance that they will choose in the future what they now deem best. Since it enables addicts to act in accordance with their rational, well-considered judgment, this strategy provides a way of dealing with their tendency to act irrationally.

Another well-known form of pre-commitment is to rely on and trust in others. Alcoholics Anonymous and other twelve-step programs stress the need for fellowship among recovering alcoholics. A more drastic way of pre-committing oneself is to enter a rehabilitation facility. In doing so, Hetfield rationally chose not only to stay in an environment in which booze is unavailable, but also chose to undergo therapy and thus rely on others to protect him from himself.

Having sobered up, Hetfield initially refused to go back on tour, because he did not want to be put in situations he associated with drinking. That a mere setting can trigger the craving for alcohol is called "cue dependence." Hetfield therefore wisely chose to avoid those situations that reminded him of the bottle. Many recovering alcoholics eventually achieve "cue extinction," disassociating these situations from alcohol. Apparently Hetfield managed to do this, and thankfully Metallica resumed touring after the release of *St. Anger*.

Hetfield thus forms a living example that it is possible for an alcoholic to break the chains of his addiction. Even though a rational human being can be turned into a slave by the effects of Sweet Amber, he nevertheless remains able to regain control and become his own master again.[17]

[17] I acknowledge financial support for this research by the Research Foundation—Flanders (FWO—Vlaanderen). Further, I would like to thank Joanna Corwin, Yvonne Denier, Helder De Schutter, Jason Eberl, Thomas Nys, Joris Van Damme, and especially Bill Irwin, whose comments on earlier versions of this chapter certainly helped me to improve it. Of course, any remaining flaws or errors are my own.

THROUGH THE MIST AND THE MADNESS

Metallica's Message of Nonconformity, Individuality, and Truth

THOMAS NYS

I was about fourteen years old when I bought my first Metallica t-shirt at a local store. A shiver ran down my spine when I put my money on the counter, my palms were sweaty, and the whole trans-action felt a bit like breaking the law. Buying this t-shirt was an unmistakable act of rebellion, a way of showing I was different from the rest. Back then I believed that wearing a Metallica t-shirt provided the perfect expression of my rebellious nature. Nowadays, I believe wearing the t-shirt provided the perfect excuse for not talking to the beautiful girls I was secretly in love with (girls who would have noth-ing to do with such a rebel). Whatever my deepest motivations may have been, Metallica's message of nonconformity was clear. Some Metallica-bashers would say their message has changed, and that they have sold out. But let's not bother with the critics. Let's return to the original message of Metallica—the Metallica of my t-shirt buying days—which was not only about being different, but also about being true to yourself, being free, and seeking the truth.

Philosophers have always disliked conformism (and conformists, in turn, have always despised philosophers). Socrates (470–399 BCE), for example, was ridiculed for his unusual behavior by Aristophanes

(448–385 BCE), who in his play *The Clouds* depicted Socrates as a madman who was hopelessly entangled in his own philosophical constructions. Or consider Diogenes (404–323 BCE), a colorful Cynic who lived in a tub and who, when Alexander the Great asked him what his deepest wish was, calmly answered: "Stand back, you block my light." From the very beginning, authority, fashion, and custom have been at odds with philosophy. Admittedly, throughout the centuries philosophy has become respectable—the domain of professors who could afford the luxury of contemplation. Nevertheless, as a critical profession, philosophy has remained highly skeptical of conformism. Even in the nineteenth century, a period in which philosophy had reached the pinnacle of its prestige, John Stuart Mill (1806–73) and other philosophers frowned upon conformity, fashion, and custom.

At first glance there is little in common between Mill and Metallica. Mill was a prototypical English gentleman: well-groomed, polite, and incredibly intelligent, whereas the members of Metallica either deliberately or unintentionally seem to shun such qualities. But when we compare the central messages of Metallica and Mill, we find the similarities truly striking. Let's begin with their shared contempt for conformity.

Nonconformity:
Do You Fear What I Fear? Living Properly

In its early days Metallica was all about rebellion. The title of their debut album is a case in point. On their tribute video to Cliff, James tells the crowd that the title *Kill 'Em All* refers to the managers and "men in gray suits" who control the music business. Metallica was clearly not afraid to bite the hand that fed them. Indeed, Metallica was pissed at the entire world. They were sick of people telling you what to do, pointing their fingers, and making you play by the rules. They hated the "posers" with big hair and makeup who tried to woo their female audience with their high-pitched voices. Metallica wanted to do things differently. They wanted to be faster and louder than any band that had gone before. They had no desire to be smooth and sexy and, as a result, they looked like shit. In fact, we all looked like shit in those days, because that just happened to be the uniform of rebellion, and we wore it with pride.[1]

The lyrics on *Kill 'Em All* read as a manifesto of the metal way of life. Metallica reached out to thousands of kindred spirits across the world and urged them to join their ranks, leaving no doubt that in joining them they would distance themselves from others. James, Lars, Kirk, and Cliff were deeply committed to what they called the "metallization of your inner soul," and you could either "jump by your will or be taken by force." Metallica's goal was to forge a bond between like-minded people by clearly separating "us" from "them." This feeling of belonging, this sense of connectedness, is prominent in various songs, but it is perhaps most straightforward in "Metal Militia": "We are as one as we all are the same / Fighting for one cause / Leather and metal are our uniforms / Protecting what we are / Joining together to take on the world / With our heavy metal / Spreading the message to everyone here / Come let yourself go." The message of nonconformity, of being different, is most clear in "Motorbreath," which gives the following advice: "Those people who tell you not to take chances / They are all missing on what life is about / You only live once so take hold of the chance / Don't end up like others the same song and dance." Being a Metallica fan required guts because you separated yourself from the flock of blind followers.

The context in which John Stuart Mill expressed his contempt for conformism (the appreciation and encouragement of conformity) was of course very different. But he was similarly worried about a tendency in people to adapt their feelings and opinions to whatever is customary. Mill observed that people were quite happy with "the same song and dance" and didn't want to stand out. As a result, something valuable was lost. People no longer had authentic feelings, lively passions, or stimulating ideas; the human race was rendered dull, weak, and without energy. As Mill described the predicament:

> [People] ask themselves, what is suitable for my position? What is usually done by persons of my station and pecuniary circumstances? Or (worse

---

[1] Looking back, the fact that we all looked more or less the same is actually quite odd, given that we wanted to bring down conformism. Nevertheless, I guess this was the whole idea behind the Metal Militia: to create an army of people that was prepared to "go against the grain until the end."

still) what is usually done by persons of a station and circumstances superior to mine? I do not mean that they choose what is customary in preference to what suits their own inclination. It does not occur to them to have any inclination, except for what is customary. Thus the mind itself is bowed to the yoke: even in what people do for pleasure, conformity is the first thing thought of; they like in crowds; they exercise choice only among things that are commonly done: peculiarity of taste, eccentricity of conduct, are shunned equally with crimes: until by dint of not following their own nature they have no nature to follow: their human capacities are withered and starved: they become incapable of any strong wishes or native pleasures, and are generally without either opinions or feelings of home growth, or properly their own.[2]

Worse still, those who actually dared to be different were punished for their eccentricity. In his famous and influential essay *On Liberty*, Mill offers a vigorous plea for individual freedom; arguing that people must be permitted to have different feelings, sentiments, and opinions; that they should be allowed and even encouraged to experiment with different ways of life. It was clear to Mill, as it was clear to Metallica, that people should break free from the deadlock of conformity and live their lives according to their own judgment. No person's wings should be clipped before they learn to fly.

Happiness and Individuality:
Do You Choose What I Choose?
More Alternatives

But why is conformity such a bad thing? Why should we abandon the comfort of fixed ideas about what is appropriate? Again, Metallica's and Mill's answers converge. One important reason is that conformity is an impediment to personal happiness: a person cannot become truly happy if she just follows the rules.

Mill was a proponent of utilitarianism, an ethical doctrine that identifies the good as "the greatest happiness for the greatest number."

---

[2] John Stuart Mill, *On Liberty*, ed. by Mary Warnock (Oxford: Blackwell, 2003), p. 136. Further references to this book are given parenthetically in the body of the chapter as references to *OL* with page numbers.

Utilitarianism is very down to earth: moral conduct should positively affect human wellbeing or, expressed negatively: we should not obey abstract principles or divine commands which do not seem to contribute to human welfare.[3]

Mill, however, was not a typical utilitarian. Most obviously he reacted against Jeremy Bentham's idea of a "felicific calculus" (*felicitas* is Latin for happiness). Bentham (1748–1832), who was a personal friend of Mill's father and who is widely acknowledged as the godfather of utilitarianism, believed that we should quantify pleasure and pain, and that the right thing to do in any given situation is to calculate which action would generate the most pleasure (or the least pain). The quality of pleasure doesn't really matter. Some people prefer pushpin whereas others fancy poetry, and there is no way to choose between them. James likes driving hot-rods while Lars prefers collecting fine art. Pleasure is entirely in the eye of the beholder—it is subjective— and the more pleasure we accumulate, the happier we become.

However, it has been argued that the central idea of utilitarianism (the maximization of happiness) is mistaken because people are often willing to forego personal pleasures for the sake of some higher cause. For example, as both James and Lars should know, having children requires numerous personal sacrifices. When it comes to balancing pleasure over pain, having children is probably not such a good idea. Yet, we do not put children on this earth for our own enjoyment, and we do not regard the work of parenting as a sacrifice. There must be a different kind of happiness at stake. The loss in pleasure is not a real loss in personal happiness. In fact, the quality of this kind of happiness (the happiness of a family) is infinitely higher than that of drinking beer. (Remember James' "more beer!" sticker on his white Gibson Explorer? If we agree that there is a qualitative difference between different types of happiness, then no amount of beer could ever compensate for the lack of a deeper kind of happiness.)

Mill was one of the first to react against Bentham's crude form of utilitarianism. According to Mill, real happiness requires *activity*, whereas pleasure can be experienced passively. Such passive enjoyment should not be equated with *human* happiness. Animals can

---

[3]   Alternatives to utilitarianism are deontology and virtue ethics. The first focuses on the concept of duty (i.e., doing duty for duty's sake regardless of the consequences), while the second emphasizes the importance of certain attitudes or dispositions.

experience pleasure and pain and it is certainly better to be a satisfied pig than a grumpy swine. But human beings are capable of more than just satisfaction or contentment. We are endowed with reason and insofar as pleasure does not require the use of reason, it is not man's highest good. Hence Mill's phrase: "It is better to be a Socrates dissatisfied, than a fool satisfied."[4] No doubt, fools can have agreeable lives (ignorance is bliss), but no person in his right mind would want to trade his difficult life of contemplation for a lunatic's state of rapture. Sometimes we look enviously at our pets ("Look at sweet adorable Whiskers lying care-free in the sun, purring like he's the happiest cat alive!"), but when we come to think about it, we should admit that however tempting it might seem, we do not want to be reduced to a purring or tail-wagging quadruped.

Robert Nozick (1938–2002), a famous contemporary philosopher, makes a similar point. In his book *Anarchy, State, and Utopia* he discusses the Experience Machine, an imaginary device which, a little like the Matrix, could fulfil all of our desires.[5] Suppose, for example, that you want to experience what it's like to be on stage in front of 60,000 people, or that you want to know what it feels like to play guitar like Kirk Hammett. No problem: you just hook yourself into the machine and it will create the perfect illusion. You will have these experiences just like Kirk has them. Nevertheless, Nozick argues that we would be reluctant to be permanently connected to the Experience Machine. We don't want to be reduced to a mindless blob. Somehow the happiness and the pleasure that we would have in the experience machine would not be earned. Happiness is only worthwhile if there is a possibility of failure, and therefore instantaneous happiness, happiness we don't have to struggle for, loses its appeal. For example, if you could make a person fall in love with you (despite your Metallica t-shirt) by giving her some secret love potion, this love, no matter how pleasurable it would be, would not be real. It would be a farce, even though the victim herself would be entirely convinced of her feelings. Somehow, we want to remain in touch with reality; we want to be active rather than passive, in control rather than under the sway of some external force or device (and *that* is why Neo chooses the red pill instead of the blue in *The Matrix*).

[4] John Stuart Mill, *Utilitarianism*, ed. by Mary Warnock (Oxford: Blackwell, 2003, 188).
[5] Robert Nozick, *Anarchy, State, and Utopia* (New York: Basic Books, 1977).

Real happiness requires autonomy and self-direction. Happiness is not just about pleasurable experiences, but about living your own life and making your own choices. Autonomy has become a key value in contemporary free societies. The state or government should not force you to become happy in any particular way; it should be neutral with regard to your personal conception of the good; and it should refrain from paternalism. The government should not interfere with our liberty of action because this would not only be an offense to our dignity, but it would also be counterproductive. Personal happiness comes in many shapes, and individuals are generally the best judges regarding their own happiness. Although other people can force you to make certain decisions, they cannot make you *endorse* these particular life choices. And since such personal endorsement is a necessary ingredient for human happiness, they should allow you to choose your own way of life.[6] As Mill puts it, a person's "own mode of laying out his existence is the best, not because it is the best in itself, but because it is his own mode" (*OL*, 141).

Hence, Mill proposed his famous *harm principle*:

> The only purpose for which power can be rightfully exercised over any member of a civilized society, against his will, is to prevent harm to others. His own good, either physical or moral, is not a sufficient warrant. He cannot rightfully be compelled to do or forebear because it will be better for him to do so, because it will make him happier, because, in the opinions of others, to do so would be wise, or even right . . . In the part which merely concerns himself, his independence is, of right, absolute. (*OL*, 94–5)

Of course, a lot depends on what counts as "harm to others," but perhaps the principle is most convincing if we interpret "harm" as a commonsense notion. For example, most of us agree that people are not genuinely harmed by the mere fact that their neighbors are gay (although they might say that they are deeply offended by such an "unnatural" lifestyle). Yet, we also agree that society should intervene if one of these homophobes suddenly decides to attack his neighbors. In free societies we agree that people should have a space of

---

[6] Will Kymlicka, *Contemporary Political Philosophy: An Introduction* (Oxford: Oxford University Press, 1990), pp. 199–237.

their own, a private realm in which they can do whatever they want as long as they do not interfere with the similar pursuits of other people. A very unsophisticated version of the harm principle was poignantly proclaimed by the Anti-Nowhere League's charismatic lead singer Animal in the song "So What!" As long as there is no clear harm to others (sheep and goats notwithstanding), no one has the right to tell a person what to do.

At first glance Metallica appears far removed from Mill's conception of happiness. Countless interviews and biographies tell us that the Metalli-boys often engaged in a debauched pursuit of pleasure more akin to the teachings of Bentham than those of Mill. Nonetheless, it is also clear that Metallica is not all about happiness and pleasure. In fact, as a musical genre, metal is not about the celebration of "shiny, happy people." Every day thousands of mothers ask their sons and daughters why the music they listen to is so dark and gloomy. A standard reply to these parental worries is that the world itself is not rosy and cheerful and that good music should reflect this shadow-side as well. As such, metal is about facing facts, and being true to yourself even if the truth is not particularly comforting.

The horror of the caged individual and the importance of choosing your own way of life are prominent themes in Metallica's lyrics. Many of their songs evoke the image of a solitary individual who is swamped, coerced, or indoctrinated by external and often malicious forces. On *Ride the Lightning* there is, of course, the title track ("Who made you God to say / I'll take your life from you!?"), "Escape," and "Trapped Under Ice" ("Wrapped up tight, cannot move, can't break free / Hand of doom has a tight grip on me"). On *Master of Puppets* these themes become truly dominant in the lyrics to the title track, "Welcome Home (Sanitarium)," "Disposable Heroes," "Leper Messiah," and "Damage, Inc." All of these songs depict the gruesome situation of a person who is either forced to do something against his will, or who no longer even has a will of his own, and is reduced to a mere pawn in the hands of others.

Consider especially "Leper Messiah," which describes how people are willingly turned into blind religious followers ("Witchery, weakening / Sees the sheep are gathering / Set the trap, hypnotize / Now you follow"). What annoys Metallica (and especially James) is not the fact that people are religious, but that they mindlessly do whatever they are told. They apparently long for the comfort of conformity: it is a kind of addiction ("Need your Sunday fix"). Mill had exactly the same concern. Religious people might have the right beliefs (although he too was very skeptical of Christianity), but their faith is rendered worthless because they are just "accidentally clinging to words." They hold their beliefs not because they are true, but because it is fashionable or customary to hold them. They just mimic the behavior of others and, as such, it is just "one superstition the more" (*OL*, 114).

The song "Escape" clearly echoes Mill in its conception of happiness. Happiness comes in many ways; true happiness implies individuality; and a person should actively endorse her conception of the good. In fact, the fade-out at the end of the song—"Life's for my own to live my own way"—could be interpreted as a mantra for autonomy and individual freedom. Apart from the element of nonconformity ("Can't get caught in the endless circle / Ring of stupidity"), there is also the idea of finding one's own truth about what makes life worthwhile: "Rape my mind and destroy my feelings / Don't tell me what to do / I don't care now 'cause I'm on my side / And I can see through you / Feed my brain with your so-called standards / Who says that I ain't right? / Break away from your common fashion / See through your blurry sight." Again, Metallica and Mill agree: we should not interfere with a person's pursuit of individual happiness (as long as she does not cause harm to others), and happiness requires individuality as a "necessary ingredient."

Truth: Moving Back Instead of Forward Seems to Me Absurd

To many people who witnessed the rise of Metallica in the 1980s, it must have seemed as if they were just a bunch of angry young men who didn't really care about anything and who were just out there to "maim and kill." They looked like loose canons without guidance or purpose, genuine rebels without cause. But after *Kill 'Em All*, the rebellion and aggression became much more focused as the enemy became more clearly defined. Metallica and its fans were no longer pissed at the entire world; they were specifically pissed at those who manipulated lives and withheld the truth. On subsequent records, from *Ride the Lightning* until . . . *And Justice for All*, Metallica was deeply concerned about various domains in which the common man was wrongfully yet ingeniously deceived. More precisely, they were highly critical of those in power. Metallica depicted the life and fate of soldiers as mere disposable heroes; there were songs about the death penalty, the environment, mental asylums, and nuclear warfare. Eventually, this culminated in Metallica's most socially engaged record to date on the downfall of Lady Justice (aka Doris). A focus on deceit, abuse, and the disregard of truth gradually emerged. Yet this new focus was not a departure from Metallica's original message.

Mill believed that conformity obstructs us in our search for the truth and our quest for progress. Conformity is not only detrimental to personal happiness, it also renders society a "stagnant pool" where the same old ideas are repeated over and over again even though they should have died long ago. Without people who dare to stand out, who dare to be different and eccentric (people like Christ, or Galileo, or Martin Luther King, or Einstein), we lose all chances for progress. Old ideas need to be challenged, to be checked against new findings and new hypotheses. Only if we allow for such criticism will we gradually ascend to the truth. That is why individuality and personal freedom are so important not just for the individual person but also for society at large. To avoid the perilous quagmire we should allow for uninhibited freedom of thought and discussion as well as the freedom of any individual to conduct various "experiments in living."[7]

Admittedly, Mill's primary target was not intentional deceit, but rather the tendency to resist new and challenging ideas that could overthrow existing societal illusions. A song like "And Justice For All," however, directly targets those people who withhold or distort the truth for their own personal gain. Yet it is the individual who is "crushed" by the hammer of justice and whose view of the truth is obscured by the powers that be. Truth no longer seems important ("Seeking no truth / Winning is all"). In "Eye of the Beholder" truth and personal happiness are connected. In fact, the lyrics to that song could be taken as a very brief synopsis of Mill's position in *On Liberty* ("Do you see what I see? / Truth is an offense / You silence for your confidence / Do you hear what I hear? / Doors are slamming

---

[7] Consider the Discharge cover on *Garage Inc.*, "Free Speech for the Dumb."

shut / Limit your imagination, keep you where they must"; "Do you take what I take? / Endurance is the word / Moving back instead of forward seems to me absurd"; "Do you fear what I fear? / Living properly / Truths to you are lies to me / Do you choose what I choose? / More alternatives / Energy derives from both the plus and negative"). The key message is that freedom of speech as we know it is actually a charade and, as such, the lyrics aptly describe the environment of conformity and censorship that Mill so vehemently reacted against.

Conclusion: Trying to Get the Message to You

The message of nonconformity, individuality, and pursuit of truth may have faded into the background with the Black Album,[8] but the message is more relevant today than ever. Nowadays, an attitude of nonconformity has become a part of the whole image-building industry and, as a result, it is just a gimmick to increase sales. It is also a position to which Metallica, due to their massive success, cannot return. Whether we like it or not, they have become mainstream and their nonconformity has been copied time and time again with the distinct purpose of copying their success as well. But with Metallica important values, like a concern for individuality and truth, lurk beneath the surface (values that are totally lacking in the copycats). It's time to revitalize this message, to stir things up a bit, and to remind people of the consequences of the "same song and dance." Because, if indeed "boredom sets into the boring mind," it's about time to bang the head that does not bang.

---

[8] I do not intend to say that this message is completely absent on the post–*Justice* albums—"Through the Never" and "The Unforgiven" being obvious examples—but only that it has became less prominent.

DISC 2

EXISTENSICA: METALLICA MEETS EXISTENTIALISM

CHAPTER 5

THE METAL MILITIA AND THE EXISTENTIALIST CLUB

J. JEREMY WISNEWSKI

When I was a teenager Metallica captured and expressed my exasperation with the world. They rejected normalcy and conformity and tackled topics you simply didn't hear about in the top 40. They had an edge that was not for the meek, defying social expectations and championing individuality. In all of these ways, Metallica was—though I only came to see this years later—an existentialist band.

Existentialism is a philosophical and literary movement that has its roots in nineteenth and twentieth-century Europe. Like most "isms," the term "existentialism" cannot be defined with precision. The root of the word, of course, is "existence"—and a concern for the uniqueness and difficulty of human existence is the central preoccupation of the existentialists. The same can be said of Metallica: the band defies definition, but all of its music deals, in one way or another, with themes central to human life.

And human life *must* be dealt with, if we are to live it. Life is marked by some rather disturbing facts, including the fact that we do not ask to be born. We simply find ourselves living, and are forced to deal with the world as we find it—with, among other things, standards and ideals that are not our own. Much of what we experience is meaningless. We are fundamentally free, though, and this presents us with one grand existential choice: what should we become? If the world has no meaning—if a certain absurdity lurks at its core—how are we to live our lives?

Metallica's songs explore the human condition in an amazingly lucid and intriguing way: the inevitability of death, the ever-presence of absurdity, and the difficulties that accompany our best efforts to be *ourselves*—these are themes that run through all of Metallica's early music. But Metallica does more than simply explore our predicament. The music also demands that we make a decision about how we are to live our lives—about how we will respond to our existential predicament. And it is this, I contend, that makes Metallica an existentialist band.

Kill 'Em All: Welcome to the Absurd

The existentialist Albert Camus (1913–60) famously claimed that the only real philosophical question was whether or not life was worth living, a question Metallica raises again and again. Even posing this question sets one apart from the crowd, for it shows that one will not simply assume that life has a value. For the existentialists, the idea that the world—that life—has some definitive meaning for all time is merely wishful thinking. If we are honest with ourselves, the existentialists contend, we must acknowledge that the world is absurd: that it exists, and that there is no reason for its existence; that it demands to be understood, but that it cannot be.

To add insult to injury (or perhaps injury to insult?), if we do manage to find some meager meaning in this absurd world, it will be wiped away by our deaths—and death is inevitable. So, here is the absurd in a nutshell: we find ourselves existing in a world we did not ask to be in. We are forced to deal with this world—to attempt to find meaning in it. But ultimately it doesn't matter if we do or do not find meaning. We will die all the same.

Thus we are presented with a choice—and no less than our lives ride on our decision. "It is essential to know whether one can live with [the absurd] or whether, on the other hand, logic commands one to die of it."[1] For some, this question is too much. They "fade to black," answering the question of life with suicide. For most, the question is one they try to ignore. The existential choice for most

[1] Albert Camus, *The Myth of Sisyphus* (New York: Vintage Press, 1991), p. 50.

involves conformity to the norms of the world into which they are thrown: they simply accept the meanings they have been told things have. For a remaining few—those not willing to die, and those not content to conform—this is not satisfactory. These others want to *express* themselves in the world—they want to assert their individuality; separate themselves from the herd. They want, in short, to *own* their own lives—to be authentic individuals who *create* meaning in a world they did not ask to be in.

The existentialist *defies* the absurd. To create a meaningful life *despite* life's intrinsic meaninglessness—this is heroic. We must engage life as art—choosing to engage in projects that have no intrinsic value simply because we *can*. In a world bereft of any transcendental meaning, we must *invent* our own meaning. It is the attempt to create meaning in the face of the absurd that dominates Metallica's *Kill 'Em All*.

The seemingly shallow songs on *Kill 'Em All* manage to make a profound existential point—a point about what we are to do in the face of an absurd world. Songs like "Metal Militia" and "Hit the Lights" help us to recognize the plasticity and groundlessness of our everyday actions: one can be a lawyer or a militia member; one can join the establishment or "kick some ass tonight." Whatever one does is unjustifiable. The absurd world offers no guidance. But we will all die, so the choice should be one that expresses individuality.

Many of the songs on *Kill 'Em All* do just that: they express a form of life—one that the members (and fans) of early Metallica chose. This existential choice involves rejecting the common standards of what one ought to do with one's life. The power of the paycheck is abandoned in favor of a synergy between band and audience ("When our fans start screaming / It's right well alright," "Late at night all systems go / You have come to see the show / We do our best You're the rest / You make it real you know"). A life of creature comforts is traded in for a life of energy and adrenaline ("Life in the fast lane is just how it seems / It's hard and it is heavy dirty and mean / Motorbreath / It's how I live my life / I can't take it any other way"). The normal activities we engage in (activities like seeing movies, watching television, and so on), are abandoned for activities that defy social expectations ("We are scanning the scene in the city tonite / We are looking for you / to start up a fight").

What initially appears shallow is just as deep as any other activity we might engage in. The world offers no definitive meaning. Our response to this absurdity can be to do what everyone else does, or it can be to express ourselves in the world. The way we respond to the absurd is *the* central existential issue. Metallica's *Kill 'Em All* offers an option other than suicide: where there was no meaning, we will create meaning. We will respond to the absurd by making our lives truly expressive of what we care about—and we will do this *despite* the absurd. The only justification for this form of life is simply *that we choose it*. "Now is the time to let it rip / to let it fuckin' loose / we are gathered here to maim and kill / 'cause this is what we choose."

Ride the Lightning: An Existentialist Anthem

A recurrent theme in all of Metallica's early music—but particularly *Ride the Lightning*—is the inevitability of death. The songs on *Ride the Lightning* serve an existential point: they reveal human finitude, the fact that human lives inevitably come to an end. The uniqueness of each individual's death serves to distinguish one human being from another. The philosopher Martin Heidegger (1889–1976) contends that death is the only thing that human beings must do alone. Because of this, death individuates particular persons. When I see that only I can die my death, Heidegger maintains, I recognize that I am fundamentally different from you. Our impending death forces us to see that we are individuals—that our existence cannot be reduced to the existence of the crowd.

Living *in spite* of the fact that one cannot escape death is one existential response to the absurd. Metallica's *Ride the Lightning* presents us with several possible deaths: nuclear holocaust ("Fight Fire with Fire"), execution by electrocution ("Ride the Lightning"), war ("For Whom the Bell Tolls"), suicide ("Fade to Black"), and plague ("Creeping Death"). But the album doesn't only present the *inevitability* of our eventual annihilation. Amid songs of demise, we find a celebration of our individual freedom—or, at a minimum, the chance we each have to find such freedom. To assert one's individuality when death lurks around every corner is a mark of existentialist thinking. Although death might well be inevitable, and life itself might have no meaning, our lives are still *ours* to do with what we will. This belief is captured in the existentialist anthem "Escape." The chorus of that song, "Out for my own, out to be free / One with my mind, they just can't see / No need to hear things that they say / Life is for my own to live my own way" is a testament to the value of individuality, despite the ever-present prospect of death.

But the "escape" of "Escape" is not an escape from death. There is no escape from death. It *is* an escape from a world that is not of one's own making. To choose life *despite* death and the absurd—to give meaning to one's own life simply because one can—this is the way of the existentialist. And "Escape" advocates precisely this: we must escape from the view of the world we have inherited. ("Feed my brain with your so-called standards / Who says that I ain't right?") We must create *our own* standards; live our own way ("Break away from your common fashion")—and in doing so, we must recognize that the common understanding of things most people have is *not* the correct one ("See through your blurry sight"). Doing this, however, is incredibly difficult—it can be thwarted at any moment.

Master of Puppets: An Existential Lesson on the Difficulties of Authenticity

Metallica's *Master of Puppets* examines, in brilliant detail, the ways in which our attempts to be individuals can be thwarted by the world— by other people, random events, and even our own actions. "Battery" depicts the way in which animal instincts can overpower us—how our destructive urges can actually take control of our lives ("Smashing through the boundaries / Lunacy has found me / Cannot stop the battery"). Even our attempts to deal with our violent impulses ("Pounding out aggression") can overtake us ("Turns into obsession").

But our animal nature is by no means the only thing that stands in the way of owning our own lives and expressing those lives freely in the world. Our own *choices* can lead us away from our freedom. Addiction—the end result of a series of choices—comes to impede our ability to *make* choices. ("Taste me you will see / More is all you need / You're dedicated to / How I'm killing you.") This is one of the painful existential lessons of *Master of Puppets*: our freedom is to be prized, but it cannot be taken for granted. One must *work* to remain free—and hence to remain fully human. We are, after all, only what we make of ourselves.

Even when we master our urges the world itself can make freedom difficult. Our obstacles are usually all-too-human. Social institutions (like insane asylums, the military, and religion) exert immense control over our options, and in some cases, even our actions. We are beaten into the status quo by common notions of what is "normal" ("Sanitarium"). We become lost in the anonymous machinery of institutions—swallowed by the roles we must play ("Disposable Heroes"). We are surrounded by messages compelling us to believe in a particular way—and we are seduced by such trickery ("Leper Messiah").

Jean-Paul Sartre (1905–80), perhaps the most famous of the existentialists, was well aware of the dangers the social world posed for authenticity (for living a life that is truly one's own). He recognized, in much the way *Master of Puppets* does, that we have a tendency to flee from our freedom, to cover it up with excuses. We do this, Sartre contends, because we are totally responsible for every aspect of our lives, and we cannot bear this responsibility. To lose sight of our total responsibility for ourselves is to fall into what Sartre calls "bad faith," a form of self-deception in which we reduce ourselves to mere things. We attempt to view ourselves (or others) as mere objects without any choice, rather than as beings who are totally free, and hence totally responsible, for who we are. "Man is nothing else but what he makes of himself."[2]

To call someone "insane" is, for Sartre, an instance of bad faith. We are what we have chosen to be. Being "labeled mentally deranged" is just that: a label. We are complicated creatures, and we cannot be reduced to one trait, or set of traits. Likewise, we are far more than any particular role that we happen to occupy. The waiter is more than a waiter, James Hetfield is more than a member of Metallica, a soldier is more than a body in the front line. "Playing soldier" is as much an instance of bad faith as is "assuring me that I'm insane." When we attempt to mold persons into particular roles ("Soldier boy,

---

[2] Sartre, *Existentialism and Human Emotions* (Secaucus and Toronto: Citadel Press, 1984), p. 15. Further references to this book are given parenthetically in the body of the chapter as references to Sartre with page numbers.

made of clay / Now an empty shell") and control their every action ("You will do what I say, when I say"), we are missing something essential about the human condition: to be human, the existentialist contends, is to be free. As Sartre bluntly puts it, "man is freedom."

Authenticity involves, among other things, avoiding bad faith—at least to the extent that this is possible. Authenticity involves seeing ourselves for what we are: free beings totally responsible for ourselves. It also involves recognizing the world for what it is: absurd, without permanent meaning. Authenticity thus precludes simply following others in our thinking about the world. Metallica is right in claiming that such blind devotion rots the brain ("Leper Messiah"). Importantly, however, this does *not* mean that one cannot believe particular things. There's no formula here. We will believe what we choose to believe—and we are utterly free to believe anything at all. If we are authentic, however, our beliefs will be truly *ours*—we will not simply latch on to some hero; we will not "join the endless chain / Taken by his glamour."

One might thus choose even a life of violence, or a life of religion, or a life in thrash metal. What is crucial is that the choices one makes are really one's own choices, and not simply conformity to some social norm. For the existentialist, the authentic life—even if it is incredibly difficult, or perhaps even fatal—is preferable to the inauthentic life. It is preferable only because truth is preferable to falsehood. In "Damage, Inc." Metallica provides us with just this Either/Or: "Living on your knees, conformity / Or dying on your feet for honesty."

Damage, Inc.: Troubling Choices

The choice advocated—to die for honesty—is obvious, but also troubling. The choice made in "Damage, Inc." seems to be one of violent retaliation: "Inbred, our bodies work as one / Bloody, but never cry submission / Following our instinct not a trend / Go against the grain until the end." The choice here is to lash out—against common expectations, but also against persons.

It is tempting to say that the choice made here is morally suspect, but this would be just another instance of bad faith. The only morality is the one we decide to have. There is no "eternal morality" that can guide us in our actions. There is only choice. If our choice is an honest one—if we make it authentically—there is little that can (objectively) be said against it. The persona behind the song (perhaps Hetfield, perhaps an imaginary narrator) seems to acknowledge precisely this: "Honesty is my only excuse / Try to rob us of it, but it's no use / Steamroller action crushing all / Victim is your name and you shall fall."

In the face of absurdity, we make choices. These choices are incredibly difficult, because there is no objective standard by which we can make them. This leads most people to flee from authenticity: the weight of responsibility is too great. To be authentic is to choose your own life, and to take utter and total responsibility for your life—and this is a terribly troubling prospect.

This troubling prospect makes *anguish* a central concept to the existentialist. We must choose, but we have no guidelines. Sartre thus claims "we are condemned to be free." To recognize the human predicament is to face this condemnation. After recognizing the ways in which the world pulls us away from authenticity and offers us stories about how we ought to behave—after it supplies us with ready-made roles we can use to define ourselves—few have the courage to simply embrace a choice as *their* choice. Few can say, with Metallica, "Fuck it all and fucking no regrets," though most can see why, in an existential predicament such as our own, there are "never happy endings on these dark sets."

. . . *And Justice for All*: A Note on Alternate Choices

But we can make other choices, too. Importantly, authenticity requires no particular beliefs, nor does it require rejecting particular beliefs. It only requires that *what* you believe is truly your own. Anguish and violence are not the only destinations of existentialist thinking—though they are certainly among the possibilities. Sartre was famously active in many social causes (he wrote a book criticizing US involvement in Vietnam, for example). So a recognition of the absurd, and the inevitability of our own death, need not relegate our lives to utter and total despair; nor need it make us violently anti-social.

Many of the songs on Metallica's . . . *And Justice for All* raise issues that are well beyond the violent retaliation of "Damage, Inc." Concerns about the environment ("Blackened"), corruption (". . . And Justice for All"), and blacklisting and discrimination ("Shortest Straw") are the order of the day—and these concerns are emphasized *with* traditional existential themes, not *instead* of them. Death still lurks around every corner, as do worries about the ways in which institutions lead us to live inauthentic lives.

Concern for individuality and authenticity is forcefully presented in "Eye of the Beholder," where we are pushed to examine the value of freedom: "Do you need what I need? / Boundaries overthrown / Look inside, to each his own." The questions in "Eye of the Beholder" are directed to the *listener*—and they are relentlessly posed. "Do you want what I want? / Desire not a thing / I hunger after independence, lengthen freedom's ring." With each question, we are asked where we stand as individuals. We are then told where the persona behind the song (perhaps Hetfield) stands. The emphasis is on authenticity.

Our existential predicament can just as easily lead us to confront social problems as it can lead us into rage and despair. Let me make this point one last time: there simply is no formula for dealing with the absurd. One must choose. There is nothing more and nothing less involved in the human condition.

Metallica's music lets us explore this condition in all of its horrid splendor. But beyond this, Metallica demands that we confront the human predicament, and make our lives our own. For this reason, we can unequivocally call Metallica an existentialist band.

A Concluding Thought: Did Metallica Sell Out?

When the Black Album was released in 1991, there were many disgruntled fans. The album wasn't like the ones that came before it, as so many of us desperately wanted it to be. Metallica had "sold out," people said. Hell, I might have said it myself.

But these accusations had been made before. "Fade to Black" and "Escape" were cited as evidence of "selling out" when *Ride the Lightning* was released. Many of us thus hoped that the post-Black

Album music would be a return to Metallica's thrashy roots. Whatever hope we had for such a return "faded to black" with *Load/Reload*. The accusations of selling out were voiced more loudly than before and by more people. Many of those who had insisted that the Black Album was *not* selling out no longer had anything to say in Metallica's defense.

But if we take seriously the idea that Metallica is an existentialist band, the idea of selling out ceases to make sense. There is no predefined standard for what one should do. To claim that Metallica has sold out is an instance of bad faith. It presumes that there is some set content to being authentic, when there is no such content. The world is absurd. When Metallica made the Black Album, heavy metal *itself* had gone mainstream. Given this, perhaps the *truly* authentic thing to do was to change the kind of music being played—to break away, once again, from the crowd.

This final point can be captured (I hope) in a joke: if the founding member of an existentialist club put up a poster, the motto would have to be: "If you join us, you're not one of us." Breaking away from thrash metal as it gained in popularity—a popularity for which Metallica itself bears a large share of responsibility—is yet more evidence for the view that Metallica is an existentialist band.

CHAPTER 6

THE STRUGGLE WITHIN
Hetfield, Kierkegaard, and the Pursuit of Authenticity

PHILIP LINDHOLM

"Reaching out for something you've got to feel / while clutching to what you had thought was real." So begins Metallica's "The Struggle Within," which poetically expresses the pursuit of authenticity described by Danish thinker Søren Kierkegaard (1813–55). The world wants to control your life by making you objectively detached from who you are and who you are meant to become. But, says Kierkegaard, another way is discovered in reaching out for something you have to feel, the way of being true to yourself, the way of authenticity. To become authentic is to passionately embrace your sense of self despite living in a world that speciously lures its inhabitants away from subjectivity and honest introspection, both of which are recurring motifs in Metallica's music.

After the "New blood joins this earth" and enters into a "fight he cannot win" in "The Unforgiven," he endures everything from the Darwinism of "No Remorse," where "only the strong survive," to the desperation of "To Live is to Die" in which the narrator asks: "Cannot the Kingdom of Salvation / take me home?" At times, we do glimpse the acceptance of responsibility for our own lives ("Nothing Else Matters"), but it often reverts back to the self-deception typified in "Holier than Thou" where "you lie so much you believe yourself / judge not lest ye be judged yourself," echoing the Gospel of Matthew (7:1).

The path to authenticity is an arduous journey, but one absolutely necessary for a life well lived. We may initially empathize with "The Invisible Kid" who is "Locked away in his brain" and bellows "I hide inside / I hurt inside / I hide inside," but even he was able to finally declare: "I'm being right here, right now." Such is our existential task.

"One" Before God

Kierkegaard is often called the Father of Existentialism, a school of philosophical thought addressing what it means to exist, to encounter and exercise freedom and, perhaps most of all, to make choices. Though existentialism has taken many forms since Kierkegaard, especially with respect to its vastly different theistic and non-theistic formulations, it remains focused upon concrete existence and its implications for arriving at "knowledge" and "truth."

For Kierkegaard, there are two types of truth: objective truth, which concerns subjects like mathematics and logic, and subjective truth, which regards ethical and religious issues. Objective truth can be understood logically by abstracting from a particular thing in order to make a general claim. By contrast, subjective truth is only comprehended through the inward passion of each particular individual, who must inquire through the first person. After all, subjective truth pertains to ethical and religious concerns, which cannot be pursued with a detached third-person perspective. Why? Because ethico-religious truth "is related essentially to existence,"[1] and it is precisely existence to which the objective third-person view is indifferent.

---

[1] Søren Kierkegaard, *Concluding Unscientific Postscript*, trans. Howard V. Hong and Edna V. Hong (Princeton: Princeton University Press, 1992), fn. 199. Further references to this book are given parenthetically in the body of the chapter as references to *Postscript* with page numbers. Kierkegaard attributes this work, like many others, to a pseudonym, but, at the risk of misrepresentation, ideas in this essay will nevertheless be attributed to Kierkegaard himself.

Metallica's "One" offers a profound lyrical meditation on human existence. Wavering between the worlds of dream and reality, the soldier can only discern that "nothing is real but pain now," and begins to truly face the harshness of his own mortality. First, he thinks "Look to the time when I'll live," but then decides to "Hold my breath as I wish for death," which is prompted by his state of dependency as one "Tied to machines that make me be." The soldier knows that he is no longer in control of his life and reflects "I cannot live / I cannot die." The war is through with him; he is now living as just a "wartime novelty," which, to him, is to not live at all. Thus, he pleads "Cut this life off from me." There is no more war or world for this soldier. There is only the singularity of his existence and its potential annihilation. In this way, he declares: "The world is gone I'm just one . . . oh please God help me."

The soldier in "One" who cries out for God's help exemplifies the move towards subjectivity outlined by Kierkegaard. The point of life is to become a "subjective existing individual" who opposes the herd mentality of society by recognizing that, before God, we are all individuals. The truth of the individual is antithetical to the "untruth" of "the crowd," and, for Kierkegaard, the most exemplary individual of all was Jesus Christ who "was crucified because he would not have anything to do with the crowd."[2] Jesus was an individual unwilling to compromise individuality all the way to the cross.

So harmful is the crowd to individuality that Kierkegaard asserts: "the thesis that 'the public, the crowd, is untruth' is a thesis of Christianity; in every generation where this thesis is not fought through to the finish, in every such generation Christianity does not actually exist" (*Journals*, 3.326). Left unchecked, the existence of the crowd necessarily entails the absence of Christianity, because the sense of distinct selfhood is lost. Therefore, the highest possible task for the Christian, and indeed for every individual, is to become a true individual before God.

---

[2] Søren Kierkegaard, *Søren Kierkegaard's Journals and Papers*, trans. Howard V. Hong and Edna V. Hong (Bloomington: Indiana University Press, 1967–8), 3.308. Further references to this book are given parenthetically in the body of the chapter as references to *Journals* with page numbers.

Lars isn't the only hard-hitter from Denmark. Kierkegaard's discussion of the individual is a harsh condemnation of his Danish contemporaries who, he claims, are "accustomed to being Christians and being called Christians as a matter of course" (*Postscript*, 588). They want to define Christianity objectively by saying "A Christian is one who accepts Christianity's doctrine" (*Postscript*, 607), but such an approach disregards the difficulty and importance of *being* a Christian.

To be sure, Hetfield is not advocating that his audience become Christians in "One." He does, though, communicate the difficulty and importance of reflecting upon existence as an individual, and moreover of being reconciled to the inevitable death to come. Kierkegaard considers such self-reflection to be a vital prerequisite to becoming an authentic individual, to becoming a Christian, since it is a move toward subjectivity.

The Struggle Within

Kierkegaard's most (in)famous claim is that "subjectivity is truth" (*Postscript*, 343). Many commentators have interpreted this as a rejection of objective truth, but he is actually making the dual argument that (1) subjective truth is most important and (2) one must come to know it subjectively. Trying to live objectively makes life a parody and people mere shadows of their true selves, like those "pale deaths which men miscall their lives." To live is to live passionately, and so frustrated is the narrator of "To Live is to Die" with those who imitate life that he declares: "All this I cannot bear / to witness any longer." We must never settle for just going through the motions as one refusing to feel. Rather, we are called to go "twisting / turning / through the never" in "pursuit of truth no matter where it lies." We are called to the struggle within.

While "The Struggle Within" will never rival the popularity of "Enter Sandman" or "Nothing Else Matters," it nicely displays Hetfield's preoccupation with existential angst and the difficulty of facing one's own demons. The song begins almost encouragingly with "so many things you don't want to do / What is it? What have you got to lose?" but suddenly turns on its vulnerable victim with "What the hell /

What is it you think you're gonna find? / Hypocrite." Part of the lyrical draw here is the ambiguity. Who is Hetfield accusing? Who is the "hypocrite" acting without thinking and constantly engaging in self-deception? Is it James himself? Is it the world?

In all likelihood it is both. Hetfield often walks the fine line between self-deprecation and judgment of a world that refuses to listen. In this way, "The Struggle Within" is a struggle Hetfield shares with all of humanity in which "home is not a home it becomes a hell ... you struggle inside your hell." We all have internal demons to which we can *either* give in ("struggle within you seal your own coffin") *or* overcome ("struggle within the struggling within"). The choice is ours, but it is a choice we must make.

The necessity of choice is a recurring theme with Kierkegaard, and particularly in his early work *Either/Or*. For Kierkegaard, and existentialism more generally, an essential distinction of humanity is its ability to choose. Each individual has the freedom to become authentic through choice, since to choose is ultimately to choose oneself, to embrace one's own potential as a free human being. In so doing, one becomes an authentic individual who has taken on responsibility for his or her own life. Unfortunately, though, people continually refuse to choose a life of choice, and thereby lose their identity; "choice itself is crucial for the content of the personality: through the choice the personality submerges itself in that which is being chosen, and when it does not choose, it withers away in atrophy" (*Either/Or*, 163).[3]

Most people would think that the importance of choice lies in its object, as in choosing good over evil. However, in *Either/Or*, Kierkegaard emphasizes not as much the object, but the manner of choice: "I may very well say that what is important in choosing is not so much to choose the right thing as the energy, the earnestness, and the pathos with which one chooses" (*Either/Or*, 167). To choose is to choose with passion—the former necessitates the latter—which means that choice must always bear a sense of personal meaning.

---

[3] Søren Kierkegaard, *Either/Or*, Vol. 2, trans. Howard V. Hong and Edna V. Hong (Princeton: Princeton University Press, 1988), p. 163. Further references to this book are given parenthetically in the body of the chapter as references to *Either/Or* with page numbers.

Kierkegaard's goal as an author is to "bring you to the point where this choice truly has meaning for you. It is on this that everything turns. As soon as a person can be brought to stand at the crossroads in such a way that there is no way out for him except to choose, he will choose the right thing" (*Either/Or*, 168). The most important thing for "the struggle within" is to choose *either* to succumb to internal demons *or* to conquer them. To deny the issue, to choose not to choose, would be to embrace an inauthentic existence replete with self-deception.

The most challenging aspect of choice is its ability to isolate the chooser. As we are told in *Either/Or*, "In the moment of choice, [the chooser] is in complete isolation, for he withdraws from his social milieu, and yet at the same moment he is in absolute continuity, for he chooses himself as a product" (*Either/Or*, 251). One cannot choose (oneself) in general, but only as a solitary and concrete individual, which makes the path to authenticity all the more painful. One must go it alone and understand that, as in "Fade to Black," even if I am "Getting lost within myself . . . No one but me can save myself." This willingness to accept personal responsibility characterizes the James Hetfield of today.

Wherever James May Roam

For most of its existence, Metallica has been led by a front man who, though dominating on the stage, remained reticent in the interview. As journalist and author Joel McIver recounts, "Anyone who has seen Hetfield interviewed (the measured tones; the shy, almost reserved manner; the storm clouds which lower on his brow if he is asked a question not to his liking) knows that his emotions are held back, deep inside."[4] James' mystique generally derives from his juxtaposition of temerity with timidity. Particularly in the early days of "Alcoholica," Hetfield was known as a party animal who deeply rejected personal intimacy, even with his own band members. As

---

[4] Joel McIver, *Justice for All: The Truth About Metallica* (London: Omnibus, 2004), p. 310. Further references to this book are given parenthetically in the body of the chapter as references to *Justice* with page numbers.

Dave Mustaine recounted in recent catch-up sessions with Lars, Hetfield was always hard to get close to.[5]

Things have changed, though, since James admitted himself to rehab in 2001. Regarding the filming of *Some Kind of Monster*, Hetfield offers a sobering account of his "pre-hab" days:

> A lot of this stems from me not being honest with myself for a long time and not wanting to stand up and express what I'm feeling or rock the boat and look like an asshole. I definitely want to do this [documentary]. I think this film is important. There are messages in it that are helpful to people. But when Lars talks about Metallica as a different person that scares me. Metallica is three individuals and three individuals have to decide what to do. I'm pretty tired of putting the band first instead of our personal feelings. (*Metallica*, 145–6)

Monster revealed a vastly different Hetfield than the one to which fans were accustomed. The scruffy rock-star beard is gone, thick-rimmed glasses adorn his face, and a deep sense of maturity continually shines through.

James has indicated that many of his demons are rooted in childhood abandonment issues. Hetfield's parents went through divorce proceedings during ages twelve and thirteen and his mother died when he was sixteen, which led him to seek refuge in music. While involvement in the scene offered a modicum of relief, it also exacerbated his tendency to withdraw. As James recounted after going to rehab, "I felt that I couldn't show any weakness. For me, I was James Hetfield of Metallica rather than just James Hetfield. And I was trying to live that lifestyle at home; I was trying to wear that mask all the time. And it's amazing how long you can wear a mask for" (*Justice*, 323). James was living the very inauthentic existence that Kierkegaard derides, and yet his lyrics championed the quest for authenticity.

One need only consider "The God that Failed" and "Until it Sleeps" to hear Hetfield express in music what he could not in conversation. "The God that Failed" was written as an outcry against the death of his mother, and "Until it Sleeps" is a rage following the death of

---

[5] Joe Berlinger with Greg Milner, *Metallica: This Monster Lives* (London: Robson Press, 2005), p. 124. Further references to this book are given parenthetically in the body of the chapter as references to *Metallica* with page numbers.

his father. Both parents refused to accept medical assistance for their ailments, which left James in 1991 to indict "the healing hand held back by the deepened nail" and then to ask in 1996, "where do I take this pain of mine? / I run, but it stays right by my side."[6]

It was not until walking out of rehearsals for *St. Anger* and entering rehab that James would finally force himself to find expression apart from music. Only then could he bring himself to tell Lars, in front of Kirk and an entire production team, "I really, deep down, feel sometimes that it's just . . . that there's some empty . . . just an ugly feeling inside" (*Metallica*, 157). This newfound capability for honest self-reflection demonstrates a definitive move towards authenticity. James has taken responsibility for his life by refusing to hide any longer behind a contrived persona, by removing the mask he once wore and accepting the introspection to which Kierkegaard calls us all. Rather than being consumed by who he is, Hetfield has chosen to pursue the individual he wishes to become.

James's existential journey has brought him a long way from the suicidal spirals of "Fade to Black" and "One." As McIver reflects: "The idea of escaping existential horrors through voluntarily ending one's own life is clearly one that had intrigued James over the years" (*Justice*, 144). But Hetfield no longer flees from internal crises; he *chooses* to confront them, and can now honestly proclaim "by myself but not alone / I ask no one." He has fled the Kierkegaardian "crowd" and sought authenticity.

Kierkegaard laments that "The world has perhaps always had a lack of what could be called authentic individualities, decisive subjectivities, those artistically permeated with reflection" (*Postscript*, 66).

---

[6] In an interview with *Playboy*, James recounted his difficulty with being a Christian Scientist as a child: "I was raised as a Christian Scientist, which is a strange religion. The main rule is, God will fix everything. Your body is just a shell, you don't need doctors. It was alienating and hard to understand. I couldn't get a physical to play football. It was weird having to leave health class during school, and all the kids saying, 'Why do you have to leave? Are you some kind of freak?' As a kid, you want to be part of the team. They're always whispering about you and thinking you're weird. That was upsetting. My dad taught Sunday school—he was into it. It was pretty much forced upon me. We had these little testimonials, and there was a girl that had her arm broken. She stood up and said, 'I broke my arm but now, look, it's all better.' But it was just, like, mangled. Now that I think about it, it was pretty disturbing." Quoted in *Justice*, 10.

Perhaps Hetfield has added one authentic individuality to the world's spare few, and, wherever he may roam, may others follow in the pursuit of honest self-reflection. Insofar as James is successful in motivating the masses, he will remain forever linked to two Danes, a drummer and a philosopher, together pounding out the message to confront "the struggle within."

METALLICA, NIETZSCHE, AND MARX

The Immorality of Morality

PETER S. FOSL

> Those who can make you believe absurdities can make you commit atrocities.
>
> Voltaire

In songs like "Leper Messiah" and "The God that Failed," Metallica charges religion with moral failure and in this way connects itself with a tradition in philosophy stretching back through thinkers like Voltaire, Hume, Lucretius, Socrates, and Xenophanes. According to these philosophers, what religions prescribe as morally "good" is actually morally bad or wrong. What religions claim to be "righteous" is instead corrupt. What they portray as "pious" is in fact perverse. What they present as "truth" is in reality deceit. Since religion has had such a wide effect on common ideas about morality in our society, what passes for sound morality across society generally is more often a putrid tangle of immorality.[1]

---

[1] Thus Metallica and their philosophical predecessors offer a moral critique of religion. Other philosophical critiques of religion are rooted in epistemology, metaphysics, and the philosophy of language. Epistemological critiques leverage their criticisms on an examination of the possibilities of acquiring knowledge about religious matters, typically arguing that one can't really "know" the sorts of things that the faithful claim to know. Metaphysical critiques hinge on ideas about what's "real" and might possibly be real, often maintaining that religious claims about divine reality are somehow flawed—that entities of the sort described by religion don't exist or can't exist. Critiques drawing on ideas from the philosophy of language address what it's possible and not possible to speak of meaningfully. They argue that religious language is literally meaningless, or at least not meaningful in the way the faithful think.

Morality and Power

One of the most important critiques of Christian morality was developed by German philosopher Friedrich Nietzsche (1844–1900). In books like *Beyond Good and Evil* (1886), *The Genealogy of Morals* (1887), and *Twilight of the Idols* (1888), Nietzsche describes the way Christian morality presents a pathological doctrine, one that ultimately weakens people, tearing down their minds, bodies, and cultures.

In a manner not terribly different from the way Metallica's James Hetfield describes it, Nietzsche depicts Christianity as a "slave morality." Originating among the members of a relatively insignificant ethnic group living under the heel of Roman rule, Christian morality found its origins in a sentiment both puny and dishonorable—"resentment" (*ressentiment*). Resenting Roman power, members of the Jesus movement argued that it's really the meek that are blessed. Resenting Roman wealth, they praised poverty and simplicity. In the face of Roman pride, Christians promoted humility. Against Roman military might, they deployed peacemaking. Since the Romans ruled this world, Christians concocted a better, truer kingdom in another world, a transcendent world beyond this one, beyond Rome.

But it wasn't enough for early Christians simply to defy Roman rule. They also produced their own distinctive way of ruling, of exerting power over others. Perhaps the most effective way Christians exerted power was by collecting the faithful into a docile "herd" through the idea that we all carry an internal debt called "sin."[2] Having convinced people of this, Christian priests proclaimed that they alone could forgive the debt, that only through the authority of their religion could human beings find consolation and salvation (John 14:6, 10:9). It was a wildly successful technique.

Aside from Nietzsche's, perhaps the most influential critique of religion was articulated by Karl Marx (1818–83). While it would be wrong to characterize Metallica as a Marxist band, there are elements of Metallica's critique that overlap with Marx's. Writing in

---

[2]   Friedrich Nietzsche, *Genealogy of Morals* in *Basic Writings of Nietzsche*, ed. and trans. by Walter Kaufmann (New York: Modern Library, 1968), §20.

the year of Nietzsche's birth, Marx famously described religion as the "opium of the people."[3] This opium, says Marx, deadens people, submerging them in a stupor that renders them unable to think clearly or resist effectively the exploitation to which they're subjected. Metallica is certainly no stranger to this insight.

Hetfield's lyrics in, for example, "Leper Messiah" describe religion alternatively as a "disease," an addictive drug, a form of mind control, and an instrument of power.[4] In an especially rich and compressed lyric, Metallica weaves together Nietzschean and Marxian themes into an evocative bundle: "Marvel at his tricks, need your Sunday fix. / Blind devotion came, rotting your brain. / Chain, chain / Join the endless chain, taken by his glamour / Fame, Fame / Infection is the game, stinking drunk with power. / We see." The song also depicts the way Christianity weakens people and gathers them into an obedient herd: "Witchery, weakening / Sees the sheep are gathering / Set the trap, hypnotize / Now you follow. / [Chorus] / Lie." "Holier than Thou" announces a kind of solidarity with the working class and threatens (religious? revolutionary?) judgment in response to the way things posing as "sacred" and "just" commonly cloak privilege and exploitation. "It's not who you are, it's who you know / Others lives are the basis of your own / Burn your bridges build them back with wealth / Judge not lest ye be judged yourself." "And Justice for All" expresses a more impotent and defeated sentiment, but nevertheless an understanding of how things really work: "Halls of justice painted green / Money talking / Power wolves beset your door / Hear them stalking / Soon you'll please their appetite / They devour / Hammer of justice crushes you / Overpower."

For all its apparent defeatism, however, there is perhaps a kind of ambiguity in that last line, "overpower"—a call to the oppressed to rise up and overpower the forces that are crushing them. But, if revolutionary inspiration's what you're after, these few half-submerged suggestions offer a pretty thin reed to cling to.

---

[3] Karl Marx, *Contributions to a Critique of Hegel's Philosophy of Right* [1844] in *The Portable Karl Marx*, ed. by Eugene Kamenka (London: Penguin, 1983).
[4] The figure of the "leper messiah" reaches back into ancient Hebrew mythology, perhaps rooted in Isaiah 53. David Bowie draws upon the image in "Ziggy Stardust" and, of course, Bowie's song "Fame" resonates here, as well.

Indeed, on balance Metallica does seem more pessimistic than Nietzsche or Marx. Their songs often seem preoccupied with the failure of religion and the failure of attempts to resist it. Perhaps this is because Metallica writes more than a century after its German predecessors, at a time when the hopes and expectations of a revolution against the religious, economic, and political institutions that dominate our contemporary world have been largely discredited or forgotten. Since both religion and revolution seem to have failed, Metallica finds itself, like so many others today, awash in despair.

The pitiful figure depicted in "One," for example, can find no comfort in religion. Left blind, deaf, mute, and without limbs through the effects of a landmine, the disconsolate veteran speaks to us now after having been used up and cast aside by his exploitive rulers. "Nothing is real but pain now," he declares. Pleading for death, he beseeches God for release, even the release of annihilation. But God brings no consolation to the abandoned soldier—just as God failed to bring consolation to James Hetfield at age thirteen when his father left the family and at age sixteen when his devout Christian Scientist mother died of cancer. This disposable hero's only reward is isolation, "hell." The oppressive forces of society (represented in "God that Failed" by the Romans who successfully nailed God to the cross and killed him) seem to have won. "Broken is the promise, betrayal / The healing hand held back by the deepened nail."

Metallica and Rebellion

But, perhaps, if we just dig a bit deeper through the provocative layers of meaning in Metallica's songs, something more than defeatism and despair can be unearthed. "The Four Horsemen" is a good place to dig. From a Christian point of view, the four horsemen of the Apocalypse (Revelation 6:1–17) are instruments of God's justice: "So gather round young warriors now / And saddle up your steeds / Killing scores with demon swords / Now is the death of doers of wrong / Swing the judgment hammer down / Safely inside armor, blood, guts, and sweat." These lyrics on their surface seem to affirm the Christian point of view, calling young men (like so much of

Metallica's work, it is male-centered) to join in striking down the wrongdoers whom God has come to judge and punish.

But, looking deeper, one finds a more subversive suggestion here. Who are the true "doers of wrong," anyway? The lyrics give us a clue in describing the horsemen as those who threaten wives and children. A more telling implication surfaces when we consider why the young warriors wield "demon swords." Mustn't they be fighting with the demons? Perhaps they are the demons?

If the horsemen are the real enemy, there can be no hope, of course, in opposing them. Ultimately, the horsemen must win. And so it seems as though defeatism permeates even the deeper layers of the song, the same sort of defeatism we find in "Phantom Lord": "Victims falling under chains / You hear them crying dying pains / The fists of terrors breaking through / Now there's nothing you can do."

But whether or not the resistance must ultimately succumb, it's important to acknowledge that "The Four Horsemen" does call for resistance. For many rebels, there's dignity in resistance, even if it offers only temporary freedom. In the phrase attributed to Mexican revolutionary Emilio Zapata: "It's better to die on your feet than live on your knees."

In fact, "The Four Horsemen" deploys a number of common heavy metal tropes to advance a message of defiant freedom. The inversion of standard ideas of good and evil, the use of demonic perspectives, and blasphemy as a form of rebellion all serve as devices to loosen the grip of Christian authority. In short, in order to subvert it, metal bands confront Christian power with its own worst nightmare.

Demonic tropes announce a defiant freedom from Christianity's control. They proclaim the successful establishment of a life beyond its reach, the achievement of a space where people don't fear Christianity—its terrifying threats of damnation, its cruel judgment, or its retribution for disobedience. Striking back at the Christian regime with dark, offensive imagery makes freedom incarnate. But how deep does this line of resistance really run in Metallica?

Metallica's inversion of good and evil in "The Four Horsemen" presents an example of what Nietzsche called a "transvaluation of all values," dismantling Christian anti-life traditions and replacing them with something life-affirming. But to what extent has Metallica really achieved a Nietzschean transvaluation? Does Metallica suffer what Nietzsche called "incomplete nihilism" (the attempt to escape

Christianity without fully transvaluing its values)?[5] Is Metallica, at the end of the day, just a Christian rock band?

Metallica, Nihilism, and Nostalgia

Nihilism, which derives from the Latin word *nihil*, for "nothing," may be defined as a cultural condition where people can't value anything, where nothing seems really right or wrong, good or bad, beautiful or ugly—where neither life nor death, neither action nor inaction seems to matter. Christianity, according to Nietzsche, actually produces nihilism. Here's how.

First, Christianity devalues the world in which we actually live by arguing that the general features characterizing our existence are bad. It's bad, according to the Christian tradition, to have a body and to experience physical desires. It's bad that everything changes, that nothing lasts forever, and that we die. It's bad that we must labor and struggle and exert ourselves in contests of power. It's bad that we don't know everything and that people hold different opinions and values. In place of this inferior world, the Christian-Platonic tradition promises a better, transcendent world beyond it.

The transcendent world Christianity promises is decorated with perfections and absolutes. Its truths and its beauties are singular, clear, fixed, permanent, and unambiguous. Its realities are unchanging, crystalline forms of being, clearly superior to our messy world of flux—or so they say.[6] The heavenly world is one of harmony, ease, tranquility, pleasure, love, and immortality. And thank God that He and His heavenly reality exist, because without them our earthly existence would be pointless and our world would be worthless. The only thing that ultimately justifies us and makes our existence worth a damn, say the Christians, is that we mean something to some heavenly Father.

[5] Friedrich Nietzsche, *The Will to Power*, ed. by Walter Kaufmann and R.J. Hollingdale (New York: Vintage Books, 1968), Book I, §28, 19.
[6] Plato's theory describing an eternal world of "forms" (*eide*), of which our world is a mere imperfect image, is perhaps the *locus classicus* of this view.

The next step in the nihilistic process takes place when the Christian model of truth and reality collapses and it becomes impossible to believe in God, god-like truth, or the heavenly reality any more. Ironically, the Christian-Platonic tradition's excessive demand for a pure, singular truth becomes self-subverting. According to Nietzsche, after carefully scrutinizing things, people finally come to acknowledge that the sort of pure, singular, universal, absolute "truth" Christianity requires can't be acquired and perhaps even makes no sense at all. Similarly, the kind of reality Christian metaphysics describes comes to look like a fantasy, and perhaps an incoherent one at that. People realize at long last, in Nietzsche's (in)famous phrase, that "God is dead."[7]

But the trouble is, says Nietzsche, that having lived for centuries under the Christian-Platonic regime people have internalized its way of seeing the world. Yes, people do come to understand that the Christian way of thinking and valuing is untenable, but they can't conceive of an alternative. (Offering such an alternative, one where people don't need to look beyond the world for something to give it meaning, is of course just the task that Nietzsche undertook.)

Christian systems of thought, despite having devalued our world, had nevertheless infused it with a derivative kind of purpose, meaning, and value. Christianity had given the world a source of value—from their perspective, its only source. With that source of value gone people find themselves at a loss, without a source of truth or meaning, unable to find value elsewhere or to give the world value themselves. Like addicts in withdrawal, people still long for a Christian-Platonic fix, but they know that no such fix is coming. About this condition, Nietzsche writes:

> Now we discover needs implanted by centuries of moral interpretation—needs that now appear to us as needs for untruth; on the other hand, the value for which we endure life seems to hinge on these needs. This antagonism—not to esteem what we know, and not to be allowed any longer to esteem the lies we would like to tell ourselves—results in a process of dissolution. (*Will to Power*, Book I §5, 10)

---

[7] Friedrich Nietzsche, *The Gay Science*, ed. by Bernard Williams (Cambridge: Cambridge University Press, 2001), §108.

Having reached this point, it's a short step (even a predictable step) to move from not valuing anything to valuing nothingness—that is, to valuing intoxication and escapism and even, in the most extreme cases, to valuing death and destruction, including self-destruction. That's why so many today have turned to drugs, to new age mysticism, to video games and television, and endless consumer consumption. That's also why it's no surprise we're plagued with murderous Islamic *jihadis* who would incinerate this world for the sake of a phony transcendent kingdom. Hardly monstrous aberrations, these are the predictable, natural offspring of the nihilistic religious traditions that have spawned them.

The popularity of films like *The Passion of the Christ* (2003) and the militarism of Christian conservatives are explicable on this model, as well. There's good reason why Mel Gibson's execrable snuff film pays scant attention to the resurrection, to the healing, to the feeding, and forgiving parts of the Jesus story. It's because, despite their protestations to the contrary, religious conservatives (Christian and Islamic, alike) really value death. Unable to find value in life any longer, their fascination turns to suffering, to explosions, to missiles and guns, to war, to suicide bombing, to blood and sacrifice, to crowns of thorns and crucifixion.

Is Metallica part of this nihilistic culture? In many ways it is (as any of us living today are likely to be). Metallica is keenly aware that our society is pervaded by lies, injustice, exploitation, and suffering. But its criticisms of this state of affairs often appear to be not thorough-going rejections of Christian truth and value, but rather disappointments with their absence from the world. Rather than rejecting God, often Metallica seems simply to lament God's failure and wish that God wouldn't fail—as if the band were wishing that the father and mother who left Hetfield on his own would return as the dependable parents they were supposed to be.

This lamenting disappointment and this wish are perhaps most clearly evident in "To Live is to Die" (Hetfield's spoken-word performance of a poem by Cliff Burton): "When a man lies he murders / Some part of the world. / These are the pale deaths which / Men miscall their lives. / All this I cannot bear / To witness any longer. / Cannot the kingdom of salvation / Take me home?"

Sick with the world and its lies, without the strength to bear it any longer, this song abandons life and, like the soldier in "One," longs for death. The pain the voice expresses is not simply the pain of destruction, exploitation, and deceit, but also the pain of abandonment—the betrayal of promises for consolation, sustenance, fairness, and truth. Metallica's response to this pain in "To Live is to Die," however, isn't revolt, resistance, or imagining new forms of truth and health. It's instead exhaustion, resignation, and death-wish (*thanatos*).

The perverse longing for death as the path to one's true home, as the route to the absent father, is classic Christian nihilism and a sign of what Marx would call alienation. The promise of such a home may be a false one, and Metallica like the rest of us may full-well know it. But the longing remains, and this longing compounds the pain—as it does in so many of Metallica's songs, as it does so often for abandoned children, exploited workers, and recovering Christians in our nihilistic culture today. Despite their recognizing the pervasiveness of this betrayal, songs like "To Live is to Die" still long nostalgically for the things that had been promised. They seem still to wish Christianity were true.

Just as we saw, however, in the case of Metallica's capacity for rebellion, there's more to the band than this. The voice of "Master of Puppets," for example, exhibits the heightened but lonely nihilistic resignation I've described ("Hell is worth all that / natural habitat / just a rhyme without a reason"). But living now a life that's "out of season" also signals what the beginning of the song heralds—that the illusory passion play of religion is over.[8]

Another clue that Metallica moves beyond nihilism is available simply by stepping back from the lyrics and listening. The angry tone, the driving guitars, the pounding drums show us muscle, testosterone, strength, and defiance. Metallica's voice is hardly the whimpering tremolo characteristic of so much of the music scene today. This band is no puddle of dissolution. Its art has drawn together and sustained a culture of fans and admirers, as well as a few philosophers, over more than two decades. It has influenced the direction and content of culture across the globe. Nietzsche would, I think, find power in this creativity.

---

[8] Metallica's characterization of its voice here as "out of season" calls to my mind Nietzsche's description of his own thought as "untimely." Friedrich Nietzsche, *Untimely Meditations*, ed. by Daniel Breazeale (Cambridge: Cambridge University Press, 1997).

There are other indications, too, that Metallica is not thoroughly nihilistic, but that it also works towards what Nietzsche would call "overcoming" Christianity. We already saw in the ambiguities of "And Justice for All" and "The Four Horsemen" a sort of call to arms against Christian oppression. Metallica's anthem "Escape" takes a step farther in that direction, marking perhaps the most Nietzschean moment in Metallica's corpus.

From its opening chords the voice of "Escape" declares its defiance and its independence from the manipulating and dangerous lies our culture presents. More importantly, however, it does so from a position of strength, without any nostalgia for things Christian: "No one cares, but I'm so much stronger. / I'll fight until the end / To escape from the true false world. / Undamaged destiny. / Can't get caught in the endless circle / Ring of stupidity."

Nietzsche observed that the end of the Christian-Platonic idea of truth would also make it possible to neutralize the Christian-Platonic poison of thinking about our world as something derivative, inferior, and merely apparent: "With the true world we have also abolished the apparent one."[9] For those with strength enough for it, the collapse of Christian-Platonic ways of thinking (the "true/false world") opens a path of escape, of escape from the debilitating and oppressive effects of those regimes entirely. The voice of "Escape" has begun boldly striding down that path.

Confirmation of this interpretation may be found a few lines later when the song affirms the same self-creative power that Nietzsche extols when he portrays life as a work of art through which people may authentically express themselves: "Rape my mind and destroy my feelings. / Don't tell me what to do. / I don't care now, 'cause I'm on my side / And I can see through you. / Feed my brain with your so called standards / Who says that I ain't right? / Break away from your common fashion / See through your blurry sight. / [Chorus:] / See them try to bring the hammer down. / No damn chains can hold me to the ground. / Life's for my own to live my own way." Here we see then not simply the critical complaints about what's wrong with the world that may lead one to interpret Metallica as a critic of

---

[9] Friedrich Nietzsche, *Twilight of the Idols* in *The Portable Nietzsche*, ed. and trans. Walter Kaufmann (New York: Viking Penguin, 1982), pp. 95–6.

Peter S. Fosl

Christianity that hasn't fully escaped its nihilistic clutches. "Escape" shows us that Metallica is also on the path to freeing itself from Christianity and achieving a life beyond it. It's a path through which Metallica offers listeners not only outrage, disappointment, and defiance, but promise, as well.

In fact, the confidence the lost little boy of "Dyers Eve" seems to have ultimately found in the angry young man of "Escape" may have ironically laid the foundation for acquiring a sense of peace with his parents and perhaps with their religion, too.[10] Hetfield's eleven-month stay in rehab while the band was producing *St. Anger* (2003) seems to have tempered his regard for the positive ways in which belief in a "higher power" may function in some people's lives. The maturity and self-possession he achieved there (evident, I think, in the film *Some Kind of Monster*, 2004) corresponds to his overcoming another sort of disease afflicting his life—alcohol abuse. Insofar as the wish to escape the world through intoxication might itself be read as symptomatic of nihilism, perhaps Hetfield's new physical health offers us the outward sign of a kind of philosophical health, too—the overcoming of Christian nihilism and the achieving of a kind of freedom from obsessing over the pain it had caused him.

The case of Metallica, then, is a complicated one. The band's work echoes with the critical theories of both Marx and Nietzsche in arguing that religion is rife with crippling deceits. In this, Metallica advances a critique of Christianity based on moral rather than epistemological or metaphysical considerations. The band nevertheless at times itself succumbs to the sort of nihilism Nietzsche predicted would flow from the degeneration of Christian-Platonic culture. But a closer look also reveals in the band's powerful music and multi-layered lyrics efforts to overcome this nihilism and free itself (and ourselves) from Christianity's pathological grip. Ironically, this overcoming of religion's pathologies may have made possible not only a healthier life outside of religion, but also an awareness of the possibility that religion may serve salutary functions, as well.[11]

---

[10] Here I'm speaking of the maturity of the narrators of the songs, recognizing that Hetfield himself was actually older when he wrote the lyrics to "Dyers Eve."

[11] I am grateful to Isaac Fosl-van Wyke, Bill Irwin, Joanna Corwin, and Eileen Sweeney for their comments, corrections, and suggestions in the writing of this chapter.

84

METALLICA'S EXISTENTIAL FREEDOM

From We to I and Back Again

RACHAEL SOTOS

Rock music has always been about *freedom*, about the expression of freedom in a variety of forms: as sexual desire, as nonconformity and rebellion, sometimes as critique, and certainly as the proclamation of new artistic possibilities. Indeed, many great artists and bands are remembered by their characteristic expression of freedom. When Elvis Presley put a white face on the seemingly dangerous pelvic gyrations of black music, he propelled himself straight into mainstream America and changed popular music forever. When snarling Sid Vicious and the Sex Pistols gave Margaret Thatcher the finger and urinated on their adulating audiences, punk rock pushed the limits of expression beyond what had been known before.

Metallica too can be considered in the light of their unique expression of freedom. And while there are many approaches one might take in such a consideration—as there are many philosophical perspectives from which one might think about freedom—freedom as the expression of *authenticity* is an approach particularly suited to capturing the essence of the band. According to philosophers in the existentialist tradition, authenticity is a kind of *lived* truth, a *truth proved in existence*.[1] Music fans, and particularly Metallica fans,

[1] Existentialism is a tradition in philosophy which encompasses a fairly wide spectrum of thinkers; some are religious, some are completely secular, some resist even

usually have a good grasp of what "authenticity" means even without having read any philosophy.

First, existentialist philosophers understand "authentic" to mean something like "truth," but not "truth" in the sense of "objective facts," but in the sense of "truth" that is personally, *existentially* meaningful, as when we speak of being "true to ourselves," or having "a true friend." Second, existentialist philosophers, like music fans, and like many ordinary, thoughtful people, draw various contrasts between *authentic* and *inauthentic* modes of life, between modes of life that are fresh, original, and interesting and those that are characterized by stereotypical clichés and mere conventionality. Artists, however, fall into a special category, as they are quite often self-conscious about the possible contrast between authenticity and inauthenticity. Artists, likely more than average people, are concerned with *original* forms of expression which are "true" to their own sense of creativity. And in this sense, artists, insofar as they are "true to themselves," live their lives like existentialist philosophers.

Metallica, in this fan's opinion, have *always* lived like existentialist philosophers because their music has *always* been grounded in a quest for an authentic expression of freedom. It is this steadfast quest that has distinguished their work through several stylistic breaks; it is what signals their widespread appeal; and it is what helps us to understand their remarkable longevity. Consider, to begin, the mark Metallica first made in history with the genre of "thrash" or "speedmetal." In the heady (headbanging) days of the early 1980s Metallica stood out for the purity and minimalism of their expression. And in the context of the rock scene of the time, this was a sure sign of authenticity. In contrast to the glamrock poseurs who expressed a quite different brand of rock freedom in playful inversions (in cross-dressing androgyny), Metallica remained unconcerned with appearances (and

being called "existentialist." In the most basic sense though all are united in the thought that individual human beings are responsible for the *meaning* in their lives. This is the root of the existentialist concern with authenticity as a *truth proved in existence*. Without extensively addressing the many fascinating philosophical debates within this tradition, I will consider Metallica in light of some key themes in four major figures: Søren Kierkegaard, Martin Heidegger, Jean-Paul Sartre, and Hannah Arendt—though she is not often classified as an existentialist.

with MTV). Metallica came as themselves and spent their energy immersed in the relentless driving power of their music, in the seemingly inhuman speed with which they played their instruments. And let it also be said that in their purity and minimalism of expression, Metallica made their mark without falling into the "clichés" of metal mythology, the "whole sexist, Satanist crap," as Lars Ulrich has put it.[2] Like Elvis, the Sex Pistols, Iron Maiden, and every other great band, Metallica has made their unique mark in history, but in their case the expression of artistic freedom is first and best understood in a stripped-down metal message: "You're thrashing all around / acting like a maniac," " 'cause we are Metallica."

This is not to say that the relentless quest for an expression of authentic freedom is a simple matter for any human being, let alone for talented musicians who meet with unfathomed success. Considering the journey of a rock band, though, is an excellent way to see the challenges of authenticity that philosophers in the existentialist tradition have identified. Decades before Metallica, indeed before the emergence of rock music itself, the German philosopher Martin Heidegger (1889–1976) and one of his French philosophical heirs, Jean-Paul Sartre (1905–80), outlined the promises and pitfalls of authenticity. The story of Metallica not only fits their fundamental schema neatly, but gives us examples that help us to grasp concretely these two philosophers' conceptions.

In *Being and Time* (1927), Heidegger's most existentialist work, the question of authenticity primarily concerns *historical* existence.[3] To live authentically is to grasp the potential to make the most of the historical condition into which one is "thrown." In Heidegger's formulation, to fail to understand oneself historically and thus to fail to recognize "one's own most possibilities," is to live inauthentically; it is to mechanically repeat the past; it is to remain with "the They,"

---

[2] Quoted in Mick Wall and Malcom Dome, *The Making of Metallica's Metallica* (Burlington, Ontario: CG Publishing, 1996), p. 23. Hereafter cited in text as *MM*.

[3] Martin Heidegger, *Being and Time*, trans. John Macquarrie and Edward Robinson (New York: Harper & Row, 1962). Hereafter cited in text as *BT*. For those interested in a further exploration of Heidegger, an excellent place to begin is the collection *Basic Writings*, ed. by David Farrell Krell (New York: Harper Collins, 1993).

the unthinking people who fail to either take responsibility or be authentically free. Although in *Being and Time* Heidegger is thinking more of politics than art, his historically grounded line of thought makes much sense of the history of art, of the "genius" of creativity and of the development of artistic genres. From this perspective, to be in a band that helps to originate a whole new genre of music—in Metallica's case, "thrash" or "speedmetal"—is precisely to recognize the possibilities of one's historical existence, to express authentic freedom.[4]

In *Being and Nothingness* (1944), Jean-Paul Sartre, writing a generation after Heidegger, upped the ante of authenticity as he gave existentialist philosophy a new psychological depth and furthered our understanding of the obstacles confronting freedom.[5] In Sartre's analysis—so well-suited to a consideration of Metallica—the task of living authentically requires constant vigilance, a real effort to understand oneself with maximal honesty and transparency. Where Heidegger in *Being and Time* primarily understood authenticity as the heroic founding of new possibilities unseen by "the They," Sartre revealed the layers of deception and inauthenticity *within* the individual self. In his famous analysis of "bad faith," he portrayed human beings in near constant states of denial as they identify with masked caricatures of themselves, because they live according to roles which have been externally ascribed to them or with which they have long since ceased to identify (*BN*, 86–118). For artists, and particularly successful artists, the dilemma of "bad faith" analyzed by Sartre is intensified for a couple of reasons. In the first place there is something we might call the "rock star syndrome." Typically, the people around the rock star—precisely because they passionately identify with the form of freedom he or she represents—come to expect certain forms of expression. As it turns out though, it might not feel "authentic" to smash one's drum set *every* night. In the second place, for an artist

---

[4] As Heidegger emphasizes in his later writings, it is just as "authentic" to maintain and preserve a tradition once it has become established as it is to grasp the possibilities of a new foundation, provided of course that one does not become homogenous and mechanized. For a further discussion of Heidegger's development, see Krell's discussion in *Basic Writings*.

[5] Jean-Paul Sartre, *Being and Nothingness*, trans. by Hazel E. Barnes (New York: Washington Square Press, 1956). Hereafter cited in text as *BN*.

who must change and grow in order to develop his or her artistic potential, remaining with what one has already achieved instead of developing new ideas and new capacities is a constant *temptation* and a danger to oneself. Thus, in an ironic sense, a steadfast concern for authentic expression might itself become an obstacle to authenticity. For what feels "true" at one point might appear as "stock" or "average" at another time. And finally, success may present an obstacle to authenticity on a more personal level; it may imply modes of living that no longer correspond to political, ethical, and cultural reality. In James Hetfield's words, "Change has to happen no matter how much people don't want to see their stable things change. As humans we have to change" (*MM*, 22).

The Power of the "We"

In a 1984 interview for the British magazine *Sounds*, Lars insisted that nothing about Metallica was planned or orchestrated, "Everything Metallica does is spontaneous; I think if we lose our spontaneity we will be in one hell of a lot of trouble."[6] As fans can read in Metallica's official fan book, twenty years later this pronouncement appears rather brash (in a good way) to the band members themselves; it sounds like the talk of "young punks" [James], of kids, "young, drunk, full of spunk"[Lars], "pumped up and ready to take on anything and everything" [Kirk] (*SW*, 5).

This punk attitude, this unchecked confidence in "spontaneous" expression, appears in hindsight as the "magic of youth." But it also reflects experiences of creativity and freedom that can be considered *philosophically*. Just because Metallica themselves did not philosophize at the very time they were busy helping to originate a new genre of music, does not mean that this spontaneous expression cannot be described in theoretical terms. A good place to start is with the account of *positive freedom* made by the political philosopher Hannah Arendt

---

[6] Quoted in Steffan Chirazi (ed.), *So What: The Good, the Mad, and the Ugly; The Official Metallica Illustrated Chronicle* (New York: Broadway Books, 2004), p. 3. Hereafter cited in text as *SW*.

(1906–75) (a student of Heidegger, incidentally). In *The Human Condition* and many other writings, Arendt argues that freedom is experienced most authentically when it is *shared* with and among other people *in the world*.[7] In the scheme of her political philosophy authentic freedom is *public* freedom. It is not the private freedom of the single individual existing in solitude, but freedom that *happens* in a shared space when people act *with* each other rather than against each other. In such moments of shared freedom—we might think of a protest or a town hall meeting—people become *empowered*. This experience of positive, shared freedom feels richer and more vital than all other forms of freedom. Importantly, this empowered feeling is not rooted in violence or omnipotence, experiences which Arendt sees as characteristic of tyranny rather than of freedom. It is an experience of the "we." The feeling of power and capacity, of the "I-can" (to use Arendt's expression), comes because one is part of something larger: one is not alone, but part of a "we."

Arendt is thinking of a specific form of *political* freedom, but there is no doubt that musical performances, particularly kick-ass ones, are experiences of an empowered "we." And certainly for all of their changes and challenges throughout the years Metallica has always been grounded in this "we" of live performance, all the more so as they have been one of the hardest working bands in rock and roll, often touring for years on end. There are numerous stories about the band that corroborate their dedication to the "we." Think of their repeated celebration of the "garage days" and the decision to follow Cliff Burton (a kind of punk rock hippie) from Los Angeles to San Francisco, a city considerably more grounded in experiences of the "we." If we consider in particular the first album, *Kill 'Em All*, it is truly remarkable how predominant the experience of the "we" is at the beginning of Metallica's journey. In the lyrics of this album the word "we" appears more times than on all the other albums combined. It appears and is repeated, again and again announcing the "we" of the newly born speed metal community. From "Hit the Lights": "No life till leather / *We* are gonna kick some ass tonight / *We* got the

---

7   Hannah Arendt, *The Human Condition* (Chicago: University of Chicago Press, 1958). See particularly chapter 5, "Action." Also helpful is the essay "What is Freedom?" in *Between Past and Future* (New York: Penguin, 1993).

metal madness . . . When *we* start to rock / *we* never want to stop . . . *We* are gonna blow this place away . . . *We* are gonna rip right through your brain / *We* got the lethal power." From "Whiplash": "*We* are gathered here to maim and kill / 'cause this is what *we* choose." From "Metal Militia": "*We* are as one as *we* all are the same . . . Leather and metal are our uniforms / Protecting what *we* are / joining together to take on the world."

It might seem that *Kill 'Em All* is "immature," both musically and thematically. In comparison to Metallica's later work their debut features less musical virtuosity and no social commentary. On the other hand, we might say that this immaturity precisely corresponds to the expression of the freedom of the "we." "Jump in the Fire," which is, of course, not about the devil, but about the "we," beckons us to join the collective in a metal baptism, moshing "down in the pit." The remarkable spontaneity that Lars spoke of is nothing other than the feeling of power and capacity, which "we" feel when the "adrenaline starts to flow."

Discovering and Developing the "I"

Metallica's subsequent albums in the 1980s, *Ride the Lightning*, *Master of Puppets*, and . . . *And Justice for All*, established the band as masters of the metal genre. Although the dynamic power of the "we" is still present in every note and drum beat, there is a remarkable new emphasis on the singular experience of the "I." In the lyrics of *Ride the Lightning* the word "I" appears in almost every song and is reflected throughout the thematic content of the album: "*I* can feel the flame . . . As *I* watch death unfold . . . *I* don't want to die" ("Ride the Lightning"); "*I* have lost the will to live . . . cannot stand this hell *I* feel" ("Fade to Black"); "*I* am dying to live / Cry out / *I'm* trapped under ice" ("Trapped under Ice").

Ride the Lightning's concern with death—in the electric chair, under ice, by suicide—might seem a morbid fixation characteristic of youth, but in fact such concern has a long history in philosophy and in Christian theology. In the existentialist tradition Heidegger stands out with his "death analyses" in *Being and Time*. According to Heidegger, reflection on one's own death is important for authentic living. In his formulation, "attunement" to the possibility of death "discloses" one's "own most possibility" and thus can return the individual from an inauthentic mode of living among "the They" to authenticity and the recognition of one's "true" possibilities in this life (*BT*, 270–311).

Heidegger is a good reference point in thinking through Metallica's mode of expression in this period because, from at least one perspective, his underlying concern in *Being and Time* corresponds neatly with an important development in Metallica's music. In Heidegger's view the "attunement" toward death and other seemingly negative experiences such as "anxiety" in fact produces an *empassioned* sense of life; from these moments of negativity, *conscience* and responsibility develop. Thus while the song "Fade to Black" is dark indeed, the overall pessimism of *Ride the Lightning* is only the flip side of a powerful activist sentiment, of a passion for life: "I am dying to live." On *Master of Puppets* and . . . *And Justice for All* the dark reflections of the "I" are analogously developed. The concern with death gives way to ruminations on addiction, hypocrisy, nuclear proliferation, environmental degradation, and social injustice—all evils to be confronted in this world. Interestingly, the darker and more pessimistic the overall themes become—as if the world were dictated by deterministic forces that overwhelm the very possibility of freedom—all the more does Metallica's forceful driving music provide powerful optimistic counters to the "dark forces." If "Master of Puppets" reminds us that something else is "pulling the strings" and "The Shortest Straw" tells us that something bad might have been drawn for unlucky you, we have at the same time, as a vital counter, the extraordinary musical virtuosity characteristic of this period. This is most dramatically the case with Kirk Hammet, of course, whose brilliant solos win him recognition by guitarists far and wide. From our perspective we might say that Kirk's talent, developed to genius, represents the living power of freedom confronting the forces of determinism.

The "Embodied Me"

Metallica's fifth album, the so-called Black Album, put the band on the megastar map. In this fan's opinion, as the Black Album is chock full of such classics as "Sandman," "Holier than Thou," "Sad but True," "The Unforgiven," and "Nothing Else Matters," it stands on its own, absolutely. As it also signals the ambition for commercial success though, it immediately raised "authenticity questions" for some diehard fans, particularly the choice of the radio-savvy producer Bob Rock. As Lars summed up some fans' horror at the choice of the producer responsible for the likes of Mötley Crüe and Bon Jovi, in 1991 it seemed Metallica was now "standing for" what they had been "going against for the last five years" (*MM*, 11).

From a philosophical perspective, Metallica and their fans have been engaged in a constant dialogue about authenticity that has parallels in the history of philosophy. First, defending the Black Album, Metallica explicitly resisted being pigeon-holed in the thrash genre. Second, they explained their own dissatisfaction with the increasingly technical and progressive direction that the last albums had taken, particularly . . . *And Justice for All*. As Kirk put it, reflecting on the supporting tour for *Justice*, "we realized that the general consensus was that the songs were too long . . . I can remember getting offstage one night after playing the [ten minute-plus] song 'And Justice For All,' and one of us saying, 'that's the last time we ever play that fucking song'" (*MM*, 23). Lars echoes this sentiment with a further analysis: "I think we spent a lot of years trying to prove to ourselves and to everyone that we can play our instruments . . . this big drum fill . . . Kirk's playing all these wild things that are really difficult." In fact though, "it's gotten so clean and antiseptic that you've got to wear gloves to put the damn thing in the CD player!" Lars insists that the decision to go with Bob Rock was because the band needed to express something "looser, groovier," some "emotion," "the shit that's in there naturally" (*MM*, 12, 9). And finally, James adds that Metallica was seeking a new sound, something "really bouncy, really lively—something that just has a lot of groove to it" (*MM*, 8).

The move from the structural complexity and virtuosity characteristic of more progressive metal to a "looser" sound, grounded in the blues base of rock and roll, can be viewed in several lights. Metallica's move reflects participation in a wider musical trend of the 1990s, a decade when groovier and funkier sounds reinfiltrated rock—recall Guns N' Roses, Jane's Addiction, and the Red Hot Chili Peppers. But insofar as the move reflects the need for a more "embodied" personal form of expression, it has striking parallels in the history of philosophy, indeed in the history of existentialism. Let's consider just one of these moments and note again the way in which Metallica have, perhaps without knowing it, *always* lived their lives as existentialist philosophers.

The first and perhaps the greatest existentialist philosopher, Søren Kierkegaard (1813–55), found his footing as a thinker and made his mark while engaged in a deep critique of Georg Hegel (1770–1831), who was generally regarded as the greatest philosopher of the time. To put it much too simply, Hegel was a philosopher in the old-fashioned style; he wrote a *monumental* system of philosophy that claimed to capture all of reality from the perspective of "Absolute Spirit." Kierkegaard found Hegel's bombastic monumental system to be a work of genius and yet ridiculous. Kierkegaard wittily suggested (in a notebook) that if Hegel had written his gargantuan *The Science of Logic* but, "in the Preface disclosed the fact that it was only a thought-experiment . . . he would have been the greatest thinker who ever lived." However, without acknowledging that his system was as an "experiment" offered by a single human being living in this world (rather than an absolute system conceived by a disembodied abstract thinker speaking for God himself), Hegel proved himself a brilliant philosopher, but ultimately "comic" and *inauthentic*.[8]

In a striking sense Metallica's need for "a looser, groovier" expression parallels Kierkegaard's original critique of Hegel. It's as if, for all of the genius and virtuosity of . . . *And Justice for All*, they had become comic and inauthentic because they had lost themselves and their own embodiment in the complex abstract system of progressive metal. What had been authentic before because it inspired the development of their musical faculties (and some truly monumental music), was now in fact an obstacle to true expression.

There's no doubt that the leap out of the system allowed Metallica new-found creative freedom. With the Black Album and *Load* and *Reload* they explored a variety of genres, from classical to country, and allowed these influences to penetrate their creative process. The band found themselves free to slow down, free for melody, free for the occasional sample. Most strikingly, and most horrific to diehard *heshers* (Californian for long-haired metal fan), they allowed

---

[8] Quoted in Roger Kimball, "What did Kierkegaard Want?" *New Criterion*, www.newcriterion.com/archive/20/sept01/kierk.htm.

themselves to strike the pose of poseurs, to play at being rock stars, even wearing eyeliner. If this is a 180-degree turn from the decade before, it is worthwhile thinking about Metallica's new megastar status and the grunge pose of authenticity. Lars, ever the master of "cutting through the baloney," reminds us that a rock star *pretending not* to want to be a rock star itself smacks of "bad faith." As he says: "Apart from the guy in Nirvana [Kurt Cobain], who'll lie to you and say, 'Uh, we don't want anyone to buy our records,' 99.9 percent of people in bands would like people to hear their music and get into their band. That is a fucking fact" (*MM*, 43).

The most outstanding transformation in 1990s Metallica obviously came for James, who was the band member most liberated by the leap from the progressive metal system. As he explains in the documentary DVD entitled *Metallica*, which follows the making of the album, his new-found permission to actually *sing* rather than simply yell, allowed him to go deeper into himself, to be both "more inward and more universal."[9] This new depth of experience is manifest in several surprising developments in Metallica's music in this period, especially in the *love* song, "Nothing else Matters," and in James' reflections on the trauma of growing up with Christian Scientist parents in "The Unforgiven" and "The God that Failed." The 1990s Metallica consistently used their new-found freedom to make music that speaks *from somewhere*, be it James' personal experience, the country roots of "Mama Said," or the single feminine voice of Marianne Faithfull on "The Memory Remains." Very much in the manner of Kierkegaard's critique of Hegel's abstract philosophizing, Metallica leapt out of the system of progressive metal and made music with personal and emotional depth.

Psychological Stagedive

The end of the 1990s found Metallica in disarray. Granted, things were much worse for other major bands of the period: Jane's

---

[9]   DVD (2001) *Metallica*, Classic Albums series 3. Limited/Metallica, a partnership. An Isis production in co-production with Eagle Rock. Directed and edited by Mathew Longfellow.

Addiction and Guns N' Roses had split up; Kurt Cobain was long dead. Metallica was still a band, but almost in name more than in spirit. Creatively repressed, Jason Newsted left to pursue his own work in Echobrain, and the relations among other band members were strained. While Metallica's general lack of pretension had always been reciprocated in the dedication of their fans, the Napster controversy opened an abyss between the masters of metal and the iGeneration. The decision to film the making of the next CD—all the while being "therapized" by a performance coach—was bold indeed. To make a "reality show" of the band at its lowest point was, to speak metaphorically, a stagedive risked from the greatest heights, without any certainty that there would be a safe place to fall. As it turned out, the documentary *Some Kind of Monster* landed Metallica even more intimately in their fans' laps, stripped of layers of pretension that two decades of megastardom had inevitably brought.

In the new media environment there are empowered communities of authenticity-hungry fans and a new form of relations that rock bands must engage. Metallica, it seems, with a slight stumble, have hooked into this new (virtual) reality with the same spirit as ever. They have stripped away the wrapping and are allowing maximal direct access to themselves and their creative process.

Some Kind of Monster stands on its own as a documentary with universal significance; it is a tragic-comic revelation of the human condition. From the perspective of Metallica's journey as a band grounded in the quest for an *authentic* expression of freedom in music it is of particular significance, for it brings us full circle to the experience of the "we" that came so spontaneously in the heady days of early speed metal. What the documentary reveals—and this is simultaneously its universal significance—is that the "we" is always something that needs to be tended and nurtured. There are of course magic moments in life when everything seems easy—when one first forms a band, when one first falls in love—but the truth of the matter is that the "we" should never be left to chance. Human relationships involve work. In Metallica's case, acknowledging the "we" meant that the most authentic thing was to allow a touchy-feely therapist (Phil Towle) to create a space for the band to come together. The payoff of this process, as we see in the movie, is that the "we" of Metallica emerges stronger than ever. Most strikingly, a *democratic* process replaces the Ulrich-Hetfield creative dictatorship, the tyranny that pushed Jason to the point of no return. Thus while there are many moments of beauty in *Some Kind of Monster*, surely among the top is, after so much grievance, Kirk's visible inspiration after James' attitude adjustment, his "opening the door" to other band members writing lyrics. The new democratic mode indeed made for a stripped-down final product, but it is the fulfillment of the promise for which Metallica has always stood. It is freedom that is authentic in the sense that Arendt describes, it is more empowered and alive because it is shared; the "I" is only truly free when it allows others to be free too.

The choice to have the video for *St. Anger* shot at San Quentin, the notorious prison, is a gesture that reflects groundedness in the quest for an *authentic* form of free expression. For what community is more authentically aware of freedom than the residents of the big house? This gesture, along with Matt Mahurin's remarkable illustration of St. Anger—an angel in a straitjacket—returns us to themes of the 1980s, to the (Heideggerian) obsession with the obstacles to freedom that heighten our existential awareness, that bring us back from "the They." Metallica's "baptism" of anger and the fact that the supporting tour was named "Madly in Anger with the World" underscore the band's wisdom and maturity. At the risk of being overly philosophical, we might say that Metallica have resynthesized the original power of the "we" with self-reflection and responsibility. Metallica is about "aggressive music with constructive energy," as Lars puts it in the DVD commentary to *Some Kind of Monster*. At the core remains, we may be sure, the steadfast quest for authenticity. "Keep on searching . . . you live it or lie it . . . keep on searching . . . / my lifestyle determines my deathstyle."

DISC 3

LIVING AND DYING, LAUGHING AND CRYING

CHAPTER 9

TO LIVE IS TO DIE

Metallica and the Meaning of Life

SCOTT CALEF

The questions come like creeping death; we begin to sense something's wrong. Something vaguely sinister is stalking us, unnamed, just beyond consciousness. Whether the doubts dawn slowly or suddenly, we wake with them; once aroused, like unwelcome groupies they refuse to leave. Why am I here? What's the meaning of it all? What have I been doing with my life? The cycle of working, commuting, eating, reading the paper, and going to bed exhausted now strikes us as meaningless and absurd. What, we wonder, is the point? To repeat the whole sequence tomorrow? To buy things? To be respectable? To distract ourselves from the questions which now press so insistently? Life is slipping away, and sooner or later we'll all be forgotten.[1] All of our accomplishments, no matter how esteemed, and all of our striving, no matter how heroic, will eventually amount to nothing. A pall of futility settles over everything. Like a nasty hangover, it ruins your mood and colors the world black.

In those moments when everything seems pointless, we have several Metallica-inspired options. One: drink a lot. Two: go on tour and have a blast (see option one). Three: go to therapy. Four (available here for the first time ever): try philosophy! We'll talk more about options one

---

[1]   We may ask ourselves, "If I could have my wasted days back, would I use them to get back on track?" ("Frantic"). But what would the right track be? And *is* there any track that's "right"? Given the inevitability of our demise and that of everything and everyone we care about, perhaps all paths are equally bleak.

and two below. For now, hopefully, we can agree alcohol doesn't really solve the problem and tends to further fuel the spiral into despair.[2] The second alternative, alas, isn't an option for most of us, and as we'll see, didn't really work for Metallica either. Option three is expensive, and let's face it: do you really want to be locked up in a room with Phil Towle twice a week? Therefore, let's begin with philosophy. After all, isn't figuring out the meaning of life philosophers' business?

Well, not exclusively. Metallica certainly have something important and constructive to say about it. Although their lyrics are frequently dark, violent, and negative, we shouldn't expect only nihilism and despair from the band. Metallica's courage and strength shine forth not only through their denunciations of social evils like war, the worst excesses of religion, or injustice, but through their willingness to be open and honest.[3]

For countless millions of fans, of course, Metallica's music itself helps give life meaning. But what's the message in that music? I'll argue that, ironically, according to Metallica there *is* no "meaning of life." Paradoxically, then, if we derive meaning from the music of Metallica we must take seriously philosophical arguments in the music that life has no meaning! Can we avoid the paradox by saying we should just enjoy the music and not think about it too much? Maybe, but Metallica suggest enjoyment isn't what makes life worthwhile either. As we'll see, for Hetfield, pleasure is inherently fleeting and constantly threatened by boredom. Our lifestyle can determine our deathstyle, but it can't generate value or meaning. Of course, Metallica might be wrong, but we shouldn't assume so until we've considered their arguments.

First, however, a word about the meaning of "meaning." Some philosophers hold that, in a literal sense, only forms of communication have meaning. Words and sentences are the primary examples. If you

---

[2] The glass of liquor I'm lifting—the "sweet amber" who "holds my hand"—"rolls me over till I'm sick. She deals in habits, deals in pain. I run away but I'm back again" ("Sweet Amber").

[3] In *Metallica: Some Kind of Monster* Lars wonders whether having cameras in the room will inhibit the group's intimacy and ability to be real. Therapist/performance enhancement coach Phil Towle, hired by Metallica's management firm Q-Prime after the departure of Jason Newsted, suggests that "it's not going to be a matter of if the cameras are in play but whether or not you guys are free enough to risk being seen by other people" (DVD at 5:29).

think about it, it makes sense to ask what the lyrics mean, but not what a guitar solo or "The Call of Ktulu" mean. Non-verbal communication through symbols, art, holding our cigarette lighters aloft, and making obscene gestures or the devil horns is possible, but only because these things stand for, or represent, something. Because lives lack "semantics," however, many philosophers think they're neither meaningful nor meaningless. Lives are like "Orion"; the concept of meaning just doesn't apply.

In a way, this is good news. After all, if the theory is correct, no one's life is meaningless and our troubles are solved! But can't things *mean* in a variety of other ways, too? A DNA sample might mean Hammett is innocent or not the father; an increase in downloading might mean Napster is flourishing and Ulrich is pissed; Newsted's departure means the band has to hold auditions, and a world tour means mucho dinero. Although (as we'll see) Metallica agree life lacks meaning, the "semantic" theory of meaning is too narrow. When we talk about the "meaning" of life, we aren't asking whether life has a definition or linguistic interpretation. We're wondering about its point, significance, or purpose, or, more negatively, whether it's futile, pointless, or vain.

So, does life have meaning in this broader sense? Although I'll eventually claim the band has a positive message (that's right, no meaning of life is a good thing!), initially they offer several plausible and depressing arguments to the contrary.

Through the Never

According to the first, life is purposeless and without meaning because, on a cosmic scale, it's insignificant. When we contemplate the vastness of seemingly infinite space and our own smallness, the brevity of our lives in the span of eternity, the certainty that everything we will ever do, write, say, sing, or strum will eventually be forgotten, we can't help but wonder whether anything matters. We yearn for answers to the riddles of life, but the universe is silent and our questions doomed to remain unanswered.

Despite a smorgasbord of distractions most of us could scarcely imagine, the members of Metallica really do experience these feelings.

James captures them perfectly on "Through the Never": the universe is "much too big to see." Because "time and space [are] never ending" we have "disturbing thoughts, questions pending" and realize the "limitations of human understanding." The question of whether life has meaning, and what the reason for it is, arises from the inescapable fact that the universe is immeasurable and its cold blackness will swallow us forever, leaving no trace of us in endless time. Because "Life it seems, will fade away . . . Nothing matters." "All that is . . . ever was [or] will be ever" is just a twisting and turning "through the never." "Who we are, ask forever." We can ask who and why we are until the never, but in the end, there's no reply. Only darkness.

Such reflections can wobble the best of us. Fortunately, they also embody questionable assumptions. For example, does the fact that humans are tiny, momentary specks in an unbounded universe really imply that life is insignificant or meaningless? "Why should the existence or non-existence of stars or planets billions of miles away make any difference to the meaning or significance of things right here?"[4] If life has no meaning, it can't *only* be because humans are small and life is short. If I stood a million miles high instead of six foot two (or if the universe shrank and I occupied a greater percentage of it) that wouldn't invest my existence with deeper meaning. Similarly, if a brief life is meaningless, why would a longer one automatically be more meaningful? How would *merely prolonging* what is meaningless generate meaning?[5] A very long life—indeed, an eternal one— can be utterly pointless. Consider Sisyphus, damned by the gods to perpetually push a rock uphill only to have it roll endlessly to the bottom each time he nears the summit. This cycle of incessant drudgery repeats *forever*, without intermission or significant alteration. Sisyphus' life and routine accomplish absolutely nothing; they

---

[4]   Christopher Belshaw, *10 Good Questions About Life and Death* (Oxford: Blackwell, 2006), p. 112.

[5]   As Thomas Nagel eloquently puts it, "would not a life that is absurd if it lasts seventy years be infinitely absurd if it lasted through eternity?" "The Absurd" in *Life, Death and Meaning*, ed. by David Benatar (Lanham, MD: Rowman and Littlefield, 2004), p. 30. Hereafter, references to *Life, Death and Meaning* will receive abbreviated citation as Benatar.

are, as Richard Taylor puts it, "a perfect image of meaninglessness."[6] Infinite longevity only aggravates his despair.[7] Consider, too, the sense of futility that accompanies the recognition that nothing I do now will matter in a million years; it will all be forgotten, and things will be as if I had never been. If nothing we do now will matter in a million years, is everything pointless? Well, if nothing I do now will matter in a million years, "nothing that will be the case in a million years matters now. In particular, it does not matter now that in a million years nothing we do now will matter"![8]

Escape

Many seek to avoid the finality of death and the hopelessness of their fate by turning to the consolations of religion. Viewed from the standpoint of time and space, our lives are but the infinitesimally brief flicker of a barely perceptible candle. But what if death isn't real and we inherit eternal life in heaven? Then the brevity of life is an illusion, not a threat depriving us of meaning. From a religious point of view, the meaning of life may be found beyond life in another world where we fully achieve the purpose which eludes us on earth. Alternatively, our lives have meaning, not intrinsically, but because of their value to God. The fruits of our striving will not be forgotten, for God appreciates our efforts, and God has an excellent memory.

For Metallica, religious attempts to find meaning beyond the limits of space and time are prone to disillusionment. The band is clear that

---

[6] "The Meaning of Life" in Benatar, p. 20. Metallica give the image of an eternally runaway locomotive: "Can't stop this train from rolling; Nothing brings me down; No, can't stop this train from rolling on and on, on, forever on and on" ("Better Than You"). If the train never stops, it isn't *going* anywhere. But then, does its movement serve any purpose?

[7] Søren Kierkegaard (1813–55) argues that "the torment of despair is precisely this, not to be able to die . . . the hopelessness in this case is that even the last hope, death, is not available . . . [when] death has become one's hope, despair is the disconsolateness of not being able to die." *Fear and Trembling* and *The Sickness Unto Death*, trans. by Walter Lowrie (Princeton: Princeton University Press, 1974), pp. 150–1.

[8] Nagel, in Benatar, p. 30.

this alternative is unavailable to thinking persons.[9] Because Metallica's critique of Christianity is discussed elsewhere in this volume, I'll here be brief. The following considerations, though distinct, build upon and reinforce one another.

First, Metallica argue that resorting to religion is intellectually dishonest.[10] It amounts to a denial of the actual conditions of life. Belief in God is not based on adequate evidence, but on a craving for psychic comfort in a comfortless world. In "The God That Failed," for example, the band criticize the devout who "Find your peace, find your say, find the smooth road on your way." The pilgrim's path may be smooth and serene, but the fact that a way is easy and tranquil is no basis for conviction. Because believers accept doctrines based on how they make them feel, religious belief is, as Freud (1856–1939) argued, an illusion. According to Freud, we believe without sufficient evidence because we *want* or *need* religion to be true so badly.[11]

Second, existence looks grim enough without religion, but religion reinforces the worthlessness of life by denigrating it for the sake of a future life by comparison to which it suffers.[12] Consequently, "home is not home, it becomes a hell, turning it into your prison cell" ("The Struggle Within"). Earth isn't home because you don't belong here. It and the body are prisons confining you until your day of death, when

---

[9] Although Metallica are frequently critical of religion and its corruptions, the views of its members are of course subject to change. Post rehab, Hetfield has apparently embraced the idea of a "Higher Power." In what follows I try to take their earlier lyrics more or less at face value. I leave it to the reader to decide whether there are forms of religion the band would find unobjectionable.

[10] "Living on your knees, conformity, or dying on your feet for honesty" (*Damage, Inc.*). "It feeds. It grows. It clouds all that you will know. Deceit. Deceive. Decide just what you believe" (*The God That Failed*). "Marvel at his tricks. Need your Sunday fix. Blind devotion came, rotting your brain" (*Leper Messiah*). "You lie so much you believe yourself" (*Holier Than Thou*).

[11] For Freud's account of religious belief as a product of wish-fulfillments, see his *The Future of an Illusion*.

[12] For Nietzsche, "To talk about 'another' world than this is quite pointless, provided that an instinct for slandering, disparaging and accusing life is not strong within us: in the latter case we *revenge* ourselves on life by means of the phantasmagoria of 'another,' a 'better' life." *Twilight of the Idols* and *The Anti-Christ* (New York: Penguin, 1990), p. 49. Hereafter, reference to this work will be cited as *Twilight*.

you flee this wretched scene to the glorious, heavenly abode awaiting you hereafter.[13] Religion thus breeds alienation.

Third, since religion emphasizes the importance of the next world over this one, we lose the motivation to fight for justice and what is right here and now. Religion thus becomes an agency of evil. It makes its followers accomplices in wrongdoing by sapping their will to oppose preventable suffering. Consider, for example, Metallica's condemnation of Christian Science in "The God That Failed": "Trust you gave, a child to save, left you cold and him in grave . . . The healing hand held back by the deepened nail. Follow the god that failed." This child could have been saved by medicine, but spiritual concerns led the parents to reject that route. They're to blame for the resulting tragedy.

Fourth, religion deflects responsibility for our lives onto a cosmic force which assumes control of our fate. It accordingly makes us weak, servile, compliant, and lacking in self-sufficiency. James sings in "Escape," although "my life ain't easy I know I'm my own best friend. No one cares, but I'm so much stronger, I'll fight until the end." Because there's no God, he has to be his own best friend; "no one cares," but this only forces him back upon himself and makes him rely on his own resources. "No one but me can save myself" ("Fade to Black").

Finally, the religious search for answers attempts to ground meaning in objectivity. Because God is all-knowing, it's thought he can provide an unbiased and irrefutable frame of reference for our lives and values. The problem stems from human fallibility. Because things that *seem* important to me may not actually *be* important, I'm an untrustworthy judge of what makes for a meaningful life. But since God's perception is perfect, if I act according to, or embody, the things *he* says are important, I can't go astray. Put slightly differently, if human life has meaning, an omniscient God presumably knows what it is. If he tells us, we can know also. Thus, according to this way of thinking, religion offers the best prospect for discovering our purpose and destiny. From Metallica's perspective, however, values *aren't* objective; "one man's fun is another's hell" ("My Friend of

[13] Christianity here embodies strong overtones of Platonic philosophy, especially as represented in Plato's *Phaedo* from 64a–67e.

Misery"). Standards are in the "Eye of the Beholder": "Look inside, to each his own . . . Choice is made for you, my friend." If something is valuable or significant, it must be valuable or significant *to* someone. You can't have value without a valuer. But once we introduce the "someone" who values, we're no longer dealing in the realm of objectivity. We're in the subjective realm of someone *to whom* it *seems* that the thing has meaning or worth. If God does exist, he's just another "beholder" in whose "eye" the thing matters. Here's a question to ponder: if God has a purpose for our lives, that might make them significant to *him*, but why should it make them significant to *us*?

No Life 'Til Leather

From the standpoint of the universe and eternity, life looks insignificant and meaningless. Avoiding this perspective with religious ideology is, for Metallica, dishonest and immoral escapism. But perhaps life shouldn't be evaluated on such an unrealistically grand scale. Measured against the immensity of the cosmos or the span of eternity, we come off looking rather unimportant. But what makes *that* the appropriate standard by which we should judge ourselves? *Of course* we won't live forever, and, yes, eventually we will be forgotten. Our whole species will one day be extinct. But if meaning can't be found in the boundless ocean of infinity, perhaps it can be found right here, in the activities, pursuits, and values commonly thought to make life worthwhile. Even if death ultimately wins, can't we still find meaning in the everyday enjoyments of life?

Metallica suggest not, and Socrates (470–399 BCE), at least, agrees. Condemned for corrupting youth and for impiety (sound familiar, Metallica fans?), Socrates insists even the great king could easily count the days and nights that were better and more pleasant than a night of dreamless sleep. "If death is like this," Socrates claims, "it is an advantage, for all eternity would then seem to be no more than a single night."[14] If annihilated, Socrates will be delivered from

[14] Plato, *Apology* 40c. The "great king" was the lord of Persia, a monarch renowned in antiquity for his magnificence and life of luxury.

troubles and find peace in eternal rest. Since life is filled with frustration, emptiness, heartache, evil, and pain, even the great king would prefer an end to it all. Despite its undeniable appeal, pleasure offers less than obliteration and the permanent extinction of the personality.[15] Ultimately, perhaps all that can be said is that "my lifestyle determines my deathstyle."

Hetfield and Socrates seem to agree, right down to the kingship example. The first verse of "King Nothing" suggests that even if our longings for wealth and honor are satisfied, we won't be content; gold and fame can't pacify the soul. "All the things you've chased" will crash down. However much we want or attain we'll always want more so that, in the end, the objects of our desire are simply unattainable. Hetfield's metaphor for this is the star in the familiar children's rhyme: Star light, star bright, first star I see tonight, "I wish I may, I wish I might, have this wish I wish tonight. I want that star, I want it now. I want it all and I don't care how" ("King Nothing"). A wish made on the evening's first star is supposed to come true. King Nothing, however, demands the wish-granting star itself; he wants to possess the power of infinite obtainment. But stars—including, of course, the wishing star—are out of reach and not for the taking. Unable to capture the star, he can't secure all he wants. Our desires inevitably exceed our grasp. Consequently, this road leads to perpetual discontent. Ironically, "the less I have the more I gain" ("Wherever I May Roam"). The world is running after money, but it won't find meaning or happiness there.

---

[15]   Nietzsche is profoundly suspicious of the pronouncements of "wise men" like Socrates on the meaning and value of life. Prior to his execution through self-administered poisoning, Socrates argues in Plato's *Phaedo* that death will enable his soul to pursue truth without bodily limitations (63e–67a). For Nietzsche, this reveals an inverted preference of wisdom over life. The love of wisdom (the meaning of "philosophy") is thus (in Socrates' case, literally) self-defeating and anti-life. Thus, Nietzsche wonders, "Does wisdom appear on the earth as a raven . . . inspired by the smell of carrion?" (*Twilight*, p. 39). Nietzsche makes much the same complaint against religion and morality, which he also considers anti-life: "all *healthy* morality is dominated by an instinct of life . . . virtually every morality that has hitherto been taught, reverenced or preached, turns on the contrary precisely *against* the instincts of life . . . it denies the deepest and the highest desires of life and takes God for the *enemy of life* . . . The saint in whom God takes pleasure is the ideal castrate . . . Life is at an end where the 'kingdom of God' *begins*." *Twilight*, p. 55.

Second, even if we get what we think we want, we may not want what we get: "Careful what you wish, you may regret it. Careful what you wish, you just might get it." Socrates argues there's a big difference between doing as we please and doing what we really want. What we truly want is always something good; no one wishes to be harmed. What we please, on the other hand, is what seems good at the moment. But when what *seems* good is really harmful, we're not doing what we want even though we're doing as we please.[16] The point is, some pleasures are counterproductive if they don't further our true good. Since a meaningful life would be a good life, the enjoyment of pleasure doesn't guarantee meaning. Pleasure can diminish meaning if it detracts from, interferes with, or works against our having a good life.[17] That's one reason we have rehab.

Third, Hetfield observes, the pursuit of what can be "bought and sold" leads to a "heart as hard as gold." Living for the satisfaction of capitalist-instilled desires makes us selfish and isolates us from the needs of others. Unable to feel or connect, we experience deeply the emptiness of life and risk becoming kings of vacant lands, Kings of Nothing.

Since wealth, fame, and pleasure "crash down" and "crumble," they provide no lasting satisfaction. Eventually, even Metallica will find rotation only on the oldies station. Barely coping in the present by basking in past glories (or worse, trying to recover them with endless "reunion" tours), few things are more pathetic than aging rockers who hang on past their prime. (Think, Rod Stewart.) The joys of sex, drink, and the rock star life in general don't last long, sometimes even until the next day, and James is sober-minded about the limits of fan loyalty and the fleeting nature of celebrity: "Fortune, fame, mirror vain . . . See the nowhere crowd cry the nowhere cheers of honor. Like twisted vines that grow, hide and swallow mansions whole and dim the light of an already faded prima donna . . . that time forgets while the Hollywood sun sets behind your back . . . Ash to ash, dust

---

[16] Plato's *Gorgias* 466b–468e.

[17] In contrast to the lyrics of Metallica, Socrates thinks values are objective. However, even if you don't believe in "objective goodness," the point can still be made that some pleasures work against our having a good life by creating a barrier to what we really want for ourselves.

to dust, fade to black . . . but the memory remains." If a memory's all you've got, in the end "you're just nothing, absolutely nothing." In sum, money, fame, power, and the satisfaction of desire are meaningless; therefore, their pursuit or attainment can't confer meaning.

James captures this beautifully in *Some Kind of Monster* when he looks into the camera and poignantly confesses:

> I'm workin' on, really hard on bein' the best dad and father and husband I can be—and the best me. I don't want to lose any of this, the stuff I have. I know it can all go away at one time. And that's a tough part of life. It's a total rebirth for me, looking at life in a whole new way. And all the other drinkin', and all the other junk that I was stuck in, it was so predictable. So boring. I'm out there looking for excitement and all the stuff, the results are the same, man. I wake up the next day somewhere, in some bed. I don't know who this person is next to me and I'm drunk, completely hung over, and have a show to do. And the result is the same. You know? When life now is, is pretty exciting. You don't know what's going to happen when you're kinda clear and here and in the now. In the moment.[18]

James confides that he's gone through a total rebirth, and so now, at last, perhaps we can begin to construct a more positive approach to the meaning of life. What are the keys to this "rebirth"? Let me suggest two. On the one hand, honesty. James doesn't kid himself by pretending that his wealth, fame, and talent guarantee any real security. He admits everything "can all go away at one time." Life and its toys are impermanent. This is the core of the two arguments against meaning already explored. According to the "eternity" argument, life is insignificant because impossibly small and brief when considered on a cosmic scale. We and everything we stand for will

---

[18] *Metallica: Some Kind of Monster* DVD at scene 19, 1:03:08. Hereafter, I dub this soliloquy of James' "the confession." So far we've considered only whether such things as money, fame, and power can give life meaning. Here, however, James discusses a different kind of good—the joys of fatherhood and companionship or, as we might say, love. Can *these* invest life with meaning? Yes and no. Their value is subjective; if someone didn't wish to marry or be a parent, their life wouldn't lack meaning in any absolute sense. On the other hand, love seems a more meaningful and worthy pursuit than, say, sex and bling. Metallica don't talk a lot about love in their songs, however, and so neither will we.

fade to black. The second argument, that the pleasures of sex, drugs, and rock 'n' roll offer diminishing returns, also derives from considerations of impermanence.[19] Pleasure by nature is short-lived and eventually, James admits, boring.[20] So, a satisfactory response to the problem of life must address its transitory nature. The second "key" is this: James' confession is deeply personal. He stresses how he's "looking at life in a whole new way" and devoting himself to being "the best dad and father and husband I can be—and the best me." Let's examine these two insights—the honesty about impermanence and the primacy of the personal or subjective dimension—in reverse order.

Eye of the Beholder

Rather than trying to find meaning by relating life to externals—the cosmos, earthly satisfaction and success, or God—Metallica suggest finding it within. There isn't one prescription for a meaningful life, and any meaning life may have isn't objective. Rather, as "Nothing Else Matters" suggests, "life is ours" and we must "live it our way." The band is adamant that we must not force ourselves into some prescribed mold. James "never cared for what they say . . . Never cared for what they do. Never cared for what they know. And I know." It doesn't matter what everyone else says or does or "knows." What matters is what we know ourselves, and *that* we know ourselves, "forever trusting who we are." The thought is echoed in "Escape": "Don't tell me what to do . . . Feed my brain with your so-called standards. Who says that I ain't right? . . . Out for my own, out to be

[19] Rock and Roll? Impermanent? Diminishing returns? Rock and Roll will never die! Why then have some of the band members been wearing earplugs on stage for years now and why is Lars producing public-service announcements for HEAR—"Hearing Education and Awareness for Rockers"?
[20] If anyone should know, it's Metallica! Kierkegaard considers boredom a primary difficulty confronting the "Aesthetic" lifestyle—a life devoted to sensuality (or, in its higher expressions, art). See his "The Rotation Method" in *Either/Or* Vol. 1, trans. David F. Swenson and Lillian M. Swenson (Princeton: Princeton University Press, 1959), pp. 279–96.

free, one with my mind, they just can't see . . . Life is for my own to live my own way." Precisely because life has no objective meaning, we're free to create our own meaning. If life had an objective meaning, the same for everyone, we couldn't invent our own without being in denial and opposition to reality. But since, for example, there's no God to determine the goal and meaning of existence, we're free to do so on God's behalf. As Jean-Paul Sartre (1905–80) puts it:

> If God does not exist, there is at least one being . . . who exists before he can be defined by any concept, and . . . this being is man . . . man exists, turns up, appears on the scene, and, only afterwards, defines himself . . . Only afterward will he be something, and he himself will have made what he will be. Thus, there is no human nature, since there is no God to conceive it. Not only is man what he conceives himself to be, but he is also only what he wills himself to be after this thrust toward existence.[21]

We occupy the role God is often thought to play; we're the source of all value and significance in the world. Although in certain moods life and the universe seem pointless, James can "redefine anywhere." The world doesn't belong to God; "it's my world [and] you can't have it." Since it's mine, I get to decide what it means and what it's for.

Where the Wild Things Are

Just because the lack of objective meaning makes possible the creation of meaning doesn't entail all efforts to find significance are equally legitimate. We've already seen Metallica reject attempts that involve acquiring as much stuff as possible or ceding control of one's destiny to deities or priests. This is where the constraint imposed by honesty comes in.

For Hetfield, the freedom to create meaning must be understood in a way consistent with philosophical naturalism. "Naturalism" is the view that only nature exists and that it's identical to the totality of physical reality. The universe has no creator, since there are no

---

[21]   *Existentialism and Human Emotions* (New York: Carol Publishing, 1995), p. 15.

Scott Calef

non-natural events or causes. According to naturalism, everything happens according to natural laws and can in principle be explained in terms of those laws. By contrast, "supernaturalists" believe nature isn't the only reality and that non-physical, spiritual realities exist too. Supernaturalists believe the universe was created by a God who occasionally interrupts the regularities of nature. God can work miracles, and when He does, those divinely caused, non-natural events can't be predicted or explained using the laws of physics.[22]

In the naturalism-supernaturalism debate, Metallica clearly identify more with the naturalists. Accordingly, the project of creating a meaningful life requires coming to terms with the fact that we are animals—biological beings subject to death—in a world where death is necessary for life itself.[23] Living in a dangerous world is exciting, and the fact that life will end is part of what makes it precious. "Those people who tell you not to take chances, they are all missing on what life's about. You only live once, so take hold of the chance. Don't end up like others, same song and dance." The "safe" way is the mindless path of conformity, the mediocre life that risks nothing great. To experience "what life's about" you must take chances. But risk, by definition, is dangerous and threatening. Paradoxically, to really live, you must be prepared to risk life itself. You must have courage. You must make peace with death.

So far from mortality making life meaningless, then, it's integral to the value it has.[24] Precisely because life is limited we must strive to be wholly present, living with simplicity and purity in the now. This suggests a solution to the problem of death, for the fear of dying—a future event, for all readers of this chapter—is largely what scares us away from chancing great things in life. Living wholly in the now is also the key to the problem of impermanence, for the only moment

[22] The accounts of naturalism and supernaturalism are indebted to Stephen T. Davis, "Is It Rational For Christians to Believe in the Resurrection?" In *Contemporary Debates in Philosophy of Religion*, ed. by Michael Peterson and Raymond Vanarragon (Oxford: Blackwell, 2004), p. 165.
[23] "I hunt; therefore, I am" ("Of Wolf and Man"). In "Creeping Death," the sparing and deliverance of the Hebrews requires the death of lambs and the "first born pharaoh son."
[24] "Energy derives from both the plus and negative" ("Eye of the Beholder"); without the "negative" the "plus" has no power, no purpose.

114

that never ceases to be—the only unchanging time—is the present. The past and future don't exist, but the now *is*. Perhaps realizing this is the "meaning" of life. The faded prima donna is pathetic because she's dwelling forever on a past that has ceased to hold any meaning or for the sake of a future comeback ("another star denies the grave"). No wonder her life is empty; it's lived in the past and future, which are nothing. Christians (the band might argue) also refer all meaning either to the annals of history and the crucifixion and resurrection of Jesus or forward to the coming age when He returns in power and triumph. Living in the past and future, their lives are rendered shallow and unreal. The forlorn thinker who worries all is pointless because compared to infinity it's insignificant also fails to live in the present; she allows the future to infect the present with its unreality, creating the perception of a void. Consumed with foreboding that she'll be forgotten in a million years, she forgets to live today.

When searching for the meaning of life, we often look for some point to the totality of our experience. However, any meaning life as a whole can have must come from outside life since the *totality* of one's experience can only be assessed in death.[25] Moreover, in assessing life—or anything else—we try to step back, adopt an objective perspective, and come to a rational conclusion about its merit. But life concerns *subjects of experience*—namely, people; an "objective perspective" eliminates the subjectivity of life and so kills the patient under examination. Put differently, we're not going to understand uniquely and intrinsically subjective people better by intentionally ignoring the subjective dimension. But objectivity strives to do just that by being neutral. Rationality applied to life thus distorts its character and misapprehends the true nature of its subject. Being in the moment, however, takes us beyond the categories of evaluation; life's value is non-rational. The point isn't to *evaluate, judge, or issue proclamations* on life but to live it; the purpose of life is life itself.[26]

---

[25] About this, the Christians are right. Nietzsche, however, argues that pronouncements about the meaning of life as a whole are unreliable. The "*value of life cannot be estimated*. Not by a living man, because he is a party to the dispute . . . and not the judge of it; not by a dead one, for another reason." *Twilight*, p. 40.

[26] This may be an implication of biological evolution, naturalism's preferred account of human origins. Beings and systems evolve based on their success or failure at realizing the goal of survival.

In his "confession" James admits his life used to be predictable and boring whereas "life now is, is pretty exciting. You don't know what's going to happen when you're kinda clear and here and in the now. In the moment." Life is boring when it repeats the past and loses its freshness. It's predictable when we contemplate what will happen and realize we already know. But when you're "clear and here and in the now," you aren't reliving the past or anticipating the future. A person living this way feels no need to ask whether life matters.

Hetfield's metaphor for these truths is the hunter, the wolf, whose senses are totally focused and who's ready for action at any instant. "I hunt, therefore I am . . . back to the meaning of life . . . back to the meaning of wolf and man." Wolves don't fear death. Jean-Jacques Rousseau (1712–78) writes, "an animal will never know what it is to die . . . the knowledge of death and its terrors is one of the first acquisitions that man has made in moving away from the animal condition."[27] Religion, especially, makes us afraid, so we'll embrace its offer of salvation and depend upon it to assuage the apprehension it has itself instilled. Because this foreboding arises from social institutions, it's conventional and unnatural. Wolves, however, are natural. They're wild, in the moment, and willing to take risks. Wolves just are; they don't question the meaning of life. They don't mistake the meaning of *life* with amassing *inanimate* objects. "So seek the wolf in thyself." James says, "I like the animalistic part of man and nature. I don't know, sometimes I look around and see all the crap that we've accumulated. I mean, what the fuck do we need all this shit for anyway? 'Of Wolf and Man' essentially brings things back to the basics, back to the meaning of life. The song illustrates the similarities between wolves and men, and there are similarities."[28] For example, wherever I may roam, where I lay my head is home. The meaning of life is here, now.

[27] *Second Discourse on the Origin and Foundation of Inequality Among Men*, trans. by Roger D. Masters and Judith R. Masters (New York: St. Martin's Press, 1964), p. 116.
[28] Chris Ingham, *Nothing Else Matters: Metallica—The Stories Behind the Biggest Songs* (New York: Thunders' Mouth Press, 2003), p. 105.

MADNESS IN THE MIRROR OF REASON

Metallica and Foucault on Insanity and Confinement

BRIAN K. CAMERON

Madness evokes fear in us, just as it provokes a seemingly necessary social response in the form of confinement and treatment. The individual's fear of insanity is the experience of a kind of dread, a subtle yet permanent anxiety over the government of reason that unfolds all the more as we sample human society. We are left, as "Frayed Ends of Sanity" suggests, "fighting the fear of fear." Society, for its part, expresses an ambivalence toward madness that, on the one hand, accepts the artistic and imaginative productions of a tortured mind and, on the other hand, seeks to constrain and confine those who deviate too far from its pattern.

For Metallica, madness and its accompanying societal response figure as an important artistic theme in a number of songs, most notably "Welcome Home (Sanitarium)" and "Frayed Ends of Sanity." Madness erupts within the span of sometimes brooding, sometimes discordant rhythms, and is left to play upon the fertile imagination. Metallica's music reveals, as madness so often does, the dark impulses we seek to repress and deny, but which struggle to engulf us in a sea of unreason. Lyrically, Metallica has sought to illuminate the social anxieties associated with madness at the same time that they have attempted to make explicit the rebellious and socially threatening aspects of insanity. Interestingly, these same themes of fear, repression, and rebellion constitute the central concerns of the French philosopher Michel Foucault (1926–84) in his writings on madness. Like Metallica, Foucault sees madness not so much as a disease to be cured, but as a threatening aspect of individuality that western society has sought to repress and deny.

Home Sweet Home

Among Metallica songs dealing with insanity, "Welcome Home" is perhaps the most revealing. Beginning with the subtitle, "Sanitarium," we are confronted not with a mental condition, but with a physical place—an institution "where time stands still." Of course, not much happens when time stands still, suggesting that life within the sanitarium is unchanging and eventless. But you can't just stick people somewhere and simply hope that very little will happen. Rather, you have to exercise a great deal of control over the smallest detail of human life to get that result, or something like it. You need people who "dedicate their lives, to running all of his," as "The Unforgiven" describes. You'll also need physical forms of restraint. Necessary are the locked doors and windows barred that impede escape and restrict the uncontrolled interactions characteristic of life on the outside. The sanitarium cannot manage what it cannot contain, and it cannot contain what it manages without extensive force. Even when the patient voluntarily submits to the treatment, as Hetfield did for rehab, he forfeits (at least some degree of) freedom in order to be made well—a curious trade-off.

Still, the primary mechanisms of control within the sanitarium are non-physical, "feed[ing] my brain with your so-called standards," as "Escape" puts it. The social incision into the individual psyche may be as subtle as applying peer pressure to induce conformity. Or it may extend further to include pharmacological and psychocognitive therapies, even electric shock treatments and surgery (like a crash course frontal lobotomy). No matter the mode, social forces are aligned to whisper things into the patient's brain in order to regain control and induce conformity. And, as in *One Flew Over the Cuckoo's Nest* (which inspired the song), we find a general willingness to deploy extensive social forces to control those who fail to conform.

But "Welcome Home" doesn't remain centered on the institution and its various forms of control. Near the end, it turns inward and reflects on the condition of the confined patient. There is, on the one hand, the "fear of living on" and, on the other hand, the seemingly twisted and paradoxical goal of killing in order to reconnect to normalcy—"seems the only way, for reaching out again." What sense can we make of this?

Total Institutions:
An Actual Master of Puppets

The sanitarium is what Foucault called a "total institution." Like the prison, it is an isolated and self-contained space where every detail of human existence is carefully studied and meticulously controlled. Set apart and isolated from the larger society, the total institution is nonetheless very much within the grasp of social powers. Against the disorder that is insanity or criminality, is the vast order of the total institution, replete with its rules, regulations, schedules, and requirements, all designed to make the patient or criminal "better" and able to reorient herself toward socially defined goals. In large part, this is accomplished by a kind of machinery of power that employs surveillance and observation to control those caught up within its all-pervasive gaze.

In the dungeon, it was the power of the king or prince that was made visible, while those within the dungeon were rendered more or less invisible and superfluous. Curiously, however, total institutions (and modern societies generally) reverse this mechanism by making those within them visible to a power that is invisible and unverifiable, essentially by means of surveillance. You'll recognize this principle if you pay attention to all those black globes in virtually every store you walk into—we are being made visible to a power that is essentially unverifiable (we never know, after all, if we are being watched).

Ideally, nothing can escape the gaze of the institutional machinery—all deviance, all abnormality, all aberrant behavior, is seen, catalogued, studied, and controlled. The total institution is therefore a kind of machinery for producing knowledge of deviance and abnormality at the same time that it is a machine for producing a power that manages and controls that deviance. It is a machine that produces knowledge of how to control bodies (rather than persons) in order to make them docile and obedient. Like the Master of Puppets, it is pulling your strings.

The total institution first came on the scene in seventeenth-century Europe. The very first sanitarium, the Hôpital Général (1656), set itself the task of preventing begging and idleness "as the source of all disorders."[1] Where previously the leper might find himself a living outcast from society—not a "messiah" but a person left to die amid a colony of the dying—the madman was now caught up within an isolated yet socially defined space. Where the leper was isolated but left alone, the madman was isolated in order to be better controlled. What accounts for this difference? "Confinement," as Foucault points out, "was required by something quite different from any concern with curing the sick. What made it necessary was an imperative of labor."[2]

In all previous ages labor was looked down upon as something that, while necessary, could not for that very reason be among our truly human powers. A person labors because he must. But what defines us as human is our capacity to be free, an idea expressed in the hopeful declaration of "Welcome Home": "I see our freedom in my sight." So what changed? The seventeenth century discovered the power of labor: the power to create a new world of things, and a new power to recreate a world of laborers.

What does this have to do with the madman? First, there was the seventeenth-century belief that laziness was the source of mental dysfunction. If we could make the sick work—rather than keep them tied—we could make them well. Or so it was thought. Second, by depriving us of the use of reason, madness stripped away what essentially separated us from animals. The mad were not animals in the literal sense, but they could no longer function in the human world. So it made sense to confine and restrain them in order to tame

[1] Michel Foucault, *Madness and Civilization: A History of Insanity in the Age of Reason*, trans. by Richard Howard (New York: Vintage Books, 1965), p. 47.
[2] Foucault, p. 46.

their animal impulses (the rage of the patient in the sanitarium, for instance).

Yet what really accounts for the historical emergence of the total institution is the understanding that madmen, if left to their own devices, would be exempt from laboring precisely because they were themselves unable to exercise the self-control necessary for them to be productive members of society. While their true numbers might be small, there were too many like them who, for various reasons, could not or would not labor. It was necessary, therefore, to take them out of their ordinary surroundings and confine them with others (beggars, the desperately poor, the marginalized) in a place where they could be made to work.

That such institutions eventually lost their connection with labor and became fully medical or penal institutions has less to do with our diminished interest in labor than with our increased ability to more precisely define (or create?) degrees of abnormality or criminality and prescribe new interventions to control these. Instead of the twofold divisions between sanity and insanity that prevailed previously, we now have a vast continuum of mental disease and disorder that justifies an equally vast array of chemical, psychological, and physical interventions. Hetfield's own alcoholism is now seen as a medical condition, a condition that carries with it an imperative to treat, cure, restore, and renormalize. In short, we have learned how to use the scientifically defined categories of psychological deviance (a form of knowledge) in order to adjust our controls over the individual (a form of power). Yet in all that we have never lost interest in controlling bodies and making them docile and obedient.

Indeed, what Foucault calls the "power-knowledge" relation is in all total institutions. We have all heard the refrain that "knowledge is power," so it should come as no real surprise that as we acquire more knowledge about deviance (which, among other things, means a failure to comply or conform), we should learn better how to control that particular deviation.

But it works the other way as well: power creates knowledge. The power to confine is likewise the power to study and observe—the patient within the sanitarium is the object of study. The sanitarium is therefore a vast factory of knowledge, a testing ground for determining what forms of control are best adapted to what kinds of patient.

And it is a factory whose products are destined to be used outside its limits, in society at large.

Not only has psychological and psychiatric knowledge made its way into our popular culture, it has likewise provided us with a justification to monitor carefully, intervene upon, subtly adjust, and restudy our children—"always censoring my every move." Now, with the aid of sophisticated psychometric tests, we can at least create some of the conditions of the total institution within our public schools. We can better control our children and form them to fit the roles they will someday play as workers, consumers, and debtors. Is it any wonder when our children scream "dear mother / dear father / what is this hell you have put me through"?

Sad, but True

What is it about the nature of madness that evokes fear and provokes confinement and control? In part, we already have an answer—madness is feared because it represents a kind of living death, a death of the human within the life of the animal. Indeed, the symbolic alignment between death and madness is a persistent cultural theme in the West, so much so that the sanitarium is a place "where time stands still. Where no one leaves and no one will." Not unlike death. But, if Foucault is correct, there is yet another explanation.

Alongside the legal-political order (the order that establishes the sanitarium and the prison) lies the moral order. In principle, the two orders run a kind of parallel course, both aiming to establish rational rule (whatever that might mean). In the legal-political order madness, like criminality, constitutes a break with that order and therefore provokes a socially necessary response. In the moral order, madness likewise represents a kind of break because it signals the possibility of scandal and immorality. Historically, the mad were thought to be unconstrained by the limits of public morality and therefore capable of virtually any act, behavior, or intention. Madness was therefore a disorder that always carried with it a kind of moral imperative—not so much a judgment *against* the madman, for his condition could be pitied, though not easily condemned. Rather, madness evoked the fear of moral disorder and provoked the moral imperative to fix, treat, or otherwise intercede in the lives of the insane.

Consider how and why lepers and madmen were treated differently. Lepers represented a threat to the individual, to the individual's immediate physical existence. Consequently, they had to be removed from society not because they could not function within it, but because they represented a danger to its members. Madmen, by contrast, represent a threat to the rule of reason, a direct challenge to the government of law and morality, to civilization itself. They might be removed and carried away in a "ship of fools" (such things actually existed), but not safely. Better that they be isolated but kept squarely within the reach of social power in order that their special "contagion" not spread too far.

Madness evoked fear, therefore, because it signaled disorder and potential chaos: it was the mirror image and opposite of the order established by reason. It provoked the response it did (confinement) because it was necessary to contain the threat rather than let it spread. And it became linked to medical science (psychiatry, in particular) because scientific descriptions of "disorder," "abnormality," "insanity," and the like, always carried with them the apparent justification to intervene by means of a "treatment" and "cure." In other words, science offered a convenient mechanism to align power-knowledge in a way that justified the exercise of vast social powers.

Of course, western cultural attitudes regarding madness were not and are not always as one-sided as this analysis might suggest. Indeed, there has always been a curious ambivalence in our attitudes regarding madness that signals yet another way in which insanity can be understood. Instead of seeing madness as the opposite of reason, it is also possible to see madness as the extreme point of reason itself. In genius we are often confronted with the possibility of both brilliance and disorder, of minds that are simultaneously situated at the extreme points of remarkable talent and remarkable deficiency. Is it possible to confine the mad genius without "tear[ing] out everything inspired"? Indeed, as Foucault notes, many of the great artistic and intellectual achievements of the West were products of the mentally unstable. And, if we extend our thinking outward to consider the deployment of reason in social systems, we realize that remarkable scientific and technological achievements that require amazing powers of reasoning might likewise result in seemingly insane consequences, like the development and build-up of nuclear forces leading to the decision to "fight fire with fire." Madness, then, may evoke fear not simply because it represents the end of order and reason, but because it represents a side of reason that we wish to repress and deny.

The Mirror Stares Back Hard: The Existential Cost of Rebellion

"Welcome Home" has little to say about the subjective experience of being insane, a subject considered in "Frayed Ends of Sanity" and a perennial obsession for other heavy metal artists like Ozzy Osbourne, Iron Maiden, and Slayer. Instead, the song focuses on the rage that accompanies confinement, the fear of living on (in confinement?), and the desire to kill.

In "The Unforgiven," "New blood joins this earth / and quickly he's subdued." So maybe it's best to consider the confinement within the sanitarium as a metaphor—a way to talk about the frustration we feel at being forced (confined) to conform to a society that "rape[s] my mind and destroy[s] my feelings." Rock 'n' roll has generally presented itself as rebellious, and Metallica has been quick to market itself as a champion of rebellion and anti-conformity. Madness is not just a possible psychological response to the pressures of modern society, it's also a kind of rebellion against the rule of rules, against the herd impulse toward conformity. We are told how to think, what to think, how to love, whom to love, how to form relationships, how to end relationships, how to stay healthy, what to eat, what not to eat, how to exercise, how to make money, how to keep our money, how to dress, how to impress, how to stay unstressed, and so on, and so on. We are "hidden in your world you've made for me." In short, we live in a society that is so fundamentally conformist and rules-bound that we often find ourselves yearning for freedom "to escape from the true false world"—madness is one such route, albeit not a happy one.

You might think that rage is a natural response to such a condition. But this would be wrong. The most immediate response to entrapment is "escape," the flight response. Frustration arises when we try and fail repeatedly; rage sets in when we come to realize that there is, or may be, no escape. The patient in the sanitarium (and perhaps we are all in the sanitarium?) experiences rage precisely because she comes to realize that there may be no escape from the pressure of being told constantly what to think, who to be, how to act, how to conform, how to fit in. As in "The Unforgiven," "this fight he cannot win."

But rebellions, no matter their justifications or causes, always exact a cost from the rebel. Resisting the blind and mindless urgings of our fellow herd creatures takes an inevitable toll upon those who resist— it can make us angry, resentful, enraged, scornful, bitter, and generally misanthropic. We might call these the "existential costs" of rebellion, since they are the costs exacted upon our lives and existence for choosing to rebel against our social nature. Perhaps this is what Hetfield meant when, in *Some Kind of Monster*, he spoke of his own boredom with the life of (rebellious) drinking and debauchery. In "The Unforgiven" he puts it this way: "They dedicate their lives / to running all of his / he tries to please them all / this bitter man he is." He becomes bitter, not because he has been told all his life what to do, but because in resisting that pressure to conform he has had to close himself off. So the mirror stares back hard, because our resistance to the pressure to conform can make us into something even more contemptible than the thing we tried not to be. And perhaps because we rebel not against a particular society, but against what is essential to the human condition—sociality—we are left with regret, "the old man then prepares / to die regretfully."

Even so, it's one thing to move toward anger and rage, and quite another to kill or have the desire to kill. In "Welcome Home" killing "seems the only way for reaching out again." Probably Metallica simply intends to suggest that the madman has the desire to kill. Why should he think killing would reconnect him with others? Metallica may have something else in mind when it suggests the connection between killing and reconnecting to normal society. Consider these lines: "they think our heads are in their hands / but violent use brings violent plans." The sanitarium is a place that requires a considerable level of force or violence to maintain its functionality. But violence, like any force, calls forth resistance. The total institution, of which the sanitarium is a prime example, applies force not so much to restrain (which is merely a precondition of it being able to accomplish its goal) but to control every aspect of the individual in order that he or she may be "cured" or "reformed." To remake the individual requires that we unmake the old, that we forcibly destroy the patient's individuality so that it can be remade along the lines deemed acceptable by society. Now I'm not suggesting that the intention to "cure" or "reform" the individual cannot be noble and good, for it surely can be and often is. I'm merely pointing out that the practice is inherently coercive, and potentially violent. And, as the song points out, "violent use brings violent plans." The nexus between killing and "reaching out" to society, therefore, may lie in the recognition that our methods of dealing with the mentally ill (and with prisoners) are essentially coercive.

Neither Foucault nor Metallica sees madness as primarily explained by the medical model of disease (even if it does have a physiological basis). In other words, neither thinks that madness is something that is merely given in nature. Like gender or sexual orientation, madness may be something that has a physiological component, but its definition, its boundaries, and our response to it are all things we superimpose upon it according to our interest to control. What, we might ask, are the costs to ourselves in imposing such control over others? The mirror stares back hard.

RIDE THE LIGHTNING
Why Not Execute Killers?

THOM BROOKS

"Ride the Lightning," what a great album title. It oozes metal power and echoes Diamond Head's *Lightning to the Nations*. Strangely, the phrase itself is nowhere to be found in the lyrics to the album, not even on the title track. What are we to make of it? The electric chair on the album cover and the story told by the song make the reference clear. From its grinding and merciless beginning to its emphatic conclusion, "Ride the Lightning" charts the fear and horror of a condemned man awaiting his execution in the electric chair. With this song, Metallica touches on a thorny issue and provides a unique point of view. The legitimacy of the death penalty continues to confound us, and too rarely do we consider the issue from the perspective of the condemned.

"Ride the Lightning" is fraught with tension and ambiguity, and so sorting out its message concerning the death penalty is difficult. On one hand it's a chilling and gruesome tale. Inspired by the song, a glow in the dark electrocution adorned the back of the "Metal Up Your Ass" shirts. That image (and perhaps the song) might seem to suggest that it's cool to electrocute someone. Then again, maybe the artwork is meant to bring home the horror of the condemned, take it out from behind closed doors and make it glow in your face. It's possible to conclude that "Ride the Lightning" is an anti-death penalty anthem. But, speaking of the song, James Hetfield has said, "I believe in capital punishment, but it was more about the idea of being strapped in the electric chair even though you didn't commit the crime."[1]

The fact that Hetfield intends to portray a man who is executed despite his innocence would seem to cut against support for the death penalty. Even more so than some inherent evil in state execution, the most common arguments against it tend to be that capital punishment is dispensed unfairly across racial and socioeconomic lines and that innocent people are sometimes executed. In recent years DNA evidence has freed increasing numbers of prisoners from death row. So Hetfield must have strong and firmly held beliefs that would cause him to support the death penalty despite the recognition that the innocent are sometimes executed.

So is that it? The song is not anti-death penalty? Case closed? The power of a piece of music may not only be our enjoyment in listening to it, but the variety of rich interpretations it offers us. Herein lies the greatness of "Ride the Lightning." If we follow Hetfield's explanation, it is a piece of music that seeks only to bring to life the raw emotions of a man lacking control in a terrible affair. But how many fans really know what Hetfield thinks and intends when they listen to the song? After all, Hetfield doesn't make a habit of telling fans what his songs are about, preferring to leave the listener alone with the lyrics. So another possible interpretation is that the song moves us to question the justifiability of capital punishment on a number of fronts. As we shall see, because of an ambiguity in the lyrics, this is the interpretation that makes the most sense for those unaware of Hetfield's professed intentions. And, in fact, the tension and ambiguity in the song may reflect Hetfield's own tension and ambivalence concerning this difficult issue.

Executing Murderers: Fighting Fire with Fire?

The song begins: "Guilty as charged / But damn it, it ain't right." Notice that the phrase "guilty as charged" is ambiguous. It could refer to the judge's pronouncement or it could be the prisoner's

---

[1] *Guitar World*, December 1998; see www.encycmet.com/songs/srride.shtml.

admission. In fact, without knowing that Hetfield intends to depict a prisoner who was wrongly convicted, it might make most sense to interpret the line as the prisoner admitting guilt. Indeed, we often use the expression "guilty as charged" to mean that we are not innocent of an accusation.

So assuming the prisoner is guilty, should we "Fight Fire with Fire"? "Do unto others as they have done unto you"? Many people believe we should. Murderers have killed someone, and they have no valid complaint against our wanting to kill them in return. A life for a life seems a valid exchange.

We know from the beginning that the condemned is facing death and flooded with fear. He says: "There is someone else controlling me / Death in the air / Strapped in the electric chair / This can't be happening to me." The lyrics are reinforced by Hetfield's unsettling rhythm guitar, Hammett's otherworldly guitar solo, Burton's darkly delicious bass lines, and Ulrich's pounding drums. Immediately we are thrown into the perspective of the condemned, feeling the growing fear and anxiety of his final moments.

But the prisoner's plea that no one has a right to kill him seems disingenuous. "Who made you God to say / I'll take your life from you!" He is in his predicament solely in virtue of the fact that he killed someone else. This plea is repeated in the bridge: "Someone help me / Oh please God help me / They are trying to take it all away / I don't want to die." We might think that's too bad. If you didn't want to die, you shouldn't have killed your victim. The song seems misguided in trying to rouse our sympathy for the murderer. Having killed someone himself, the condemned is hypocritical in saying only God has the right to take life.

But maybe this view of the condemned man is too harsh and too simple. The song doesn't paint the picture of a homicidal maniac. On one interpretation at least, we have a man "guilty as charged" and repentant, begging for God's help in freeing him from his "frightening dream." The condemned man isn't hypocritically claiming it's OK for him to kill. He has come to the realization that killing is wrong: only God can take life, not human beings. He has come to terms with his wrongdoing; he is a new person and not who he was before. But still we might think that this doesn't matter. Why should we care that he is a changed person when what matters is that he is a murderer who deserves his punishment?

Metallica's unique blend of roaring guitars and revealing lyrics opens up new possibilities and keeps us thinking. The intensity of the condemned man's anguish and the sincerity of his plea moves us to consider whether his execution is warranted. An eye for an eye and a life for a life may seem perfectly reasonable in abstraction, but there is a difference when we have a real person before us who is about to "die by our hands." The condemned man is clearly repentant, but is repentance relevant to whether or not we execute this man? He may well have visited fear upon his victim, but who are we to visit fear upon him? Do two wrongs make a right?

The classic theory of punishment is "retributivism," which holds that criminals should be punished to a degree equal to what they deserve. This theory feeds upon our everyday intuitions. After all, who could disagree with a system where criminals get what they deserve? Nevertheless, it's far from clear how we should use this abstract theory in real life. We often think that punishment should somehow "equal" a crime. But it's not easy to determine the values of crime and punishment. For example, how many days' imprisonment is "equal" to a robbery? How much of a fine is "equal" to illegal parking? We seem to be satisfied with crimes and their punishments so long as our intuitions agree with our practices. In other words, we may have no idea how many hours of community service is "equal" to a public disorder offense, yet we might be satisfied with someone having to perform 100 hours of service as a result of his crime. Our intuition of whether justice is best served in a given case helps us determine whether a punishment fits with a crime. We simply do not have any obvious way to calculate the particular punishment for any particular crime.

That said, murder seems strangely different. We might not be able to punish "like for like" with other crimes, but we can with murder. For example, it's unclear how exactly we should punish a thief like for like. Do we steal money back from the thief? With murderers, it's clear. We can punish them like for like—we can execute them. This view is captured well by the eighteenth-century philosopher Immanuel Kant (1724–1804), who says:

> Whatever undeserved evil you inflict upon another within the people, you inflict upon yourself. If you insult him, you insult yourself; if you

steal from him, you steal from yourself; if you strike him, you strike yourself; if you kill him, you kill yourself.[2]

Kant's view is that criminals should be punished equal to what they deserve. The punishment for murder is the easiest to determine. When a murderer kills an innocent person, the murderer has destroyed something of infinite worth. The only thing the murderer has of infinite worth is his own life. Thus, the only punishment that will be equal to the wrongness of his crime is his execution.

So because equal and proportionate punishment seems obvious for murder we might think it is obvious that murderers should be executed. But we need to think about this more carefully. If murder is the worst crime and death is the worst punishment, then the punishment fits the crime. But, then again, maybe the worst punishment is being tortured, hung, drawn and quartered, before being bled to death in front of an angry mob. Why not set this worst punishment "equal" to murder? There is a simple answer: most people find this kind of thing barbaric and evil. The murderer may have performed a grave deed, but there is no need to stoop to his detestable level. We do not impose the worst punishment imaginable on the worst crimes imaginable because we do not want to treat people—even murderers—in that way. It has nothing to do with making a punishment "equal" to crime. It is instead about fit: a punishment should fit our intuitive sense of what is legitimate and justified for a crime.

Of course, it is true that not everyone shares this intuition. Some people believe that perhaps we ought to torture criminals. Using more "barbaric" punishments might bring about a deterrent effect. More lives might be saved if harsher punishments were used. Yet there is simply no evidence to suggest that executing murderers by whatever method has a deterrent effect. In fact, the opposite is true. When we execute murderers, states can expect a slight *rise* in the murder rate. That is, murders tend to *increase* rather than decrease

---

[2] Immanuel Kant, *Metaphysic of Morals*, ed. M. Gregor (Cambridge: Cambridge University Press, 1996), p. 105 (6:332). See my "Corlett on Kant, Hegel, and Retribution," *Philosophy* 76 (2001): 561–80; "Kant's Theory of Punishment," *Utilitas* 15 (2003): 206–24; and "Is Hegel a Retributivist?" *Bulletin of the Hegel Society of Great Britain* 49/50 (2004): 113–26.

after executions. This phenomenon has been called the "brutalization effect."[3]

We might also argue that the murderer deserves harsher punishments, such as torture and death, because he killed someone dear to us. But we live by the rule of law. Murderers have broken a public law and deserve public justice. Think about a world where people managed criminal justice on their own, a world in which we all acted as judge, jury, and executioner when wronged. On our own, we may well err in knowing how we were wronged, who wronged us, or what the appropriate punishment might be. We would not be concerned with public justice, but with the satisfaction of our own blood-lust. The rule of law offers protection and promises. It offers a system that rich and poor, young and old can call on to correct wrongs they have suffered. We do not individually decide anyone's fate. This is a matter for the state. The rule of law is about satisfying public justice, not private vengeance. It is right that our punishments are neither cruel nor unusual, no matter the plea of grieving families.

The Use of Death

"Ride the Lightning" helps us see that even if the murderer killed someone and even if he seems disingenuous when he demands we have no right to kill him, perhaps we really don't have a right to kill him. Killing people, even murderers, might not be justified. Perhaps we should not "Fight Fire with Fire" after all, especially if we empathize with the horror of the condemned and his claim of redemption. The entire second verse brings this to life: "Wait for the sign / To flick the switch of death / It's the beginning of the end / Sweat, chilling cold / As I watch death unfold / Consciousness my only friend / My fingers grip with fear / What am I doing here?"

We despise the person's crime, but we empathize with his plight. The song puts us in the condemned man's shoes. Walking down the corridor. Strapped into the chair. People rushing around us preparing

---

[3] See William J. Bowers and Glenn L. Pierce, "Deterrence or Brutalization: What is the Effect of Executions?" *Crime and Delinquency* 26 (1980): 453–84.

the scene. We sit and wait. Waiting for an unknown horror, the advent of our death. Nothing to live for, not even perhaps another minute. Anticipation. The kill.

Executing a murderer is almost always an event unlike the murder itself. Murder is not usually planned meticulously. Victims are not usually told exactly what time their death will come and by what means. But the condemned man knows these things. It's almost as if he dies twice. He first dies knowing there is no hope, no future. His execution date is set. A black cloud of despair hovers. He dies a second time with the execution. He fears death not only at the moment of his death—as his victim may have done—but every day, as he sits on death row awaiting his turn. This point is spelled out well by the philosopher Jonathan Glover:

> Many of us would rather die suddenly than linger for weeks or months knowing we were fatally ill, and the condemned man's position is several degrees worse than that of the person given a few months to live by doctors. He has the additional horror of knowing exactly when he will die, and of knowing that his death will be in a ritualized killing by other people, symbolizing his ultimate rejection by the members of his community . . . For reasons of this kind, capital punishment can plausibly be claimed to fall under the United States constitution's [*sic*] ban on "cruel and unusual punishments."[4]

The murder victim probably didn't know her life was about to end. Perhaps it came swiftly in a raging whirl. By contrast, the murderer knows precisely when he will die. His death will be a ritual. A witness gallery will fill with people; prison staff will offer a last meal, a final prayer, and administer the means of his death. All will be known in advance. It is cruel to let a man—even a murderer—live in angst for years knowing that each morning his death approaches ever more swiftly.

Because it reduces us to barbarians, death is not a justified punishment for murderers. The murderer's punishment is not proportional to his crime; he suffers more than his victim, dying twice. The prisoner in "Ride the Lightning" is right to say we have no right to kill him, even if he killed someone himself.

---

[4] Jonathan Glover, *Causing Death and Saving Lives* (London: Penguin, 1977), p. 232.

Instead of a Conclusion

If we shouldn't execute murderers, what should we do? "Ride the Lightning" is silent on the way forward, and so too is this chapter. But how much can we expect from one song and one essay? Perhaps the silence and ambiguity is a good thing. After all, it leaves us thinking.[5]

[5] My most sincere thanks to Joanna Corwin and Bill Irwin for their many helpful suggestions which have improved this chapter.

CHAPTER 12

LIVING AND DYING AS ONE

Suffering and the Ethics of Euthanasia

JASON T. EBERL

The arena is dark and the stage is empty . . . suddenly an explosion . . . then another, and another! Your heart is racing, but your eardrums are still intact to hear Hetfield strum the first few chords of "One." The war zone quiets down in the darkness to let you know that you've entered the "dark night of the soul," a night when only your *self* seems to exist.[1]

"One" (the song and video) uses Dalton Trumbo's film *Johnny Got His Gun* to explore what life is like when a man (Joe Bonham) lies limbless and "tied to machines that make me be." He has a fully conscious mind, but is unable to communicate until someone picks up that he's nodding "S-O-S" in Morse code. None of us can fully imagine what life in such a state of limbo—a state of suspension between this world and the next—would be like. But the music of "One" makes us feel some of what Joe feels: the sounds of the war that leads to his near-demise; the quiet solace of being alone with himself; finally the frantic rhythm guitar and pounding drums that provide the soundtrack for the terror Joe must feel, enduring his existence as a nearly disembodied mind.

---

[1] St. John of the Cross, *Dark Night of the Soul*, trans. E. Allison Peers (New York: Doubleday, 1959).

This is not just fiction. Many people actually live a life "locked-in" to their own selves and their own experiences of pain, loss, and utter disconnectedness from the world around them. And like Joe, some would prefer death to continued existence.

"Welcome to Where Time Stands Still"— The Nature of Suffering

When Joe first awakens after being nearly bombed out of existence, he is disoriented, without a sense of time or place, and unable to perceive the world around him. It even takes a while for him to realize that all his limbs have been amputated. This realization, along with the absence of external stimuli, leads Joe first to question his mental status—"I don't know whether I'm alive and dreaming or dead and remembering"[2]—and then to conclude that "nothing is real but pain now." It's not merely physical pain that Joe experiences, but *suffering*, which "ordinarily refers to a person's psychological or spiritual state, and is characteristically marked by a sense of anguish, dread, foreboding, futility, meaninglessness, or a range of other emotions associated with a loss of meaning or control or both."[3] Suffering is a psychological state that goes beyond the mere perception that one is in pain.

Joe's fictional plight depicts several forms of suffering that also characterize the experience of many persons who are terminally ill or otherwise seriously and irreversibly debilitated. For one, they may feel separated from other people. Joe's experience of this separation is severe, but even those who aren't "locked-in,"[4] as Joe is, nevertheless sometimes retreat into themselves when confronted with terminal

[2] Unless otherwise cited, all quotations which are not Metallica's lyrics are from Dalton Trumbo's film *Johnny Got His Gun* (World Entertainers, 1971).
[3] Daniel Callahan, *The Troubled Dream of Life: In Search of a Peaceful Death* (Washington, DC: Georgetown University Press, 2000), p. 95.
[4] Joe's medical condition is not entirely fictional. Patients who suffer from "locked-in" syndrome may be fully conscious, but are paralyzed except for voluntary eye movements, which is analogous to Joe's ability to nod his head to communicate using Morse code.

illness: "Getting lost within myself / Nothing matters no one else" ("Fade to Black"). This retreat from the world can magnify one's despair to the point of contemplating suicide. For many patients, this desire to turn inward may be due in part to their feeling ashamed of their disabled and dependent existence. Joe wonders, "Will anybody ever come to visit me? I hope not. I really wouldn't want anybody to see me like this."

In tragic irony, this withdrawal from others actually can have the undesired effect of alienation from *oneself*: "Missing one inside of me . . . I was me, but now he's gone." As Aristotle observed, we are "social animals"[5]—human beings naturally seek association with each other. German philosopher Georg Hegel (1770–1831) took this idea a step further by describing the ways in which a person comes to develop her own self-conscious identity through *recognition* by others: "Self-consciousness exists in and for itself when, and by the fact that, it so exists for another; that is, it exists only in being acknowledged."[6] Joe feels this loss of recognition when he observes, "All they want is to push me back into the darkness down here, so they won't ever see me again," and complains, "Inside, I'm screaming and howling like a trapped animal, but nobody pays any attention to me." This experience reflects a truism Joe's father notes: "Each man faces death by himself, alone." Metallica echoes: "Now the world is gone and I'm just one." It's exacerbated by the seemingly *endless* nature of Joe's current state. He must live "on through the never" without even the ability to measure the passage of time. He says at one point, "I don't know what year I'm in and I'm trying to get back into time . . . all I think about is time."

Joe and others in similar situations also suffer from the loss of their previously *active* lifestyle. As Metallica and their fans assert, "When we start to rock / we never want to stop again" ("Hit the Lights"). It's almost impossible for active people to imagine life tied to a single room, a single bed. But even more significant is loss of *control*. Immanuel Kant, John Stuart Mill, and many other philosophers have

---

[5]   Aristotle, *Nicomachean Ethics*, trans. by Terence Irwin (Indianapolis: Hackett, 1999), 1097b9.
[6]   G.W.F. Hegel, *Phenomenology of Spirit*, trans. by A.V. Miller (Oxford: Oxford University Press, 1997), §178.

argued since the dawn of the Enlightenment in the seventeenth century that a person's self-identity and self-worth are largely dictated by one's degree of *autonomy*—the capacity to determine one's own actions and, within certain natural limits, how one's life will unfold.[7] But instead of functioning as autonomous *agents* in control of their behavior and, to some extent, their destiny, terminally ill patients must live with their future determined by their present condition—they've become *victims*.

This leads to another form of suffering. A person who previously enjoyed an *integrated* life of mind and body functioning in harmony now perceives herself as deficient. She is only a mental entity whose body is her "holding cell." The body and mind have not been separated. Rather, the mind is trapped in a broken body which, in many cases, must be maintained artificially. This may have the effect of reducing the person to a *thing*. When he's first brought into the military hospital, Joe is labeled "Unidentified casualty #47." After his initial surgeries, he's stored in a utility room to save valuable space in the hospital ward; one doctor declares, "He can't tell the difference." Once he's aware of his situation, Joe describes himself as "a piece of meat that keeps on living" and "like some freak in a carnival show."

Such reduction of a patient's personhood entails an acute loss of *dignity* and severely affects the patient's perception of his life's value. Conversely, as Joe's captain asserts when viewing an enemy soldier's body from the trenches, "Death has a dignity all its own." Even Joe's physician sees no *intrinsic* value to his life—no good reason in and of itself for his life to continue—and solemnly pronounces his judgment: "There's no justification for his continued existence unless we learn from him how to help others." Joe appears to be truly a "thing" insofar as his life seems to have only *instrumental* value for others.

---

[7] See Immanuel Kant, *Groundwork for the Metaphysics of Morals*, trans. H.J. Paton (New York: Harper and Row, 1964), pp. 114–16; John Stuart Mill, *'On Liberty' and Other Writings*, ed. Stefan Collini (New York: Cambridge University Press, 1989).

"Harvester of Sorrow"—Is There
Any Value to Suffering?

It's no surprise that someone in Joe's situation (or someone who suffers from a terminal or severely debilitating illness) may see no value in his continued existence: "Hold my breath as I wish for death." But a suffering person doesn't necessarily *want* to die; rather, he may be "dying to live," simply wanting to end his suffering. Joe prays: "Oh please God, wake me."

But is escape from suffering the only real alternative? Could some meaning or value be found in a suffering person's life that could provide her sufficient solace not to wish for death? It's clear that suffering has no *intrinsic* value; no one seeks suffering for its own sake. Rather, if suffering is to have any value, it's only because it may serve some greater purpose. A simple and clear example is enduring the pain of the dentist's drill in order to have healthy teeth. Dental health is the desired goal and the pain suffered is simply a negative side-effect of the treatment necessary to achieve this goal.

Various reasons, based on both religious and secular values, have been given to support suffering's potential instrumental value.[8] Different religious traditions have embraced the *spiritual* value of suffering. In some traditions, suffering is seen partly as a punishment and a means to atone for sins: "I'm your pain while you repay" ("Sad But True"). But Pope John Paul II emphasized the spiritually *healing* nature of suffering: "Suffering must be for conversion, that is, for the rebuilding of goodness in the [sufferer], who can recognize the divine mercy in this call to repentance."[9] This is not to imply that a person suffers because, and to the extent that, she does bad deeds; but the recognition that everyone fails in some respect to be completely good opens the door for suffering's healing role.

---

[8] Much of what follows is drawn from my presentation "Recognizing the Value of Suffering in Caring for Terminally Ill Patients," delivered at "Suffering and Hope," an interdisciplinary conference sponsored by the Center for Thomistic Studies at the University of St. Thomas in Houston, Texas in November, 2005.
[9] John Paul II, *Salvifici doloris* (Rome: Vatican Polyglot Press, 1984), §12.

For an interminably suffering person, ending her life may seem to be the only way left for her to exercise autonomy. But one can also exercise control over one's own fate by searching for the possible meaning and value of suffering, rather than denying such a possibility: "When I have options to my suffering, suffering is greatly reduced. A sense of impotence, a lack of control over my own destiny, aggravates suffering or, sometimes, can convert pain to suffering."[10] An exercise of autonomous self-determination can also lead to a richer, more integrated experience of one's own selfhood: "In our response to the mystery of suffering, we define ourselves, find our integrity and ultimately shape our ethos."[11]

Consider also that suffering can cause separation between the sufferer and others:

> Suffering, in a sense, separates persons from community. Suffering persons tend to withdraw into themselves and to feel alienated from a community going on with its daily lives and tasks while they suffer. When communities ignore those within their embrace who are suffering and when they treat them uncaringly or callously the integrity and solidarity of community is shattered. (Loewy, p. 13)

Recognizing the universal suffering of all humanity, though, allows for a universal response to suffering in *solidarity*. By communally recognizing the limits of human life and the universal experience of suffering, a collective response can be made by all persons. Autonomy at the level of the individual does not disappear, but is exercised in communion with all other individuals. In this way, the solidarity of the human community is formed and expressed not only in the universal passive experience of pain, suffering, and death, but also in an active response to such experience: "The suffering individual and the community in which such suffering occurs cannot be separated.

---

[10] Erich H. Loewy, *Suffering and the Beneficent Community: Beyond Libertarianism* (Albany: SUNY Press, 1991), p. 11. This presumes that a patient is able to exercise self-control and autonomy, as opposed to being mindlessly swept up in unbearable suffering. Further references to this book are given parenthetically in the body of the chapter as references to Loewy with page numbers.

[11] Theodore Fleischer, "Suffering Reclaimed: Medicine According to Job," *Perspectives in Biology and Medicine* 42 (1999), p. 475.

When community supplies solidarity and purpose, suffering is transmuted" (Loewy, p. 6).

"Into Distance Let Me Fade"— The Ethics of Euthanasia

But not everyone can reach out and claim the potential values of suffering. For such people it appears that the only real option left is for their life to end: "I have lost the will to live / Simply nothing more to give / There is nothing more for me / Need the end to set me free" ("Fade to Black"). The most controversial way of ending such a life is *active euthanasia*, or "mercy killing." This is what Joe asks for when he nods his head in Morse code: "Kill me. Over and over again—kill me!"[12]

Voluntary active euthanasia puts an end to pain and suffering, and is also seen by some as the ultimate exercise of autonomy. It's an escape from the undignified nature of one's current life and, if there's some sort of afterlife to follow, a return to one's true nature. Furthermore, any escape from the imprisonment of one's own mind or one's own consuming suffering may be deemed worth pursuing.

Although the primary motive for active euthanasia is compassion, it may be a misplaced compassion insofar as the act of killing a terminally ill or debilitated person might communicate, however unwittingly, a message that a vulnerable person's life is inherently valueless. Whether such a message is perceived by the person herself, which may not follow if she is asking for death, or by others witnessing her

---

[12] We should note, though, that Joe first asks if he can be put in a carnival show where people can see him so that he can bear witness to the ravages of war "just like a wartime novelty." It's only after that initial request is denied that he asks for death. This goes to show that Joe, like many other suffering persons, does not wish for death *per se*. Rather, he seeks to transcend his suffering by fulfilling some instrumental purpose—in this case, demonstrating the cost of war and raising the question of whether such violence is worth it in the end. When fulfilling this purpose is denied to him by the "powers that be" he then questions whether his continued existence is worth it.

plight, a vital concern is that an *objective* devaluing of human life is occurring nevertheless.[13]

Another form of euthanasia commonly prescribed, since active euthanasia is morally questionable and thus banned in all US states but Oregon,[14] is so-called *passive euthanasia*, which involves withholding or withdrawing life-sustaining treatment. Joe's condition requires artificial support and he complains about being "fed through the tube that sticks in me," so that "in pumps life that I must feel." The *passive* nature of Joe's dependence on machines erodes his autonomy and dignity and amplifies his victimization. Such a state could be described as "unnatural" and therefore as a *bastardization* of human life. Those who witness Joe's plight must "face the thing that should not be." When the military physician in charge asks the chaplain if he can offer some words of comfort to Joe, the priest responds: "He's the product of your profession, not mine." It's unclear whether the priest is referring to the military or the medical profession (or perhaps both), since the person he's responding to is both an officer and a physician.[15] Assuming that he's referring to the medical profession, this statement calls to mind the unnaturalness of Joe's present state and his victimization at the hands of medical technology.[16] It's thus not surprising that Joe and others in similar conditions would ask to "cut this life off from me," even if it means that death will quickly follow.[17]

But is there a moral difference between the two forms of euthanasia—active and passive? Since passive euthanasia is widely practiced

---

[13] See John Kavanaugh, *Who Count as Persons: Human Identity and the Ethics of Killing* (Washington, DC: Georgetown University Press, 2001), p. 137.

[14] The state of Oregon legalized physician-assisted suicide through its "Death with Dignity Act," which went into effect in 1997.

[15] The priest, too, wears a military uniform as a chaplain; but his military allegiance wouldn't preclude him from invoking more important values based on his primary religious vocation.

[16] It's likely that he's referring to the military as well given the overall anti-war sentiment of Trumbo's film (and the book it's based upon) and Metallica's lyrics.

[17] It's worth noting the change in lyric when Metallica performs "One" live on the *S&M* album with the San Francisco Symphony Orchestra. The altered lyric is "cut this *shit* off from me." The significance of the change is that the original lyric implies Joe's intention for his life to end; whereas the revised lyric implies his intention merely to withdraw artificial life-support, with his death as a foreseen "side-effect."

while active euthanasia is illegal in all but one US state, on what basis could the former act be morally justified while the latter isn't? The American Medical Association states its position thus:

> [Active] euthanasia is fundamentally incompatible with the physician's role as healer, would be difficult or impossible to control, and would pose serious societal risks . . . Physicians have an obligation to relieve pain and suffering and to promote the dignity and autonomy of dying patients in their care. This includes providing effective palliative treatment even though it may foreseeably hasten death. Even if the patient is not terminally ill or permanently unconscious, it is not unethical to discontinue all means of life-sustaining medical treatment.[18]

"Effective palliative treatment" includes the use of narcotics, such as morphine, and other powerful sedatives that may have the side-effect of hastening a patient's death—usually by suppressing respiratory activity. There is, however, a pertinent distinction between *intentionally* ending a patient's life, as in active euthanasia, and hastening a patient's death as a *side-effect* of ameliorating her suffering.

The validity of this distinction rests on the moral principle known as "double-effect." Basically, this principle states that an action taken to produce some consequence, which is good in itself, may be permissible, even if the action produces a foreseen consequence, which is typically morally impermissible. This holds provided that the relative value of the impermissible consequence does not outweigh that of the good consequence, and provided that the production of the impermissible consequence is not *directly intended* as the goal or the means by which the good consequence is brought about.[19] So a physician may directly intend to alleviate a patient's suffering, while, at the same time, allowing the foreseen consequence of death being hastened as a result of the palliative measures. Discontinuing life-sustaining treatment would also be morally permissible provided that the physician's direct intention is *only* to alleviate the patient's

[18]   AMA Council on Ethical and Judicial Affairs, *Code of Medical Ethics*, E.2.20–1.
[19]   See P.A. Woodward (ed.), *The Doctrine of Double-Effect* (South Bend, IN: University of Notre Dame Press, 2001); Jason T. Eberl, "Aquinas on Euthanasia, Suffering, and Palliative Care," *National Catholic Bioethics Quarterly* 3 (2003), pp. 331–54.

suffering, and not to end her life as a means of releasing her from suffering.

"Back to the Meaning of Life"—The Vegetative State and Euthanasia

Joe is at first mistakenly diagnosed as "decerebrated" and, as such, unable "to experience pain, pleasure, memory, dreams, or thought of any kind." He is consigned to a life in which he "will be as unfeeling, as unthinking, as the dead until the day he joins them." The capacity for self-conscious rational thought is in some way dependent upon the functioning of the brain's cerebral cortex. Although consciousness itself may not be identical or reducible to neurons firing in the cortex, it's not at all evident that consciousness can persist in the absence of cortical neural activity (at least in *this* life). In (mis)diagnosing Joe's permanently unconscious condition, the attending physician declares: "The cerebrum has suffered massive and irreparable damage. Had I been sure of this I would not have permitted him to live."

Joe's misdiagnosed condition is not fictional. There are a number of cases of people in a *persistent vegetative state* (PVS). Unlike Joe and others who are terminally ill, PVS patients do not suffer *per se* due to their unconscious state. The most famous case is that of Terri Schiavo, who died in March 2005 after her husband decided to discontinue artificial nutrition and hydration. At the time of her death, Schiavo had been a PVS patient for fifteen years.

Some philosophers and bioethicists, following Enlightenment philosopher John Locke's *psychological* account of personal identity,[20] emphasize that cerebral functioning is required for the peculiarly "personal" activities of conscious rational thought and volition. They thus argue that a human being's death, as a *person*, occurs when the

---

[20] See John Locke, *An Essay Concerning Human Understanding*, ed. P.H. Nidditch (Oxford: Clarendon Press, 1975), Book II, Ch. 27, §9. An explanation of Locke's account is provided in my "Why Voldemort Won't Just Die Already: What Wizards Can Teach Us About Personal Identity" in David Baggett and Shawn E. Klein (eds.), *Harry Potter and Philosophy* (Chicago: Open Court, 2004), pp. 200–12.

cerebral cortex becomes irreversibly non-functional.[21] This "higher brain" concept of death is the basis for arguing that PVS patients are no longer persons and therefore should be considered dead. Other philosophers and bioethicists, however, hold the "whole brain" concept of death, which defines a person's existence as coincident with the human organism that constitutes her. The "lower brain" (including the cerebellum and brainstem) regulates a human organism's vital metabolic functions of circulation and respiration. So only with irreversible cessation of the brain's functioning "as a whole"—cerebral cortex, cerebellum, and brainstem—does death occur.[22]

Even though PVS patients arguably should still be considered *persons* with the same moral standing as you or I, it's clear that they can no longer pursue the "goal of life," if such a goal entails more than simply being alive and requires self-conscious rational thought and volition. A PVS patient's life is one of "suspended animation"— he may live, but only as a "frozen soul, frozen down to the core" ("Trapped Under Ice").

If we accept the "whole brain" concept of death and find active euthanasia morally unacceptable, then it would not be permissible to directly intend to end a PVS patient's life, for he remains a living human person. Nevertheless, his severely debilitated and irreversible state (assuming a correct diagnosis)[23] doesn't imply an ethical duty to maintain his life if other values are at stake. According to St. Thomas Aquinas (ca. 1225–74), the fundamental value of life must be balanced against what's of *ultimate* value:

> It is inherent in everyone by nature that he loves his own life and whatever is ordered toward it, but in due measure, such that these things are

[21]   See, for example, Robert Veatch, "Whole-Brain, Neocortical, and Higher Brain Related Concepts" in R. Zaner (ed.), *Death: Beyond Whole-Brain Criteria* (Dordrecht: Kluwer, 1988), pp. 171–86.

[22]   See, for example, James Bernat, "A Defense of the Whole-Brain Concept of Death," *Hastings Center Report* 28 (1998), pp. 14–23.

[23]   Like Joe, a number of PVS patients have been misdiagnosed in recent medical history. See K. Andrews, L. Murphy, R. Munday, and C. Littlewood, "Misdiagnosis of the Vegetative State," *British Medical Journal* 313 (1996), pp. 13–16; N.L. Childs, W.N. Mercer, and H.W. Childs, "Accuracy of Diagnosis of Persistent Vegetative State," *Neurology* 43 (1993), pp. 1465–7.

loved not as if the end were determined in them, but insofar as they are to be used for the sake of his final end.[24]

For Aquinas, a human person's "final end" is knowledge and love of God, which can be pursued only if he is capable of self-conscious rational thought and volition. If the irreversible cerebral damage a PVS patient suffers precludes the exercise of these capacities, then he can pursue his final end only after death (assuming that post-mortem life awaits him).

While a PVS patient remains a living human person, the value of his biological life relative to his ability to pursue goals that are consciously willed has been mitigated by his irreversibly unconscious condition. As a result, measures to prolong his life that are *futile*—in terms of failing to provide for some measure of recovery—or are unduly burdensome are not morally mandated. Discontinuing such measures constitutes *passive* euthanasia, because the patient's death is a foreseen negative consequence of the directly intended act of not continuing futile medical treatment.

"Exit: Light / Enter: Night"— What Happens to Joe?

We know how Joe's story ends: a nurse attempts to euthanize him by cutting off his breathing tube. Is this active or passive euthanasia? It looks, at first, like an ethically justified form of passive euthanasia, because she is merely removing an artificial means of life-support— akin to Terri Schiavo's feeding tube. But it's not simply the physical action as such that determines the nature of an act. Rather, a moral act is judged primarily by the intention that underlies it. In this case, given Joe's expressed wish to be killed, it appears that the nurse's intention is to kill Joe by cutting off his (artificial) airway—thus constituting active euthanasia.

---

[24] St. Thomas Aquinas, *Summa theologiae*, IIa–IIae, q. 126, a. 1. See Jason T. Eberl, "Extraordinary Care and the Spiritual Goal of Life," *National Catholic Bioethics Quarterly* 5 (2005), pp. 491–501.

Since the nurse is stopped, Joe is forced to slip back into his conscious, but disconnected, state. Without moral approval for actively euthanizing Joe, the only option left is simply to keep him going until he suffers some naturally fatal condition—for example, cardiac or respiratory arrest. Following the principle of double-effect, his physician could place a "do not resuscitate" order on his chart. This means that resuscitative efforts—such as CPR or an artificial respirator—would not be used and the foreseen consequence of his death would be allowed to occur without undue interference. Thus, instead of employing further medical techniques and technology to "save" Joe, he can be "let go" and finally allowed to say, "Death greets me warm, now I will just say goodbye" ("Fade to Black").[25]

[25] I am grateful, as always, for Bill Irwin's excellent editorial assistance, helpful comments from Candice Alaimo, Joanna Corwin, Eileen Sweeney, and Jennifer Vines, and the Schopenhauer-inspired insights of fellow head-banger, Daniel Burroughs.

CHAPTER 13

FADE TO BLACK
Absurdity, Suicide, and the Downward Spiral

JUSTIN DONHAUSER
AND KIMBERLY A. BLESSING

> There is but one truly serious philosophical problem, and that is sui-
> cide. Judging whether life is or is not worth living amounts to answer-
> ing the fundamental question of philosophy.
>
> Albert Camus[1]

"Fade to Black" is a controversial song in two ways. First, the ballad
was seen as a "sell out" by some of the more hardcore fans of *Kill
'Em All*. Second, the song is about suicide. Other chapters in this
book deal with the question of whether or not Metallica sold out. So
in this chapter we'll deal with the issue of suicide.

In a 1991 interview, James Hetfield talks about writing "Fade to
Black."

> I wrote the song at a friend's house in New Jersey. I was pretty
> depressed at the time because our gear had just been stolen, and we
> had been thrown out of our manager's house for breaking shit and
> drinking his liquor cabinet dry. It's a suicide song, and we got a lot of
> flack for it; kids were killing themselves because of the song. But we

---

[1] Albert Camus, *The Myth of Sisyphus: And Other Essays*, trans. by Justin O'Brien
(New York: Vintage Books, 1955), p. 3.

also got hundreds and hundreds of letters from kids telling us how they related to the song and that made them feel better.[2]

When we consider the lyrics of "Fade to Black" we quickly realize that whatever inspired this song has less to do with the pain of being in Jersey and more to do with being alive. "Fade to Black" is a song about the inevitability of death, the absurdity of life, and the consequent feeling of despair that sets in once we recognize these cold and dark realities. It's that cold feeling of despair and hopelessness that presents death as a warm alternative to living; hence suicide seems a compelling way to opt out.

It's pretty unlikely that merely listening to the song caused kids to kill themselves. Instead, what resonates with fans is that many of us have felt the same despair, loneliness, or loss of a sense of who we are and where our lives are headed. Maybe some have even gone so far as to contemplate suicide, or at least start thinking about death as a welcome relief from life. No doubt "Fade to Black" is a suicide song. But simply singing about suicide doesn't necessarily induce it, and the effect that it can have on its listeners might be cathartic, not necessarily catastrophic. In offering his theory of tragedy in the *Poetics*, the ancient Greek philosopher Aristotle (384–322 BCE) described *catharsis* as the purging of the emotions of fear and pity that are aroused when viewing tragic drama. Perhaps "Fade to Black" and other Metallica songs can actually purge us of the negative emotions that might incline us towards suicide.[3]

Why Fade to *Black*?

The color black, or the absence of light or color, is commonly associated with death. And death represents the absence, or end, of life

[2] "Guitar World Interview 1991: Metallica about "Fade to Black," *Encyclopedia Metallica*, www.encycmet.com/songs/srfade2b.shtml (2006).
[3] See especially chapters 6, 9, and 13 in *Aristotle: Introductory Readings*, trans. Terrance Irwin and Gail Fine (Indianapolis: Hackett, 1996), pp. 319–25. See Robert Fudge's chapter 1, "Whisper Things into My Brain: Metallica, Emotion, and Morality" in this volume for more on this topic.

(at least this life as we know it in this world). In the end (of at least this life), there is nothing. Nothingness itself is impossible to conceive of, because to conceive of "nothingness" is to conceive of something. When we try to make sense of nothingness, it's always in terms of something else, or "somethingness." For example, we might think about an empty beer mug, or the nothingness in the mug. But then we are thinking of something, namely the mug. When we try to conceive of complete nothingness we might try to think of [an] empty space, but even that is something, not nothing. If we think of nothingness in terms of all black (or all white), then fading to black comes as close as we can to imagining the process of fading to nothingness.

"Life it seems will fade away." In other words, all living things gradually vanish into nothing. A later song, "Blackened," which is largely about "the death of mother earth" through environmental pollution and nuclear devastation, also deals with death in black imagery. In the first verse, Hetfield sings: "Blackened is the end / winter it will send / throwing all you see / into obscurity." Here too blackness is symbolic of death, or the end of all being. Death and darkness certainly aren't foreign notions to metal fans. But was there death and darkness before metal?

What's More *Metal* than the Musty Stench of Corpses?

The darkness of metal lifestyle would have been very appealing to German philosopher Arthur Schopenhauer (1788–1860). In fact, Schopenhauer had a great influence on a famous musician, German composer Richard Wagner (1813–83). Although Schopenhauer counsels self-denial, this son of a wealthy merchant family was renowned for his vanity, self-indulgent lifestyle, chronic petulance, and most infamously his pessimism: "Even as a child of five or six, my parents returning from a walk one evening, found me in deep despair."[4]

---

[4] Alain de Botton, *Consolations of Philosophy* (New York: Pantheon Books, 2000), p. 171.

Usually when we think of pessimism and optimism it has to do with either a negative or positive attitude towards things—pessimists are "glass-half-empty" kinds of people, whereas optimists see the glass as half full. In philosophy, pessimism is the metaphysical theory that this is the *worst* of all possible worlds and optimism is the metaphysical theory that this is the *best* of all possible worlds. Metaphysics deals with the fundamental nature of reality and is one of the oldest branches of philosophy. Yet what might be called "worst-ism" and "best-ism" are relatively recent theories. The English word "optimism" came from the French *optimisme* in the mid-eighteenth century. French thinkers of this period first used this term to describe the position of another German philosopher, Gottfried Leibniz, in his *Theodicy* (1710). (Leibnizian optimism is most memorably rebutted in Voltaire's great satire *Candide*, which was published in 1759.)[5] The first recorded use of the antithetical term "pessimism" was in 1819, when it was used to name the metaphysical system of Schopenhauer's book *The World as Will and Representation*.

Using terms and imagery that metalheads can truly appreciate, this darkest of dark philosophers describes life as a downward spiral, in an essay titled "On the Vanity of Existence," from his bestseller *Essays and Aphorisms* (1851).[6]

> Yet what a difference there is between our beginning and our end! We begin in the madness of carnal desire and the transport of voluptuousness, we end in the dissolution of all our parts and the musty stench of corpses.

According to Schopenhauer, we're born to die. In the meantime, we're driven against our control by some blind urge to propagate and perpetuate this cycle of living to die, with no promise of personal immortality or eternal salvation. He explains that because the present moment is all that exists, and all that is real at any and every given instant, "Our existence has no foundation on which to rest except the transient present." Schopenhauer reasons further that if every present moment is continually passing out of existence, or if existence is a

---

[5] Of course, nothing is better than reading the (very short) book, but check out the DVD of Leonard Bernstein's comic operetta, *Candide*.

[6] Translated by R.J. Hollingdale (London: Penguin, 1970).

constant dying, then one's life, the future, and in turn all of humanity is in the process of being reduced to nothingness. Because we exist toward no end, or nothing, we shouldn't exist at all: ". . . something which ought unconditionally to exist, would not have non-being as its goal." Knowing that we are doomed to pass out of existence, or "crumble to dust," *that* we go on living at all seems silly. Schopenhauer cheerily concludes that since death is the aim and purpose of life and since everything as we know it will eventually become nothing, all of human existence is in vain.

Metallica sometimes shares this stark view of the human condition. In this mosh pit of human existence, we're all eventually and inevitably Fading to Black: "Life it seems, will fade away / Drifting further everyday." So why retain the will to live at all? "Getting lost within myself / Nothing matters no one else / I have lost the will to live / Simply nothing more to give / There is nothing more for me." Even though early Metallica and Schopenhauer share the same pessimistic outlook on life, Schopenhauer is not led to the same conclusion as the narrator of "Fade to Black," who has lost "the will to live." For Schopenhauer, the Will is the ultimate and only thing that is real, and the Will-to-life is not vulnerable to choice or human desire.

Schopenhauer comes out of a tradition initiated by the metaphysics of German philosopher Immanuel Kant (1724–1804), according to which there are two different ways that we can experience any object. Take our beer mug; we can think about the mug in terms of how it appears to us (*phenomena*), or as it is independently of any human mind perceiving it (*noumena*). According to Kant, human knowledge is limited to appearances, while things-in-themselves are thinkable but not actually knowable. I can't know the beer mug as it is, independently of how it appears to me. Instead of thinking of our knowledge as conforming to objects as they exist in reality, Kant envisioned that objects in the world conform to our ways of knowing them, through certain categories of understanding, or concepts, like substance and causality. In other words, as conscious subjects we come to the world equipped with these concepts which help us to understand and unify this buzzing and blooming confusing world of perceptual experience. Although we can't come to know things-in-themselves (*dinge-an-sich*) independently of how they appear to us, the objects of our representations conform to the concepts we have of them in a way that is sufficient for knowledge.

Schopenhauer's *magnum opus* begins "The world is my idea." The world that we experience (the phenomenal world) is a world of "ideas" or "representations." And all phenomena, which include the things that we observe in the world around us, as well as those things that we observe in our own world of our mental states, are simply manifestations of the underlying reality that is the Will, which can roughly be equated with Kant's unknowable thing-in-itself (*noumena*). When each of us is consciously aware of what is going on inside of us, we are in touch with the Will, which is the ultimate basis on which all phenomena, or "representations," are founded: "This and this alone gives him the key to his own phenomenon, reveals to him the significance and shows him the inner mechanism of his being, his actions, his movements."[7] Hence, the world *as* will and representation.

If Schopenhauer is right, and the Will is the key to all existence, then one can't "kill the Will." Schopenhauer's Will is a force of striving, or being, that is blindly directed towards ends, but doesn't have rationality or consciousness like our individual will. When any individual has lost her will-to-live, she might desire, and perhaps choose, suicide as a way to hasten the reality of death. But for Schopenhauer this act of suicide wouldn't bring about complete annihilation. Instead, this act of suicide paradoxically affirms the Will-to-life, which is the inherent drive within us to stay alive. Does all of this seem absurd?

Live, Shit, Binge, and Purge

In *The Myth of Sisyphus* existentialist philosopher Albert Camus (1913–60) explains that "the Absurd" lies in a relation or contradiction between the rational human being, who desires that things have coherence and make sense, and the world, which does not cooperate with our desire for coherence. In other words, absurdity arises from our demand for rationality and our search for meaning in a world that just doesn't care. As Camus sums it up:

---

[7] *The World as Will and Representation* (1819, republished 1851), trans. by E.F.J. Payne (New York: Dover, 1969), Section 18.

> I said that the world is absurd, but I was too hasty. This world in itself is not reasonable, that is all that can be said. But what is absurd is the confrontation of this irrational and the wild longing for clarity whose calls echo in the human heart. The absurd depends as much on man as on the world.

For Camus, the meaninglessness realized by the narrator of "Fade to Black" arises from the expectation that the universe owes us something. We find the world an unbearable place only because we believe that the world should be fair. But the world isn't fair, and Camus points out that it isn't the world's fault that we don't belong to it. "Understanding the world for a man is reducing it to the human, stamping it with his seal. The cat's universe is not that of the anthill." Cats don't live in anthills; just like no self-respecting metalhead frolics at the roller-disco. But it's our continual desire to make the world our home, coupled with our metaphysical demand for coherence, rationality, and purpose in a world that isn't our home, which is the Absurd. As Camus says:

> I can negate everything of that part of me that lives on vague nostalgias, except this desire for unity, this longing to solve, this need for clarity and cohesion . . . I don't know whether this world has a meaning that transcends it. But I know that I do not know that meaning and that it is impossible for me just now to know it . . . And these two certainties—my appetite for the absolute and for unity and the impossibility of reducing the world to a rational and reasonable principle—I also know that I cannot reconcile them.

Still, we might take some comfort in realizing that the world is fair in its unfairness. For Camus, the world is equally indifferent toward all creatures.

Like Schopenhauer, Camus emphasizes death as inevitable: "Death is there as the only reality." Still, both philosophers agree that suicide is not the only option. For Camus, it is possible to recover from the feeling of meaninglessness that inevitably sets in upon recognition of the absurdity of the human condition. As Camus says:

> Weariness comes at the end of the acts of mechanical life, but at the same time inaugurates the impulse of consciousness. It awakens the consciousness and provokes what follows. What follows is the gradual

return into the chain or it is the definitive awakening. At the end of the awakening comes, in time, the consequence: suicide or recovery.[8]

The narrator of Metallica's "Fade to Black" doesn't recover. Instead, he gives in to suicide. "No one but me can save myself, but it's too late / Now I can't think, think why I should even try." He has thus lost the will to live. Camus' absurd hero does better:

> The absurd man thus catches sight of a burning and frigid, transparent and limited universe in which nothing is possible but everything is given, and beyond which all is collapse and nothingness. He can then decide to accept such a universe and draw from it his strength, his refusal to hope, and the unyielding evidence of a life without consolation.

Once reason makes us conscious of the opposition between ourselves and all of creation, we have recognized the Absurd, which then provides a Rule of Life. For Camus, the answer can't be suicide. Suicide leaves behind the Absurd, as it forfeits one pole of the relation, namely, the person. To learn from the experience or conception of the Absurd, one must live: "Living is keeping the absurd alive."

Like Schopenhauer, Camus might aver that the certainty of our death can have a profoundly debilitating effect, but he suggests a way to embrace life in spite of its ultimate absurdity: "if I admit that my freedom has no meaning except in relation to its limited fate, then I must say that what counts is not the best of living but the most of living."

> To men living the same number of years, the world always provides the same sum of experiences. It is up to us to be conscious of them. Being aware of one's life, one's revolt, one's freedom, and to the maximum, is living, and to the maximum.

To live a life to its absolute fullest, in spite of its limited span in time—to *choose* to live—is to maximize our freedom, which is distinctively human, and initiates the greatest revolt, which is utterly heroic. "Thus I draw from the absurd three consequences, which are

---

[8] Schopenhauer says that throughout our lives we will suffer from passing states of what he terms *desengano*, or "disillusionment."

my revolt, my freedom, and my passion. By the mere activity of consciousness I transform into a rule of life what was an invitation to death—*and I refuse suicide.*"

"No one but me can save myself . . ."

Against Schopenhauer and Camus, couldn't one view suicide as relief from the pain and suffering that accompanies the cosmically insignificant life? "Deathly lost, this can't be real / Cannot stand this hell I feel / Emptiness is filling me / To the point of agony." At this point, death would seem a warm and welcome greeting, so why not "just say goodbye"? Or perhaps suicide could be viewed as the ultimate act of freedom: "I refuse to give in to fate, and will seize it of my own will."

In his short essay "On Suicide," Schopenhauer acknowledges that "there is nothing in the world to which every man has more unassailable right than to his own life and person."[9] After recounting his dissatisfaction with various theological and religious arguments against suicide (largely from the Judeo-Christian tradition), he expresses what he takes to be the only valid reason to condemn suicide: "suicide thwarts the attainment of the highest moral aim by the fact that, for a real release from this world of misery, it substitutes one that is merely apparent." For Schopenhauer, the son of a man who was alleged to have committed suicide (he was found floating in a canal beside the family warehouse), suicide is at worst a "mistake," but hardly a crime or moral wrong. As he says:

> Suicide may also be regarded as an experiment—a question which man puts to Nature, trying to force her to an answer. The question is this: What change will death produce in a man's existence and in his insight into the nature of things? It is a clumsy experiment to make; for it involves the destruction of the very consciousness which puts the question and awaits the answer.

---

[9]   In *Studies in Pessimism*, trans. by T. Bailey Saunders (East Lansing, MI: Scholarly Press, 1973), p. 43.

Beyond being some sort of metaphysical mistake, suicide itself is rendered absurd. Experimenting with suicide can't possibly offer relief, or any sense of satisfaction, as suggested by the lyrics of "Fade to Black." For if the suicidal person is successful, he or she wouldn't be conscious to experience the comfort of death's warm welcome.

Listen to Your Mama

Schopenhauer and Camus both recognize the meaninglessness and absurdity of the human condition, yet both advise against suicide, for it provides neither relief from our suffering nor the freedom to engage in existence. For these reasons, suicide is *no* escape. Camus suggests that suicide is for wimps: "To abolish conscious revolt is to elude the problem." On the contrary: "That revolt gives life its value." Going on in spite of absurdity is heroic. If death and absurdity are the enemy, then committing suicide is to surrender to the enemy. To fight bravely for one's freedom, in the face of ultimate loss, promises attainable salvation and release from the torments of absurdity.

In an interview with *Guitar World* (December 1998), Hetfield embraces this revolutionary spirit while defending himself against allegations that the lyrics of "Fade to Black" were pro-suicide.

> Yeah, well, you can kind of rest on the whole "well, this is art, so fuck off," freedom-of-speech thing. But when you're up there on stage, anything you say can be taken literally, and you have to be conscious of that. There's a real sick feeling of power when you're on stage: you can start a riot or put everyone to sleep if you wanted . . . On the other hand, as soon as you start being "responsible" with your lyrics, you start fucking with your integrity. Writing is therapy for me, so fuck everyone else, you know?[10]

"Fade to Black" appears to counsel "saying goodbye," or suicide. In this context, perhaps the act of saying goodbye could be seen merely as an attempt to let other people know that you are choosing to die.

---

[10] *All Metallica.com*, www.allmetallica.com/info/interviews/guitar98.php (2006).

But even this wouldn't bring about the desired result, as suggested by Camus' famous character from *The Fall*,[11] Jean Baptist Clamence:

> Don't think for a minute that your friends will telephone you every evening, as they ought to, in order to find out if this doesn't happen to be the evening when you are deciding to commit suicide, or simply whether you don't need company, whether you are not in a mood to go out. No, don't worry, they'll ring up the evening you are not alone, when life is beautiful. As for suicide, they would be more likely to push you to it, by virtue of what you owe to yourself, according to them.

When you give in and commit suicide, you won't teach the world a lesson. You won't go out serenaded by a glorious barrage of 10,000 blazing guitar solos immersed in the glow of a pyrotechnic blast. Rather, you will likely be alone and frightened. Camus writes: "Martyrs, *cher ami*, must choose between being forgotten, mocked, or made use of. As for being understood—never!"

We've seen how and why two of philosophy's heavy hitters advise against suicide. And Metallica isn't endorsing suicide either. How absurd. Instead, "Fade to Black" seeks to help its listeners entertain the possibility. Why? Because, as Hetfield suggests, it makes us feel better. It provides a purging or catharsis of negative emotions. And that's the thing with good art, including music. It transcends the particular and speaks to some universal truth about human existence. In his essay "On Aesthetics," Schopenhauer writes that music—the most powerful of the arts and the only one that is not concerned with the material world—speaks to the "weal and woe" of the human condition:

> Music is the true universal language which is understood everywhere, so that it is ceaselessly spoken in all countries and throughout all the centuries with great zeal and earnestness, and a significant melody which says a great deal soon makes its way round the entire earth, while one poor in meaning which says nothing straightaway fades and dies: which proves that the content of a melody is very well understandable. Yet music speaks not of things but of pure weal and woe, which are the only realities for the *will*: that is why it speaks so much

---

[11] Trans. by Justin O'Brien (New York: Vintage Books, 1956).

to the heart, while it has nothing to say *directly* to the head . . . For expression of passion is one thing, depiction of things another.[12]

For Schopenhauer, the aesthetic appreciation of works of art offers one way that we can escape the trapping of the universal Will, which brings about all the misery and suffering of the world.

But maybe we'd do better to end with a bit of wisdom from the metal gods themselves. Listen to what "Mama Said": "Son, your life's an open book / don't close it 'fore it's done."

[12] In *Essays and Aphorisms*, p. 162.

DISC 4

METAPHYSICA, EPISTEMOLOGICA, METALLICA

CHAPTER 14

BELIEVER, DECEIVER
Metallica, Perception, and Reality

ROBERT ARP

"Off the Veil, Stand Revealed"

I love to scream these words from the first verse of "Bad Seed": "Come clean / Fess up / Tell all / Spill guts / Off the veil / Stand revealed / Show the card / Bring it on / Break the seal." When I'm finished screaming I'm usually left thinking about the difference between what I perceive to be the case, what is *veiled*, and what really is the case, what is *revealed*. What makes up a person's "reality?" Is reality all just "My World," my own collection of perceptions and ideas, or is there a world outside of me? If there is a reality beyond my perceptions, I want to be secure in my knowledge of that reality. Along with Hetfield, I want to know "Is that the moon / or just the light that lights this dead end street? / Is that you there / or just another demon that I meet?"

Certain themes and subjects recur repeatedly in Hetfield's lyrics. Consider these: parental and governmental lies and deceptions; misperceiving my own mind and the minds of others; and the concern that my perceptions do not match up with some part of the world. All of these boil down to the realization that what I *perceive* to be the case is not always what *really* is the case.

"These Things Return To Me
That Still Seem Real"

Most of us take for granted that there is a world of things existing outside of our minds, regardless of whether we are perceiving them or not. It seems obvious that other people, material objects, the solar system, even mathematical relations like the Pythagorean theorem, exist "out there" beyond our perceptions of them. And such things would continue to exist even if they were not perceived by us.

But take a moment to think about what you are aware of when you perceive other people, material objects, and the like. For example, right now you're reading this chapter. You see the page in front of you, you feel the smooth cover of the book, and you can close your eyes and form an image or idea of the cover. Notice that we can talk about three different kinds of things in this example. There is you, the *perceiver* who has the perceptions and ideas. There are *your percep- tions* of the page and cover that take the forms of sight, feeling, and ideas. And there are the *external objects of your perception*, the actual page and cover.[1]

Consider figure 14.1. These three kinds of things are present at a Metallica show like the one immortalized in "Whiplash." There are members of the band, like Hetfield, who are the perceivers. There are Hetfield's perceptions, which include the "feeling of a hammerhead," the "exploding" sensations of adrenaline and heat, the sound of the

---

[1]   In the history of western philosophy, this three-part distinction can be traced back, at least, to Plato (427–347 BCE) in his famous work *Republic*, Book VII, where he talks about the allegory of the cave. In this allegory, Socrates asks his listeners to imagine someone (the perceiver) chained in a cave facing a wall. At first, the only things the person sees are shadows on a wall in front of him (the perceptions), which are produced as a result of things and people moving around behind him in the firelight (the external objects of perception). The person breaks free, turns around to see things in the firelight, and eventually makes his way out of the cave to see things clearly as they really are in the sunlight. The allegory is supposed to represent one's ascent from ignorance to knowledge, but it also can be viewed as a movement from perception to reality. Plato's *Republic* can be found in Edith Hamilton and Huntington Cairns (eds.), *The Collected Dialogues of Plato* (Princeton, NJ: Princeton University Press, 1961). For an excellent introduction to Plato's *Republic*, see Julia Annas, *An Introduction to Plato's Republic* (Oxford: Clarendon Press, 1981).

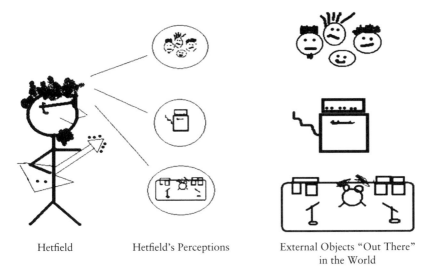

| Hetfield | Hetfield's Perceptions | External Objects "Out There" in the World |

Figure 14.1

"Marshall noise," the sight of the crowd headbanging, and the ideas he has of the show, other towns, other gigs, "hotel rooms and motorways." Finally, there are the external objects of Hetfield's perceptions, which include the other members of the band, the crowd itself decked out in leather and spikes with heads "bobbing all around," the stage, and the Marshall amp emitting a noise that is "piercing through your ears."

"Barred Reality"

Returning to the example of you and this book, certain questions arise. Can I really get beyond my own perceptions to have access to the page and cover *themselves* as they really are?

Maybe all that I can perceive are my own perceptions? How can I be sure that the external objects of my perception are really there, or that how they present themselves to me in my perceptions matches up with or corresponds with how they really are? After all, I can't step outside of my own perceptions and look at myself in relationship to external objects to see if, in fact, my perceptions correspond with these external objects. Am I "locked inside" of my own world of sense perceptions? If so, how do I know that there really is a world out there beyond my perceptions?[2]

These questions and their surrounding issues have led some thinkers to hold two philosophical positions that often (but not always) go together, *epistemological idealism* and *metaphysical antirealism*. Epistemology is the area of philosophy concerned with the sources and justification of knowledge. An epistemological idealist thinks that one's perceptions or ideas (thus, *idea*lism) are the only source of knowledge.[3] Thus I can never tell if my perceptions correspond with the external objects of my perception; the perceiver is forever barred from access to the objects of perception. It's as if my mind is like a pair of sunglasses that I can never take off to see the world as it actually is. Hetfield's lyrics hint at this possibility when he wonders whether the moon is a streetlight or some person is just a demon in "The House Jack Built."

Metaphysics is the area of philosophy concerned with the nature and principles of what really exists. A metaphysical antirealist thinks that there is no real world outside of one's perceptions or ideas; it's all just "My World."[4]

Metaphysical antirealism and epistemological idealism can be contrasted with *metaphysical realism* and *epistemological realism*, which

---

[2] In the history of western philosophy, distinguishing among me, my perceptions, and the external objects of perception became especially prominent for philosophers during the Early Modern period (ca. 1600–1800). The thinker usually looked to as the father of modern philosophy, René Descartes (1596–1650), makes this distinction in his famous work entitled *Meditations on First Philosophy*. Other philosophers during this period, such as Leibniz, Spinoza, Locke, Berkeley, Hume, and Kant, are all concerned with the distinction and its implications for perception and reality. Important parts of these thinkers' works can be found in Roger Ariew and Eric Watkins (eds.), *Modern Philosophy: An Anthology of Primary Sources* (Indianapolis: Hackett, 1998). Also see the commentary in Garrett Thomson, *Bacon to Kant: An Introduction to Modern Philosophy* (New York: Waveland Press, 2001).

[3] Good introductions to epistemology include Robert Audi, *Epistemology: A Contemporary Introduction* (New York: Routledge, 2003); and Matthias Steup, *An Introduction to Contemporary Epistemology* (Upper Saddle River, NJ: Prentice-Hall, 1995).

[4] Good introductions to metaphysics include Michael Loux, *Metaphysics: A Contemporary Introduction* (New York: Routledge, 2002); and Peter Van Inwagen, *Metaphysics* (Boulder: Westview Press, 2002).

hold there is a world beyond the perceptions in our minds (metaphysical realism) and we can have knowledge of it (epistemological realism).[5]

Consider this rock 'n' roll twist on an old question: "If a guitar falls onto a stage floor and no one is around to hear it, does it make a sound when it crashes to the stage floor?" Sound requires a thing to *make* a noise as well as a thing to *hear* the noise. According to a realist, the guitar's crashing to the stage floor would produce sound waves whether there was anyone or anything around to perceive or pick up the sound waves. So, technically, the guitar crashing to the stage floor would not make a sound if no one or no thing with the capacity to hear were present. But it still would produce sound waves that could be picked up by a person or thing with a capacity for hearing sounds. On the other hand, the antirealist would have us believe that if there were no perceivers, there would be no sound waves produced. Not only would the guitar not make a sound, but there would be no guitar! After all, there's no one there to perceive it.

By contrast, realists believe, for example, that Pythagoras *discovered* and *formulated* the theorem that $a^2 + b^2 = c^2$ for a right triangle, rather than *wholly invented* it. They also believe that the theorem would be what it is and exist as what it is regardless of whether it was ever known by any mind. In fact the realist believes that right now, out there in reality, there are all kinds of things waiting to be discovered by the human mind. Despite the fact that the mind can be quite creative in its imagination, and despite the fact that there can be many different ways of perceiving, there is still some reality out there beyond the mind and its perceptions. To think that "reality" is constituted by the mind and its perceptions, as the antirealist does, is misguided according to the realist.[6]

---

[5] For discussions of epistemological and metaphysical realism, antirealism, and idealism, see the articles in William Alston (ed.), *Realism and Antirealism* (Ithaca, NY: Cornell University Press, 2002). Also see John McDowell, *Mind and World* (Cambridge, MA: Harvard University Press, 1994) and E.J. Lowe, *A Survey of Metaphysics* (Oxford: Oxford University Press, 2002).

[6] For discussions of this sort, see Nicholas Rescher, *Objectivity: The Obligations of Impersonal Reason* (South Bend, IN: University of Notre Dame Press, 1997); also Robert Arp, "The Pragmatic Value of Frege's Platonism for the Pragmatist," *Journal of Speculative Philosophy*, 19 (2005), pp. 22–41.

"My Eyes Seek Reality"

Most people are epistemological and metaphysical realists, Hetfield included, if his lyrics are any indication of his view on the subject. Despite the fact that Hetfield's mind is full of perceptions he has imagined—like the scenarios of being "trapped under ice," languishing in a sanitarium, or being strapped to the electric chair—he seems to take it for granted that his perceptions do, at times, accurately represent real-world objects. Sure, there are moments when Hetfield can be mistaken about whether his perceptions represent real-world objects accurately, but he believes that his perceptions still can accurately represent external objects. The fact that Hetfield is aware of and concerned with the deception, concealment, and confusion he perceives in himself, others, and the world, shows that he thinks there is a real world beyond his perceptions that can be known accurately. The deception, concealment, and confusion arise from a discrepancy in the relationship between his perceptions and the real world he perceives.

Now, we have to be careful here. Hetfield communicates in his lyrics that he *thinks* or *believes* that there is a real world out there to be discovered, and he thinks that it can be accurately represented in his perceptions. Whether there is, in fact, an actual world out there is an open question. But it seems that Hetfield, like most of us, takes it for granted and just assumes that there is a real world beyond our perceptions. Hetfield combines epistemological realism with metaphysical realism. It would seem that he, as well as the various narrators in his songs, think that it is possible for perceptions to represent external objects of perception accurately, and this is so because there is, in fact, a real world of external objects that exists whether perceived or not. When Hetfield is deceived by a person presenting him or herself as someone other than who they are, he believes there is someone real, out there, doing the deceiving. At the same time, Hetfield believes that it is possible for that person to "stand revealed, show the cards" so that his perceptions of that person accurately represent the real nature of that person. In "Master of Puppets" the narrator complains "Master, Master / you promised only lies" after he realizes that he has been deceived about the nature of the whole cocaine experience. Again, he thinks that there is a real object of his perception out there in the world, cocaine, and he believes that its harmful effects are no mere perception of his mind.

"My Own World"

One unfortunate consequence of holding to idealism and antirealism is solipsism, from the Latin words *solus*, "only" and *ipse*, "self." If a person can only be aware of his own perceptions, and he is forever barred from knowing whether his perceptions match up with any external objects of his perception, then it would appear that he is alone in reality. It's as if he is "locked inside" of his own world of perceptions, never knowing whether there is even a world out there beyond the perceptions. This view is illustrated in figure 14.2. Think of Hetfield as being locked inside the room of his own mind, kind of like someone trapped inside of a movie theater. Now imagine that there is a movie screen inside the theater, representing Hetfield's or anyone's perceptions, that is connected to a movie camera on the

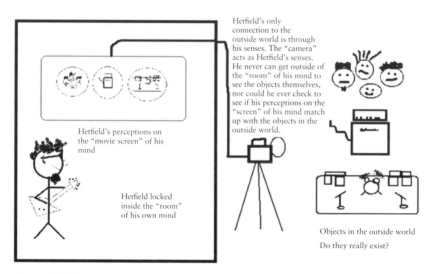

Hetfield's perceptions on the "movie screen" of his mind

Hetfield locked inside the "room" of his own mind

Hetfield's only connection to the outside world is through his senses. The "camera" acts as Hetfield's senses. He never can get outside of the "room" of his mind to see the objects themselves, nor could he ever check to see if his perceptions on the "screen" of his mind match up with the objects in the outside world.

Objects in the outside world
Do they really exist?

Figure 14.2

outside of the theater that views the outside world. The camera represents a person's five senses. A perceiver, like Hetfield, only has access to his own perceptions on the movie screen of his mind. He could never get outside of the room of his own mind to see if his perceptions match up with some external world, let alone know whether such a world even exists![7]

Hetfield's narrators hint at being alone in the universe in songs like "The Frayed Ends of Sanity," "The Struggle Within," "Dirty Window," and "The House Jack Built." But, in those same songs, there is someone or something outside that either has caused, or can save the narrator from, his pain and confusion. The title of the song "My World" would seem to indicate a solitary existence. But the first line screams, "The motherfuckers got in my head," indicating a belief that there are other minds (and hence other people) out there in reality. Further, the fact that Hetfield is a songwriter who thinks that his songs will have an effect on listeners shows that he believes there are other minds outside of his own. His very desire to have his listeners empathize with him indicates that he is no idealist or antirealist. Granted, he writes songs about how he "stands alone" or is "trapped inside." But these words express what life appears to be like at certain times, *not all of the time*. Life itself is not one huge collection of "standing alone" or "trapped inside" perceptions for Hetfield.

In fact, it could be argued that since life can seem solitary at times, but not at others, all of life cannot be just a series of perceptions with no corresponding reality. How would one know what a perception is if it were not for some reality with which it could be compared and contrasted? Just as one could not even understand what things like pain, selfishness, or love would be like without understanding their corresponding opposites of pleasure, altruism, or hate, so too, how

---

[7] In the history of western philosophy, David Hume (1711–76) figures prominently in suggesting the idea that the mind may be nothing other than a collection of perceptions, and that one may be considered a theater-goer, viewing the "perceptions successively making their appearance." See Hume's *A Treatise of Human Nature*, Section 4, parts of which can be found in Roger Ariew and Eric Watkins (eds.), *Modern Philosophy: An Anthology of Primary Sources* (Indianapolis: Hackett, 1998). Also, George Berkeley (1685–1753) seriously entertains the idea that we may be trapped inside of our perceptual reality, with no access to the external world. He argues for such a position in *Three Dialogues Between Hylas and Philonous*, significant parts of which are reprinted in Ariew and Watkins' anthology.

could one even begin to understand what a perception is if it were not contrasted with reality? This perception/reality contrast is an important part of several Metallica songs. In "Ride the Lightning" the convict incorrectly perceives that he is in some frightening dream, but is "wakened" to reality of the impending execution by his own "horrid scream." In both "Shortest Straw" and "And Justice For All" someone incorrectly perceives that they will receive "fair" treatment under the law, but the reality of this lie ultimately is made "crystal clear." In "Dyer's Eve" naïve childhood perceptions are replaced with the reality of painful adult awareness of these naïve perceptions, as well as awareness of parental deception and concealment.

"The Struggle Within"

Hetfield's lyrics often express emotion fueled by skepticism. There is a general mistrust of people, especially those in positions of authority; there is also a suspicious attitude about whether perceptions are reliable.

Skepticism can take on a good, philosophical form, and it can take on a bad, irrational form. The good, philosophical form of skepticism demands that people back up claims with reasons and evidence that any rational person can accept. In essence, a good philosophical skeptic has a solid understanding of the basic principles of sound reasoning. The bad, irrational form of skepticism is basically an attitude of general mistrust of people and events. An irrational skeptic is akin to someone who has felt burned, hurt, or scorned by people or unfortunate events in life and who, as a consequence, carries around a cognitive "chip" on his or her shoulder that manifests itself in a kind of "never trusting anyone or anything ever again" mentality. In essence, this attitude colors everything that the bad skeptic perceives, making for a skewed view of reality. A lot of the skepticism in Hetfield's lyrics seems to stem from a "struggle within," with coming to grips with the particular people and events that hurt him. But if we admit there are times we can trust others—"trust I seek / and I find in you"—or trust that events will unfold as we perceive them to unfold, then it does not follow that *everyone* is out to get me or that my perceptions are deceiving me all of the time. Now, of course, there are times when an event does *not* unfold as we perceive it, or a person *really* is out to get me, or I *am* mistaken about what I perceive. But, cultivating the good, philosophical form of skepticism should help us to distinguish "appearances" from reality so that we can live our lives to the fullest, free from as much frustration and pain as is possible.

CHAPTER 15

TRAPPED IN MYSELF
"One" and the Mind-Body Problem

JOANNA CORWIN

> James was talking to me about the idea of what it would be like if you were in this situation where you were basically like a sort of living consciousness, like a basket-case kind of situation; where you couldn't reach out and communicate with anyone around you, where you had no arms, no legs and couldn't obviously see, hear, or speak or anything like that.
>
> Lars Ulrich, *2 of One*[1]

. . . And Justice for All is vintage Metallica—ferocious music and lyrics that pull no punches. When Todd MacFarlane created his Metallica action figures, he immortalized the thrash idols as they appeared on tour for this album. It should not be forgotten though, that Metallica had come up through the underground and gained their legions of fans through relentless touring and unparalleled live performances. Their success was won almost entirely without airplay.

There was, however, one single off of *. . . And Justice for All* that could be heard on the radio. I can still remember people who knew I was a fan telling me, "Hey, I really like that 'One' song!" Metallica also released a video for "One" and with it received unfounded criticism for "selling out." The "One" video is pure Metallica—edgy, uncomfortable, brutal. It stood in marked contrast to the decadent, glam productions typical of the times.

[1] *Metallica: 2 of One* (New York: Elektra/WEA, 1989), VHS.

While MTV regularly aired "One" (even outside *Headbanger's Ball*), they usually played the shortened, "Jamming" version. The full-length video for "One" showed band performance intercut with scenes from *Johnny Got His Gun*, the movie that served to focus Hetfield's inspiration for the song. Featuring a limbless, senseless veteran begging for his life to end, "One" stunned the world. Surely it was due to its confrontational content (and not just its increased length) that the full-length version rarely aired.

Johnny Got His Gun (a book by Dalton Trumbo that he himself later made into a film) tells the story of Joe Bonham, a soldier in World War I whose body is blown to bits.[2] Left without limbs and missing most of his face, Joe cannot communicate and so appears to be a vegetable—physically alive but essentially brain dead. Yet in actuality Joe's mind is fully functional. As Lars explains in the interview included on *2 of One*, James contemplated the scenario of a human in total isolation, essentially just a mind, trapped in a body and trying to get out. To fuel Hetfield's imagination, Metallica's management team of Cliff Burnstein and Peter Mensch recommended Trumbo's book and movie, respectively.

Philosophers have long contemplated the paradox dubbed the "mind-body problem," that the human being is an interactive composite of both mind and body and yet is one. How can a nonphysical mind interact with a physical body? René Descartes (1596–1650), the philosopher who first raised the mind-body problem, also coined philosophy's most famous phrase in his "I think, therefore I am."

To be honest, the story of Joe as Metallica tells it does not map precisely onto philosophy's mind-body problem. "One" does not provide an esoteric consideration of how mind and body interact. But through the extreme case of Joe, whose body supports the existence of his mind and yet traps it, Metallica struggles with the same tensions philosophy tackles when attempting to explain the interaction between mind and body.

---

[2] Dalton Trumbo, *Johnny Got His Gun* (New York: Bantam Books, 1970), pp. 99–100. Further references to this book are given parenthetically in the body of the chapter as references to Trumbo with page numbers. Dalton Trumbo, dir., *Johnny Got His Gun* (World Entertainers, 1971), VHS, 111 min. Many Metallica fans have seen the movie, but you should definitely read the book!

I Can't Remember Anything, Can't Tell If This Is True Or Dream

Descartes' aim was the same as all philosophers—to gain knowledge about the nature of reality. But his method was different—to strip away all of his preconceived notions in order to arrive at what he could know with certainty, "clearly and distinctly."[3] Most of our thoughts about reality begin from sensory impressions of the world outside our minds. Descartes wonders whether these perceptions are real or just dreams. How could we tell the difference? "Considering that all the same thoughts we have when we are awake can also come to us when we are asleep, without there being any of them, at that time, that be true, I resolved to feign that all the things that had ever entered my mind were no more true than the illusions of my dreams" (*Discourse*, 51). So in search of greater certainty Descartes decides to doubt what his senses tell him.

In forsaking his senses Descartes becomes like Joe, our veteran in "One"—without sight or hearing. He abandons the body and turns inward, to his mind. But without any information coming through the senses, what remains? Descartes realizes he can know something without failure—he exists. After all, in order to doubt everything there must be some *thing*—some existing entity—doing the doubting. This was the solid foundation stone of knowledge Descartes was searching for, and it would serve as his standard for certainty:

> But, immediately afterward, I took note that, while I wanted thus to think that everything was false; it necessarily had to be that I, who was thinking this, were something. And, noticing that this truth—*I think, therefore I am*—was so firm and so assured that all the most extravagant suppositions of the skeptics were not capable of shaking it, I

---

[3] René Descartes, *Discourse on Method*, trans. and ed. George Heffernan (Notre Dame, IN: University of Notre Dame Press, 1994), p. 35. Further references to this book are given parenthetically in the body of the chapter as references to *Discourse* with page numbers. In outlining his method, Descartes vows "never to accept anything as true that I did not evidently know to be such: . . . and to include in my judgments nothing more than that which would present itself to my mind so clearly and distinctly that I were to have no occasion to put it in doubt."

judged that I could accept it, without scruple, as the first principle of the philosophy that I was seeking. (*Discourse*, 51)

Similarly, the very first word of "One" is "I." Joe has self-awareness. Yet the question "What is real?" remains. "Can't tell if this is true or dream," Hetfield sings. While Descartes is on a quest for answers, Joe is in a struggle for sanity. As Trumbo describes it, "This latest thing, his inability to tell dreams from thoughts, was oblivion. It made him nothing and less than nothing. It robbed him of the only thing that distinguished a normal person from a crazy man" (Trumbo, 99). Like Descartes, Joe has a breakthrough when he realizes he can distinguish his own thoughts and must remain focused on them. He realizes that the only way to keep his grasp on reality is to think and therefore to be. "No more dreaming about the past. That means no more of anything but thinking thinking thinking. He had a mind left by God and that was all" (Trumbo, 99–100).

Descartes too recognizes the importance of staying focused. "This alone is inseparable from me. I am, I exist—that is certain. But for how long? For as long as I am thinking. For it could be that were I totally to cease from thinking, I should totally cease to exist. At present, I am not admitting anything except what is necessarily true. I am, then, in the strict sense only a thing that thinks; that is, I am a mind, or intelligence or intellect, or reason . . . But for all that I am a thing which is real and which truly exists."[4]

Now the World Is Gone, I'm Just One

Joe was left virtually with only his mind when an explosion rendered his body practically useless. And so far, Descartes has established that we are at least minds, or, what he calls "thinking substances." "Substance" is what some philosophers call the basic building block

---

[4] Descartes, *Meditations on First Philosophy* in *The Philosophical Writings of Descartes*, vol. 2, ed. and trans. John Cottingham, Robert Stoothoff, and Dugald Murdoch (Cambridge: Cambridge University Press, 1984), p. 18. Further references to this book are given parenthetically in the body of the chapter as references to *Meditations* with page numbers.

of being, or the "stuff" which exists. [5] According to Descartes, thinking-substance is *not* material, not physical. By contrast, "extended substance," things that take up space are material, are physical. Our bodies are extended-substance, but so far in Descartes' investigation we only know that we think, therefore we are thinking-substance. And in fact, for Descartes, *thinking* by itself is the essence of human-being. Thinking is what makes us what we are.

For Descartes, the essence of our existence is our minds to the exclusion of our bodies. Not only do I know that I am, that I exist, because of my thinking, but in fact *thinking* is what I am. If thinking defines the human being, then all we need are minds, not bodies. Our essence is immaterial. "I am not that structure of limbs which is called a human body. I am not even some thin vapor which permeates the limbs" (*Discourse*, 52–3). Ultimately, "it is certain that I am really distinct from my body, and can exist without it" (*Meditations*, 54).

But *is* our essence really just thinking? Joe is without limbs and does still think, but he doesn't feel like he is living a complete life. Far from it. "Hold my breath as I wish for death!" Descartes' notion of a disembodied mind seems to suggest a sort of unencumbered freedom, a very refined nature, an almost ethereal existence. In contrast, James describes a "living consciousness" as a "basket-case kind of situation," which invokes hopelessness and despair. Metallica suggests that mind alone is not enough—we need our bodies to truly be *human* beings.

I'm Waking Up I Cannot See

One problem with isolating mind from body is that our minds need an object of thought—something to think about. What content is available to a mind alone? Other than "I am, I exist," Descartes recognizes two others things that he can know purely through the

---

[5]   In the history of philosophy, substance was contrasted with attribute or property. Attributes are the things which make generic being—substance—into each specific being. Kirk Hammett is human, male, with dark curly hair, and an amazing talent for the guitar. But strip all those attributes away and what is left? Many philosophers have maintained what is left is a "substance" in which all those properties reside.

mind without the aid of bodily senses, namely God and mathematical objects. Consider an octagon. You see them every day as "Stop" signs. But senses aside, you might also know from geometry class that the sum of the angles in an octagon is equal to 1,080 degrees. Do you *see* that when you stop at the corner? No, you grasp mathematical truths and thus know the properties of geometrical objects through your mind alone. To illustrate this, Descartes suggests you consider a chiliagon, which is a thousand-sided figure. We cannot picture the chiliagon in our head clearly enough to "see" it and count the sides, yet we can *know* what a chiliagon is. Thus we can consider abstractions like geometrical objects without the senses (*Meditations*, 50).[6]

Joe, who is deprived of his senses, also finds he still has mathematics, specifically numbers. When we last saw Joe, he was striving to create a reality for himself and not become lost in the fantasy of dreams and memory. He realized the way out was to keep "thinking, thinking, thinking," but about what? Without sense perception, Joe's mind is not presented with any new material upon which to think! All he can really do is think about thinking, so he fixes his mind on tracking the passage of time. His ambitious undertaking is to count— seconds, minutes, and hours, and thus find some sort of framework for his isolated existence. Joe counts furiously, eventually falls asleep, loses his place, and must start anew. He does this day after day, as if his life depended upon it, for really, killing time is all that he can do (Trumbo, 125–31). What kind of existence is that? What sort of life does an isolated thinking-substance live? A "life in hell."

Oh, Please God, Help Me

We cannot rescue Joe from his prison; the damage is done, irreversible. But perhaps we should go back and save Descartes. If we cannot trust our senses completely, can we trust them at all? For all we know, says Descartes, we are part of a cruel joke, created such

---

[6] Descartes is not only a philosopher, but was also a brilliant mathematician and the founder of "analytic geometry." You've studied this—plotting points and creating curves on X-Y axes (which is geometrically expressing algebra) was his invention. Hence X-Y axes are also called "Cartesian coordinates."

that everything we perceive to be real is not! If this were true, our creator would be some kind of demonic deceiver (*Meditations*, 28).[7] This is at least remotely possible, so we will have to prove otherwise before we can put trust in our senses and accept what we learn through our bodies.

Using reason alone Descartes proves that there must be a God. The idea of God in his mind is so perfect that only a perfect God could have produced it. And, after all, where did he, Descartes, come from? Answering "his parents" or any source less perfect than God begs the question: "Where did they come from?" Ultimately, the answer has to be God (*Meditations*, 24–36).

We doubted the senses because we know they can be wrong. That led us to question whether in fact they can *ever* be right. What if our creator is a cruel joker or demonic deceiver and made us such that we *always* misperceive the world? But the God whose existence Descartes just proved is perfect and thus cannot be a deceiver—since willingly deceiving is malicious and is thus contradictory to a perfect being (*Meditations*, 37). It follows that we can trust what is "clear and distinct" to us, including most of our sense perceptions. Of course, we will sometimes make mistakes, but that is only because our free will is unlimited while our sensory abilities are limited—we can only see so far, so clearly, and so on. Finally, we arrive back in the world, with clear and distinct knowledge about the nature of reality. We can take the blindfold off and start using our senses again.

Deep Down Inside I Feel To Scream, This Terrible Silence Stops Me

Unfortunately, Joe cannot simply remove a blindfold. The hero of Metallica's "One" is left in isolation with nothing to do but chase thoughts around in his head, with no ability to get anything out. Joe is virtually left for dead. In the video for "One," we hear the voice of a doctor from *Johnny Got His Gun*: "It is impossible for a de-cerebrated individual to experience pain, pleasure, memory, dreams,

---

[7] Or perhaps the artificial intelligence that has humanity plugged into *The Matrix*.

or thought of any kind. This man will be as unfeeling, as unthinking as the dead until the day he joins them." Unless Joe can find a way to reach them, the people around him will continue to take him for a vegetable.

Without a body we are without a vital aspect of human life, the ability to communicate our thoughts. For Descartes, we are in essence our minds, and thinking is what makes us human. Yet Descartes also understands that there is a connection between mind and body, since he knows speech is a physical manifestation of thought. Those who cannot speak will find another way to communicate. As Descartes observes, "men who, being born deaf and dumb are deprived . . . of the organs serving others in speaking are in the habit of inventing for themselves various signs by means of which they make themselves understood" (*Discourse*, 81).

This is exactly Joe's escape. The climax of the "One" video comes when Joe finally breaks down the communication barrier. As testimony of his functioning, resourceful, and in fact desperate mind, Joe taps out Morse code using his head. He sends the signal "S-O-S" repeatedly, his silent screams finally finding a way out. Thus Metallica shows us it is never enough to simply *have* thoughts; it is basic to human life to *express* them. The hell James dares us to consider in "One" is not just losing the use of our body for its own sake, but in addition the threat of silencing the mind. Thinking-substance alone is not enough; a mind requires a body to communicate its thoughts and thus complete itself.

Nothing Is Real But Pain

Descartes proved we are thinking-substances as well as bodies or extended-substances. Thus, philosophy has dubbed his theory "substance dualism." Many philosophers object to Descartes' ontology, arguing if "substance" is that which absolutely underlies all existence, why would there be two kinds instead of one? And if there are two absolutely distinct kinds of being, how can they possibly interact with each other? Descartes simply states: "Nature . . . teaches me, by these sensations of pain, hunger, thirst and so on, that I am not merely present in my body as a sailor is present in a ship, but that I am very closely joined and, as it were, intermingled with it, so that I and the body form a unit" (*Meditations*, 56). No further explanation is provided.[8]

Descartes picks the sensations of pain, hunger, and thirst because they highlight the interaction of mind and body. Hunger is a need of the body and can be felt in the stomach. But "hunger" is also an idea—a concept used by the mind to signify the sensation of the body that tells us we need to eat.

Metallica's "One" also highlights the interdependence of mind and body, presenting the horror of a mind virtually without a body— what does remain of the body serves as a prison for the mind. While Joe does not feel hunger or thirst because he is fed through a tube, regulated such that he never reaches the point of hunger, "Nothing is real but pain now." Here Hetfield highlights one of the very same examples Descartes used to show the intimate connection of mind and body. Pain is the body's way of telling the mind some harm has come to the body. "Pain" does not make sense for a mind alone. Joe's body makes its complaint to his mind, which registers pain, the body in distress. Yet because there is "not much left of me," Joe cannot move to help himself; he cannot cry out for help from another.

Can't Look Forward To Reveal

According to Descartes the union between mind and body is *not* like that of a sailor on a ship, "but rather . . . it is necessary that it [the mind] be more closely joined and united with the body, in order to . . . constitute a true man" (*Discourse*, 83). The separability of mind and body means in principle that the mind or soul (Descartes uses the terms interchangeably) can live on after the death of the body. "One understands much better the arguments that prove that our soul is of a nature entirely independent from the body, and, as a consequence, that it is not at all subject to die with it, then . . . one is naturally led to judge from this that it is immortal" (*Discourse*, 83).

[8] Descartes believed there was an actual physical locus for mind in the brain, "or perhaps just one small part of the brain," the pineal gland. This is not to say that Descartes thought mind is identical with brain, however.

Metallica shows us that to participate in the full range of human experience, and "look to the time when I'll live," we require both body and mind. In "One" we find that a mind without a functioning body is "an absolute horror." The limitations on Joe's body—and not his mind—have Hetfield howl, "Hold my breath as I wish for death" and then "Oh please, God, wake me!" So does Metallica agree with Descartes that a mind entirely freed from a body would then awaken to its own life? Does Joe's immortal soul have an afterlife for which he begs deliverance? Or is James simply expressing what the movie describes as the absurdity of "a piece of meat that keeps on living," since only God can hear Joe's cries?

The chorus alters slightly to "Oh please, God, help me!" just before the song enters its thunderous breakdown of crashing rhythms and a ripping guitar solo. From there it goes into a violent coda, each stanza marked by a single exclamatory word, followed by a sharp break and then a litany of woes sung in a harsh staccato. "Darkness!" is the first. The very briefest pause creates a gap, reinforcing the sense of isolation in the following "imprisoning me!" Joe is not involved in a contemplative meditation like Descartes, he is fighting for his very being. "I cannot live / I cannot die / Trapped in myself / Body my holding cell."

The next section bludgeons, "Landmine!" In Metallica's live performances the musical break is filled with a blindingly bright pyrotechnic display and a sonic boom that could leave you blind and deaf. On the surface level, these effects mimic the explosion that left Joe incapacitated. Yet the entire show serves as dark, defiant sarcasm: we are not Joe; we experience sensory onslaught as we see the flash and hear the boom. We feel more alive than ever as we are then pummeled with "Has taken my sight / taken my speech / taken my hearing / taken my arms / taken my legs," and perhaps most importantly, "Taken my soul." If Joe is already robbed of his soul, then it appears Metallica departs from Descartes' view that the soul is akin to mind or thinking-substance, and that the soul lives on without the body. Rather, it appears the soul is that which animates us and makes us who or what we are. Indeed, perhaps the soul exists more in the complete functioning of mind and body together, where two become one.[9]

[9] Heartfelt thanks to Bill Irwin, Chris Barr, David Hassell, and those who helped by reading my drafts.

CHAPTER 16

IS IT STILL METALLICA?
On the Identity of Rock Bands Over Time

MANUEL BREMER AND DANIEL COHNITZ

Bill owns a copy of *Kill 'Em All* and Ted owns a copy of *St. Anger*. Do Bill and Ted own albums by the same band? Both albums are by Metallica, so the answer should be obvious: yes, Bill and Ted own albums by the same band. But, unfortunately, things aren't that simple.

Things Not What They Used To Be

The mere fact that the covers of both CDs state that they are by Metallica is not enough to prove that the CDs are by the same band. Band names are neither *necessary* nor *sufficient* for a band's identity.[1] They are not *necessary* because a band can change its name and still be the same band. They arc not *sufficient* because a band just having the same name now is not enough to establish that it is still the same as that band in the past.

Consider, for example, that Eddie, Alex, David, and Michael played around Pasadena in the early 1970s under the name Mammoth.

[1] A *necessary* condition has to be met for something to be the case, a *sufficient* condition guarantees that the thing in question is the case. We are looking here for conditions that are individually necessary and jointly sufficient for band identity.

When the band became Van Halen it didn't change; it just got a new name.[2] So having the same name is not *necessary* for being the same band. Mammoth with Eddie, Alex, David, and Michael is the same band that toured and recorded under the name Van Halen through 1984.

Having the same name is also not *sufficient* for being the same band. The Van Halen example also makes this clear. In the early 1970s there were two bands with the name Mammoth. In fact this was the reason why Eddie and the boys renamed their band Van Halen. Obviously, having the same name didn't make both Mammoths identical.

I Was Me, But Now He's Gone

Maybe having the same members is what makes bands identical over time? Maybe having the same band members is both necessary and sufficient for being the same band? This would mean that the band that recorded *Kill 'Em All* is not the same band that recorded *St. Anger*. *Kill 'Em All* was recorded with Cliff Burton on bass, whereas *St. Anger* was recorded with Bob Rock on bass (though Rock was not technically a band member).

Replacement isn't the only way a line-up can change. Another way is *budding*, which occurs when a new member is added to a group[3] that was making music without him before, without the new member replacing anybody. Consider, for example, when Black Sabbath at last recognized Geoff Nichols (who played keyboard on some of their albums) as a band member. Fission and fusion are two other possibilities. *Fission* occurs when a group is divided into (at least) two groups, as was the case with Saxon, which divided into "Saxon" and "Oliver/Dawson Saxon." *Fusion* occurs when two (or more) groups

---

[2] Consider also Deep Purple, which was named Roundabout during its first tour, and Black Sabbath, which was originally named Earth. If you're like us you may have had the annoying experience of buying a record from the wrong band, just because it had the right name.

[3] We use "group" here to refer to any collection of persons, thus "group" is not necessarily synonymous with "band." We do this to give a neutral, non-question begging description of the case at hand.

join into one, as with Guns N' Roses. The band took its name from two bands that members came from: LA Guns and Hollywood Rose. Finally, consider loss and separation. *Loss* occurs when one or more group members leave without being replaced. For example, Karma To Burn recorded an instrumental record without their singer. *Separation* occurs when all members stop playing together and part ways.[4]

In looking for a criterion for the trans-temporal identity of rock bands, we are looking for a principle that would tell us in which of these cases (and under which additional circumstances) a band would continue to exist and when it would cease to exist.

One

Philosophers concerned with *trans-temporal identity* (or *identity over time* in general) ask whether some object at one time is the very same object as an object at some other time.[5] Imagine that Metallica go on a world tour to promote their latest album. Among the equipment they carry from gig to gig is Lars Ulrich's drum kit. Of course, Lars' drum roadie, Flemming Larsen, has to replace parts due to daily use

---

[4] There might also be more complicated cases. The original Black Sabbath members often claim in their interviews that when they played together there was this unseen fifth member which made the experience so special. Thus, when Ozzy was sacked, they lost in fact two members!

[5] Note that this question is, contrary to first appearances, neither the same as the question whether two distinct things are identical (this object and that object), nor the question whether this object is still identical with the *same* object a while ago. Both questions are nonsensical. The first question has a trivial answer: no two distinct things are identical. The second also has a trivial answer: everything is identical with itself; hence also identical with itself a while ago. Everything stands in the relation of identity to itself and not to anything else. Having said that, it might seem simple to state what the trans-temporal identity of rock bands consists in. It seems that every problem about trans-temporal identity of entities of some kind falls into two parts. First, the problem of whether the entities in question are of that kind (in our case, rock bands) and then the problem of whether they are identical, which seems then to be quite trivial and totally uncontroversial. As we will see, this is far from being the case.

and abuse. One day he has to replace a cracked cymbal, another day he replaces only a screw or a drumhead, sometimes he has to replace a whole tom, and so on. After a long world tour, Flemming has replaced each and every part of the entire drum kit, such that during the last gig of the tour not a bolt in the drum kit remains from the first gig of the tour. However, from one show to the next the drum kit remains the same. The fact that Flemming had changed a screw or a drumhead didn't mean that Lars' drum kit went out of existence and that some new drum kit was there on stage. The drum kit underwent a continuous replacement of parts, just as during our lives we undergo a steady replacement of cells. Our body remains the same body through the changes and so does the drum kit. At the end of the world tour Lars plays the last gig on the same drum kit that he played the first gig. If the drum kit of the first gig of the tour is identical with the drum kit of the second gig (despite minor replacements), which is identical with the drum kit of the third gig, and so on . . . , then the drum kit of the first gig is also identical with the drum kit of the last gig.

Now, a little twist to the story. Imagine that Flemming didn't throw away the used drum parts. On the last day of the tour, behind the stage, he reassembles them. The drum kit behind the stage is as complete as the one on stage (although it's a bit crooked). Moreover, it is a drum kit with the exact same parts as the one that Lars played the first gig of the tour. What now? We said in the story before, that the drum kit on stage is identical with the drum kit Lars played the first gig because its changes and replacements were continuous and gradual. Do we have to revise this statement? Is the drum kit on stage no longer the same drum kit as the one that Lars played the first gig of the tour, because there is *now another* drum kit (the one behind the stage) that is identical with the drum kit of the first gig? This would be strange. Whether or not some object is identical with another object should not depend on the existence or non-existence of a third object. For our purposes here, we call this the *Nothing Else Matters Principle*: whether a later entity is identical with an earlier entity can depend only on facts about *these two* and the relation between them. It cannot depend upon facts about any other entity. Finally, note that it can't be that both kits are identical to the kit from the first gig. Only one of them can be.

To Live Is To Die

We can phrase our concern as the problem of what relation different temporal stages of some band have to stand in to be temporal stages of the *same* band. For example, the band Metallica during their 1988 *Monsters of Rock* tour with Van Halen and the Scorpions is one temporal stage. The band Metallica during the *Escape from the Studio Re-Visited* tour in 2006 is another temporal stage. The relation we are looking for is the *unity relation for rock bands.* Having such a relation would provide us with criteria for *possible band histories.* Thus, in defining the unity relation for rock bands, we ask what could happen to a band without causing the band to cease to exist. Are things like fission, fusion, budding, renaming, replacement, and separation just radical changes in a band's history, or do they cause a band to cease to exist?

Although philosophers have so far largely ignored the problem of finding the unity relation for rock bands, they have had a lot to say about the unity relation for other things. The British philosopher John Locke (1632–1704) was among the first to give a systematic treatment of trans-temporal identity. Locke also pointed out that we have to be careful when making identity statements. Whether an entity is identical with some other entity may depend on what exactly we intend to speak about: "it being one thing to be the same substance, another the same man, and a third the same person."[6] Do we want to know whether the same atomic particles were in the studio during the recording of *Kill 'Em All* and the recording of *St. Anger*? Do we want to know whether the same collection of persons was present? Or do we want to know whether the same rock band made the recordings? These three questions, Locke would argue, might have different answers, although rock bands consist of persons and persons of atomic particles. As Locke put it, identity must be "suited to the idea," otherwise we will end up in confusion.

---

[6] John Locke, "Of Identity and Diversity," in John Perry John (ed.), *Personal Identity* (Berkeley: University of California Press, 1975), pp. 33–52.

Crash Course In Brain Surgery

We can explain Locke's point with the help of some science fiction. Imagine that a person named "Mave Dustaine" is jealous of Kirk Hammett and would like to have his place in Metallica. With the help of evil scientists he develops a technology to transplant brains in a few minutes' time. In a well-chosen moment during a Metallica tour, when all band members are sleeping on the bus, Dustaine abducts Hammett and takes him to the lab of his evil scientist friends. In a secret operation the scientists take Kirk's brain from Kirk's body and Mave's brain from Mave's body and exchange the brains. After that, they bring Hammett's body back to the tour bus and Dustaine's body to Dustaine's house. The next morning, Dustaine's body awakens, claiming to be Kirk Hammett (and soon ends up in a mad house singing "The motherfuckers got in my head / Trying to make me someone else instead"). Back in the Metallica tour bus, Kirk's body awakens. To the astonishment of everyone, he has forgotten how to play almost all of his solos, but he can play many songs by a band called Degameth. Is it really Kirk who woke up in Kirk's bed with Kirk's body but with Mave's memories?

If we were asked whether the same *human being* that went to bed in the Metallica tour bus also woke up in the Metallica tour bus, we would presumably say yes. Despite the replacement of an organ (namely the brain), it is otherwise the same organism, with the same DNA profile, still participating in the same continuous life. If instead we were asked whether the same *person* woke up in the Metallica tour bus who also went to bed there, our answer would be no. It is Mave Dustaine who woke up in Kirk Hammett's former body. As Locke would say, the unity relation for *persons* does not neatly coincide with the unity relation for *human beings*.

The Memory Remains

But what is the unity relation for persons, if it is not having the same living body? Locke explains that the unity relation for persons must have something to do with the memories and intentions of persons.

The person who woke up in Kirk Hammett's body is Mave Dustaine, because he remembers Dustaine's life, has Dustaine's intentions and interests and his character traits. As Locke expressed it, personal identity consists in "the sameness of a rational being; and as far as this consciousness can be extended backwards to any past action or thought, so far reaches the identity of that person." Let's see whether these considerations help us with our problem of finding the unity relation for rock bands.

Memory or testimony *alone*, as Locke had it in his original theory of personal identity, does not guarantee identity of rock bands.[7] Tony Iommi, despite his saintly status as the inventor of heavy metal, erred when he considered the later stages of Black Sabbath the same band (or a continuation of the same band) that played together in the 1970s. There is no first person authority (or band member authority) about a band being the same band. Therefore, sometimes fans complain that a band should have changed its name.[8]

But nevertheless, a broadly Lockean theory is likely to be about right for rock bands. Contents of the minds of the band members, namely their intentions and their musical orientations, should matter for trans-temporal band identity. To see this, notice that bands are social groups of a certain kind. And as the philosopher John Searle points out, social groups are more than just a bunch of people.[9] The beliefs and intentions of people are relevant to the question of whether they form a social group.

Imagine that Lars, Kirk, James, and Robert had by sheer coincidence met at a bus stop, say in the early 1970s, before they were even aware that they were all interested in music. The fact that they all had been together at some spot wouldn't have been sufficient to transform them into a social group. Without all having the intention to do the

---

[7] And it hardly solves the question about personal identity, either. Hetfield makes this point nicely in "Dirty Window," when he repeatedly asks "Am I who I think I am?"

[8] In fact the Black Sabbath case may be a case of imposed identity. Usually a record company does not care about style continuation or somebody, even Tony, doing a solo album—they want to have people buy records by exploiting their loyalty to a name tag.

[9] John Searle, *The Construction of Social Reality* (New York: Free Press, 1995); "Collective Intentions and Actions," in Cohen, Morgan, and Pollack (eds.), *Intentions in Communication* (Cambridge, MA: MIT Press, 1995), pp. 401–15.

same thing, a collection of people is not a social group, and certainly not a rock band. They must also have the intention to do something *together*.

Now imagine, again say in the early 1970s, that Lars, Kirk, James, and Robert arrive at a music store and each starts to play his instrument. Each sees and hears what the others are doing, and is so impressed that each one forms the thought "I want to make music with these guys." Again, this is not sufficient to make them a social group. They must, at least, also have the *common knowledge* that the others want to make music with them, and that the others know that every single one wants to join in, and that every single one knows that the others know this, and so on. Some philosophers, for example Margaret Gilbert, have argued that even that wouldn't be sufficient for them to be a social group and hence to be a rock band.[10] They must also have a "joint commitment." Lars, Kirk, James, and Robert must commit themselves as a "plural subject" to make music together. If that is true, and rock bands are something over and above a collection of people, the unity relation of rock bands will probably not coincide with the relation of being the same collection of persons.

My Lifestyle Determines My Deathstyle

This all strongly suggests that the identity relation for rock bands is independent of the people that make up the band, just as the unity relation for persons is independent of the body that makes up the person at a specific point in time. We should reject the *Person-Theory of Rock Band Identity*, which holds that the rock band-stage at some time belongs to the same rock band as another rock band-stage at some earlier time if and only if the first stage consists of the exact same persons as the second.

We will have to find an alternative criterion. Bands aren't mere collections of people, not just some social group. The most important property of a rock band is that it produces music in some way or other. This is so essential for a band that it should be part of our

---

[10]   Margaret Gilbert, *On Social Facts* (Princeton, NJ: Princeton University Press, 1989).

criterion. At the same time, a band is clearly not defined by a specific set of songs or a specific style. Metallica, like many other bands, have developed musically, and we need to account for that in our criterion.

So let's consider the *Musical-Style-Theory of Rock Band Identity*: A rock band-stage at some time belongs to the same rock band as a rock band-stage at some earlier time, if and only if it is style-continuous in musical expression with the earlier stage to a high degree and there is no other rock band-stage style continuous with that to any higher degree.

This criterion allows for replacing band members, provided that replacement does not radically change the style of musical expression. The criterion allows for *development* in the style of musical expression. Bands, after all, develop their style with time, and usually do not thereby cease to exist. We included the proviso that the style continuity must be to the highest degree, to make sure that of the many rock band stages at a time that play in a similar style, the closest one in style gets picked out and is identified with the predecessor.

No Remorse for the Helpless One

But as it stands the *Musical-Style-Theory of Rock Band Identity* is inadequate. It allows too much. The problem with the theory as stated is that no band could ever cease to exist as long as there is some band with a similar style (making the Backstreet Boys' menace "As long as there be music / We'll be coming back again" less threatening, since it would merely express a trivial truism). We could fix this by excluding fusions of rock bands explicitly or by giving strict criteria for what it means to be style-continuous to a "high degree" (thereby restricting possible musical development of a band again). But that fix would give us the wrong judgment in other cases.

Consider a band such as the Atomic Punks, which plays only cover songs of the earliest Van Halen records (from the David Lee Roth era). The Atomic Punks in 2006 are obviously style-continuous with Van Halen in 1978. Moreover, they are style-continuous with Van Halen in 1978 *to a much higher degree* than is the band named Van Halen in 2006. Today's Van Halen does not play the old songs in the old style anymore. Atomic Punks would now be identical with early Van Halen, whereas the band that toured under the name Van Halen in 2005 with Eddie, Alex, and Michael would not. This is certainly an unwelcome consequence. No member of the Atomic Punks ever was a member of early Van Halen or played regularly in a band with a player that was a member of early Van Halen or with a player that was a player in a band with a player that was a member of early Van Halen or . . . you get the point.

We could try to fix the problem by demanding that the later band-stage may not be a cover band, which would, alas, render the whole definition circular. After all, a cover band *is a band that is not the original band*, thus we would need a theory of trans-temporal band identity to determine this. But a theory of trans-temporal band identity is what we are after, so we cannot simply presuppose it in its very definition.

And even if we could exclude cover bands in a non-circular way, there are certainly bands that play, for example, in the style of early Metallica, writing songs on their own in that style (and thus do not cover), and would therefore still be better style continuers of early Metallica than the "real" Metallica of today are.[11]

Sad But True

These last arguments seem to give sufficient evidence that we cannot completely ignore the line-up of a band and that we should revise our theory in that direction. We have hinted already at how we might get the missing part into our condition of identity. Let's first define line-up connectedness: A rock band-stage is line-up connected with an earlier rock band-stage if and only if at least one person that is a member of the later stage is also a member of the earlier stage.

So every rock band would have to include at least one founding member, but for some cases this seems too strict. There are legitimate bands that do not include any of the founding members. The heavy metal band Accept that recorded *Eat The Heat* in 1989 did not include

[11] Some bands—typically in the case of reunions—spoil our days by being their own cover band. (Remember the Sex Pistols going on tour again with their old songs after decades?)

a single member of the original 1976 Accept line-up. Intuitively we would, however, still want to say that *Eat The Heat* was recorded by the same band that once won the third prize in a band competition in Düsseldorf. We can help ourselves by defining *line-up continuity* on top of *line-up connectedness*. A rock band-stage is line-up continuous with an earlier rock band-stage if and only if there is a continuous chain of line-up connected rock-band stages that connects them. This way we need a proper genealogy, but not necessarily a founding member.

Now let's articulate our revised theory, the *Revised Musical-Style-Theory of Rock Band Identity*. A rock band-stage at some time belongs to the same rock band as an earlier rock band-stage if and only if it is (a) line-up continuous, and (b) style-continuous in musical expression with the earlier stage to a high degree, and (c) there is no other rock band-stage that is also line-up continuous and style-continuous with the earlier stage to any higher degree.

Eye of the Beholder

Although the *Revised Musical-Style-Theory of Rock Band Identity* is much better than our earlier attempts to define the trans-temporal identity of rock bands, it is still far from perfect. What happens in the case of fission, when for example one band member leaves and starts a new band with others and continues the original style to the exact same degree as the "remaining" members do? An example (in fact several examples) for this can be found in the confusing history of Deep Purple. Consider also the history of Black Sabbath and Ozzy Osbourne. After the split between band and lead singer both offspring radically departed from the original style. And on some tours there were at least two original members playing in Ozzy's band, but only Tony Iommi playing with Black Sabbath. Think also of when David Lee Roth left Van Halen and started a solo career and when Dave Mustaine was kicked out of Metallica and founded Megadeth. Our revised condition would force us to say that the band that recorded *Killing Is My Business . . . And Business Is Good* and the band that recorded *Kill 'Em All* are both identical with the band that recorded *No Life Till Leather*.

We could add to our theory the requirement that line-up connectedness should also be to the highest degree, thus if only one member forms a new band that is style-continuous with the old band, but a lot more members of the old band continue playing in a similarly style-continuous way, the higher number of people from the old band would decide the matter in their favor. But what happens if a band splits exactly in half? And do all members of a band have the same weight in this?

We could try by declaring that a band simply ceases to exist if there are two successors that are style-continuous to the exact same degree and also line-up continuous to the exact same degree. Although this would get us out of trouble with the Metallica/Megadeth case, it would clearly violate our *Nothing-Else-Matters Principle*. Must we give up the *Nothing-Else-Matters Principle* or must we give up our revised identity condition? How shall we ever solve this?

Arrogance and Ignorance
Go Hand in Hand

Trying to state a good definition for trans-temporal rock band identity is discouraging. When philosophers are discouraged because of failed attempts to analyze something, they often claim either that the issue is intrinsically "un-analyzable," or more radically that whatever we tried to analyze does not in fact exist. With the issue here, defining the trans-temporal identity of rock bands, both of these strategies might have some appeal.

According to the first strategy to explain away the problem (we call it the *Simple View*), philosophers should simply insist that the trans-temporal identity of a band is just a brute simple fact, like the identity of your beloved cat or dog. Sometimes bands continue to exist, sometimes they don't, but whether they do or not isn't a function of any of the other properties of the social group that makes up a band and that we have considered so far. Whether or not different temporal band stages belong to the same band is totally independent of the members they have, their musical development, their name, and their attitude. It's just a further simple fact about bands, not possible to analyze, nor—in any way—in need of analysis.

The claim of the *Simple View* sounds totally mysterious. Philosophers who cannot accept mysteries like that would rather opt for the second strategy and argue the fact that our further definitions all failed is less proof for the "un-analyzability" of some further fact about rock bands, but rather a proof that rock bands don't really exist! This view could be called *Eliminativism*. Although the talk of rock bands is handy in many everyday situations, they just don't belong to the basic furniture of the world. If the identity conditions for rock bands are not clearly stateable then that is because they are just not there, and since there is *no entity without identity* (as the philosopher Willard Van Orman Quine once remarked), there aren't any rock bands. It might sometimes be a useful fiction to speak about rock bands, but it isn't more than that.

Right Here I'll Stay, With A Bullet In My Back

Although, as we have said, both strategies might have some appeal in this discussion, we find both to be unsatisfactory (at best). In fact, although the non-existence of rock bands (which we find hard to believe) or the simpleness of the identity relation (which we find too mysterious) might be explanations for the fact that we were as yet unsuccessful, they in no way are the only possible explanations. We'd rather blame it on the infancy of the study of the metaphysics of rock bands and other such social groups. Instead of being discouraged by our failure to come up with the ultimate solution, you should instead feel motivated to pursue this inquiry further. "You can do it your own way / If it's done just how I say."

DISC 5

FANS AND THE BAND

CHAPTER 17

METALLICA DROPS
A *LOAD*
What Do Bands and Fans
Owe Each Other?

MARK D. WHITE

For many longtime Metallica fans *Load* felt like a slap in the face. Some may have seen it coming with the shorter, simpler song structures of the Black Album compared to . . . *And Justice for All*'s progressive metal epics. Some date the shift much earlier, to *Ride the Lightning*'s refined production and songwriting as compared to *Kill 'Em All*'s rough directness. Some would trace it to editing "One" for radio and MTV, or to the death of Cliff Burton (without necessarily blaming Jason Newsted). But to my metal-soaked ears, *Load* was a uniquely abrupt change in musical style, one that rightly triggered backlash among the loyal members of the metal militia.

Our hardcore, underground metal band gained fans and popularity with every album, but primarily through word-of-mouth and the metal press. They charged into the mainstream with the Black Album (or perhaps even the video for "One"), but without deviating too much from their original style. But *Load* seemed like a desperate plea for alternative rock radio success (reinforced by headlining Lollapalooza), at the expense of their true metal roots (though to their credit, and very tellingly, they retained them live for the most part). Other thrash gods also changed: Megadeth went alternative with *Risk*, which was soundly rejected. Slayer leaned towards nu-metal with *God Hates Us All*, but not very drastically (and mostly due to production, not songwriting).

And Testament actually went in the other direction, towards a more death metal-based sound. How should we the fans feel about these changes? To paraphrase a common bumper sticker: what would Lemmy do?

Longtime fans felt hurt, violated, *wronged*. We felt that we *deserved* more of the classic thrash we loved, that we were *owed* something for our years of devotion, and for all of the money we spent on albums, concerts, t-shirts, and paraphernalia. We defended the band to the naysayers, we were loyal to the band while they were coming up, and how did they repay us? With weak alternative rock and slick MTV videos. Thanks a lot.

In short, we *deserved* better! Well, that's where philosophy comes in, particularly *moral philosophy*, which studies issues of "should" and "should not," "right" and "wrong," "owing" and "deserving." So, wearing our moral philosophy hats, we can ask: was Metallica *morally* wrong to change direction so drastically with *Load*? Or, to put it another way, did Metallica have a *duty* to its fans to maintain its long-established musical style?

Introducing Immanuel Kant, Master of Duties

Ask any ten moral philosophers about "duty" and at least nine are sure to bring up Immanuel Kant (1724–1804), one of the most influential philosophers of all time. (If the tenth doesn't mention Kant, he'll probably say, "Hey, whatever, dude . . . so do you want whipped cream on your mocha?") One of Kant's main ideas was that what makes an action right or wrong doesn't depend on what happens after you perform the act (its consequences), but instead something in the act itself. For example, if someone steals your "Ride the Lightning" t-shirt, the "wrongness" of that theft does not depend on how much you loved the shirt or how often you wore it, whether you met your girlfriend at that show or broke up with her there. The act was wrong because theft is wrong. In other words, we have a *duty* not to steal other people's stuff—especially Metallica stuff! We also have a duty not to (deliberately) hurt other people, kill other people—the standard "thou shall nots." The difference with Kant, compared to most other moral philosophers, is that these things are wrong regardless of their consequences. For example, according to Kant, attempted murder is just as wrong as murder, since the person did try to kill someone, whether he succeeded or not.

Kant called duties concerning murder, theft, and other major issues *perfect duties*, because they hold "perfectly" or absolutely. These are sometimes called "strict" duties, because we don't have any choice whether to obey them, or how much or how often to obey them—we just do (if we're moral people). Aside from special cases like self-defense, you shouldn't kill people—not a little bit, not once in a while, not even when someone insults your taste in music—just don't.

So does that mean that I'm a good person if I just avoid hurting others—I don't kill, I don't hit, I play well with others? Well, Kant would say you're not a bad person if all you do is avoid doing bad things, but you're not a really good person either! It figures that if there are perfect duties, there must also be *imperfect duties*, or "wide duties," ones that aren't so demanding and actually do leave some wiggle room. "Be nice to others" is a great example of an imperfect duty—it doesn't tell us exactly what to do, but instead what we should do in general. "Cultivate your talents" is another—it doesn't tell us whether to practice a Beethoven violin piece or the riff to "Blackened," just as long as you're practicing. (Kirk has played more than a little classical music in his day, so go ahead and do both!)

So, did Metallica have any sort of duty (perfect or imperfect) to maintain its original, NWOBHM-meets-Motorhead-meets-thrash style, and did they violate that duty with *Load*? How do we know that a duty exists? Kant came up with a rule that he thought captured commonsense morality in a nutshell. It's called the *categorical imperative*, and books have been written on it, but the main point is very simple (*Enter Sandman* simple). One way to put it is like this: you shouldn't do something that you can't imagine everyone doing at the same time (what philosophers call *universalization*). Kant would explain the rule "do not steal" this way—if everyone stole what they wanted, then no one's stuff would be safe, including the stuff you stole! It also explains the rule "do not lie"—if everyone lied whenever they wanted to, then no one would believe anything anyone said, and lies would be useless (since they depend on people believing each other in the first place). Both of these examples are based on contradictions: theft and lying each defeat themselves through destroying the concepts of ownership and communication that they depend on.

Does this mean Metallica has a duty to maintain their original style for the true fans? Let's put it this way: is there anything contradictory about every band being able to change its style whenever it chooses? What if, along with *Load* and Megadeth's *Risk* (an equal sin against the metal gods), we imagine that Slayer recorded a polka album (*Accordion of Death?*), Testament pulled a Rod Stewart with an "American Songbook" CD, and Exodus released a tribute to *NSYNC? Now *that's* a picture of hell, but Kant never said that anybody had to like such a situation. It has to be inconsistent or self-contradictory in some way to be wrong, so even if this scary alternate universe may force us to play our Warrant CDs again, it doesn't imply any duty not to change musical style.

There might be another way to justify such a duty. Kant also wrote of a somewhat looser standard, one that doesn't depend on logical inconsistency (such as the lying and theft examples do), but on "inconsistency in the will" instead. Take "do not kill," for example: philosophers who study Kant have noticed that there's nothing inconsistent about killing, as long as you don't do it *too much*! Some people would die (maybe just bands that release *NSYNC tributes), but most people would live. So we don't have a problem because everyone dying would leave no one to kill (or be killed). "Inconsistency in the will" means that you can't rationally imagine such a world, and no one can imagine living a world that condones haphazard, random murder. This is also the way that imperfect duties such as "help others" are explained—there's nothing logically inconsistent about a world in which no one helps anyone else, but no one could actually imagine living like that.

Will this give us the duty we need to condemn *Load*? I'm afraid not, because this way of putting Kant's categorical imperative doesn't rely on what we want or like, but merely what we can possibly imagine. (There's a fine line between the two, which Kant scholars are still debating.) A world in which Slayer plays polka and Exodus plays *NSYNC may be too horrible for words, but it is not unimaginable in the way that a world of rampant murder is. (But again, it's a fine line.)

So What (Have We Found So Far)?

Let's see what we've got: it doesn't look like Kant would have condemned Metallica for making *Load*, at least not as a breach of duty to their longtime fans. In fact, he may have pointed out several duties that Metallica had to other people that may have supported the decision to change their musical style. (Hey, philosophers are supposed to be objective—I don't like it anymore than you do!) First, the guys in the band are not teenagers anymore—they have wives and children to support, and you can't buy diapers with musical integrity alone. (As it turns out, *Load* and *Reload* together sold barely half as many copies as the Black Album, but we can safely assume they were meant to sell big.) Also, Metallica is not just four guys with instruments, it's a huge business that employs an army of roadies, guitar and drum techs, lawyers, accountants . . . all of whom depend on the band's fortunes to support their own families. Fans often forget that fact when they criticize a band for carrying on after the death of a member (such as Metallica did after Cliff died). If the band is successful at any level, they have a lot more people to think about than the fans, or even themselves. (Led Zeppelin is one of the few megabands that actually did call it quits after a member died—most soldier on, for better or for worse.)

But Metallica also has important duties to one more group of people—Metallica! Kant wrote of many duties that people have to themselves. Unfortunately, many of them—like "cultivate your talents" and "be true to yourself"—get so much play in *Chicken Soup for the Soul*, Oprah, and posters with kittens hanging from trees, that we cease to take them seriously. But Kant regarded them as very important to leading a full life. So if our guys really wanted to shift from true metal to alternative hard rock, if that was where their muses were leading them, whether it led down the road to riches or not, they had a duty to do just that. After all, would we want our favorite band to make music that they really didn't want to make, just to make us happy? How good do you think that music would be, if their hearts just weren't in it? AC/DC may be happy recording album after album in the same style—I know I'm happy with it, and I'm sure millions of grown men who secretly wear schoolboy short pants would agree (not that I ever . . .). But just because Angus and Malcolm are happy doing that doesn't mean every band will be, especially if their artistic drive is leading them elsewhere.

Do the Fans Have Any Duties to Metallica?

Let's turn this argument around—all this time we've been considering duties that Metallica may have to its fans. But what about duties the fans may have to the band? Settle down, settle down, I'm not going to talk about the duty not to download *Master of Puppets* illegally from the Internet—another chapter in this book is about that. But remember, "do not steal" is a perfect duty, and therefore a definite "no-no." (And don't do drugs. Listen to your mother. And don't do drugs. Most importantly—why don't you have *Master of Puppets* on CD already!?)

What I'm asking is if fans have any duties to their favorite band to stick with them while they change musical styles—call it a duty of loyalty if you like. U2 and Madonna fans seem to be loyal through all of their shifts from pop to dance to electronica to (in U2's case) rock. (Would Madonna's fans stick with her if she recorded a *Kill 'Em All*?) Another band I love, Deep Purple, had a significant change in style when Steve Morse replaced Ritchie Blackmore on guitar in the mid-1990s. Two more different guitar players could not be found, and the band's music naturally changed. Those who didn't like the change—myself included—were criticized by other fans for not being "loyal to Purple." Some sounded like Forrest Gump, saying "Purple is what Purple does," meaning that whatever the five guys currently in Deep Purple did was what "Deep Purple music" was, no matter what their music was in the past. This may apply to a band like U2, changing musical colors with the leaves, but sorry, not Purple—and not Metallica.

Let's play devil's advocate (I'm sure metal bands have a few of these on retainer). Metallica has given us so much, right? They've recorded fantastic albums that gave us sore necks for years, terrific cover tunes that may have introduced us to the forgotten NWOBHM bands of yore, killer live shows that even in the modern era rarely disappoint, and, perhaps most importantly, a band to rally around when the evil forces of hair metal, grunge, and boy bands seemed ready to steal our denim jackets and tight black jeans forever. Don't we owe them something, perhaps just some faith, when they want to try something new? Shouldn't we stick with them, while we hope that they'll return to their senses and beat us brainless again with the ultimate galloping riff and killer drum fills?

Kant didn't write about loyalty as such, but we can make a good case for a duty of loyalty. It's hard to imagine a world in which no one was loyal, even if there's no logical contradiction, so we can say that a duty of loyalty exists (at least in some circumstances). But surely we can't be expected to be loyal to everyone, all the time, even if they don't deserve it. If loyalty is a duty, it would have to be an imperfect duty—loyalty isn't something you can define precisely enough to be a perfect duty (like "do not steal"). And remember that imperfect duties have some "wiggle room" built in, so an imperfect duty of loyalty would not be absolute—you could choose when to be loyal (and when to stop being loyal), as well as to whom to be loyal.

So, when should we be loyal? I'm loyal to my friends, but I won't be for long if they're disloyal to me. I'll hold my extra Metallica ticket for a good friend, but I probably won't do it again if he decides at the last minute to see Madonna instead. The duty of loyalty would seem to require loyalty in return; one-way loyalty is spelled S-U-C-K-E-R. (One of my favorite Kant quotes is: "one who makes himself a worm cannot complain afterwards if people step on him."[1]) But what if my friend decided to see Madonna to try to fix things up with his girlfriend, and I think she's really good for him? He still bailed on the show, but I might still be loyal to him in the future because his disloyalty had a good reason behind it. (Motivation was a very important issue to Kant too, but we can't get into that now.)

Loyalty After *Load*?

Let's put this into the context of Alternica and *Load*—should we, the fans, remain loyal to the band after this stinging betrayal of their (and our) metal roots? Maybe we should ask why they did it—remember,

---

[1] *The Metaphysics of Morals*, trans. and ed. by Mary Gregor (Cambridge: Cambridge University Press, 1996), p. 188.

the right motivation can change our opinion about even the most heinous act. If *Load* was the result of an honest desire to explore new musical directions, and was not designed (unsuccessfully, as it turns out) to rake in buckets of money, then we might be inclined to stick with them. But if it was a strategic move planned to reap massive commercial success, then it's hard to see how we owe them any loyalty, since in that case, their choice was aimed toward pleasing new fans, without regard for their old ones. If this is true, then Sell-out-ica shifted their loyalty, relieving the fans of their duty to be loyal in return. They also betrayed their values as metal fans themselves. What would James and Lars have thought if Diamond Head or Mercyful Fate had sold out to hopes of radio success? In essence, Metallica sold out their values of integrity and "going against the grain until the end" as much as their music, and we fans had every right to withdraw our loyalty.

That leads us to another question regarding the duty of fans to be loyal: "to whom to be loyal?" Specifically, do we owe loyalty to the music, or to the people that make the music? Fans of the new Deep Purple sound said "Purple is what Purple does." Likewise, some Metallica fans will say "we're loyal to James and Lars, and whatever they do is Metallica and should be appreciated." By contrast, others, usually the old-school fans, will say "we're loyal to the music we fell in love with, and as long as Metallica kept making that music, we were with them." (Some new fans, who discovered Metallica with *Load*, could even be in this group.)

The first group of fans are loyal primarily to the band and the people in it, and the second are loyal primarily to the music (and to the band as well, as long as they make the music the fans like). The first group have more in common with fans of pop music, where the pop star's celebrity usually overwhelms her music. Pop fans will stick by a Madonna or a Britney no matter what style of music is on her latest album. But metalheads have a different standard—the style of music is the most important thing, and the people recording it are admired for that music (and rejected when the music changes too much). As much as it hurt—and I consider *Rust in Peace* to be one of the greatest metal albums ever—many fans like myself gave up on Megadeth after *Risk*, their version of *Load*. (If there's a book like this about Megadeth someday, I'll call that chapter "*Risk* Sells, But Who's Buying?") But since Dave Mustaine woke up (dead—bada bing!) and started making metal albums again, they've earned back our loyalty—not because he's Megadeth (though these days he essentially is), but because he's making Megadeth music again. (*The System Has Failed* is a very ironic title—the Megadeth system definitely worked for Dave with that one, even without Dave Ellefson.)

We Can Be Loyal, But Not *That* Loyal!

After all this, let's give Metallica the benefit of the doubt regarding the motivation behind *Load*, that it was what Ktulu called them to do (and not their bank accounts). And let's say we do feel an obligation to be loyal to the band that gave us nearly a decade of headbanging bliss. There's still one more issue here: how *much* loyalty do we owe Metallica? Or, to put it another way, how *long* do we have to be loyal? After all, *Load* was not a one-time mistake—they did follow it up with *Reload*, not *Remaster of Puppets*, . . . *And More Justice for All*, or *Kill 'Em All Again*. *St. Anger* was yet another change of direction and sound, but not in the right direction as far as the old-school fans are concerned.

Some of those old-school fans may have given up after *Load*, some may have thrown in the towel later, and some may still be sticking it out (or just seeing them live). Remember that loyalty is an imperfect duty at best, and each of us can decide how much or how long to stay loyal while still fulfilling that duty. Let me wear my economist hat for a little bit. When we decide how loyal to be, part of that decision is based on how much it costs us, or how much of a sacrifice we have to make to remain loyal. I used to buy all the European CD singles, even for the first few releases off *Load*—at that point, it was more out of loyalty than to get yet another alternate take or rough mix of a song I didn't like. How long was I supposed to keep doing that?

What would Immanuel Kant say? Kant is often misunderstood on the issue of making sacrifices for duty, but what he actually said is very reasonable. Take the example of helping others: you should not sacrifice so much that you require help yourself. (Don't give away your last Metallica ticket, or you'll have to beg for one!) When you have an opportunity to help someone, without making too great a sacrifice to your own well-being, then you should do so.

Let's step back and put this into perspective, though: we're talking about supporting a rock band by buying their CDs, concert tickets, and merchandise, not sending money to disaster victims or feeding the homeless! (No danger of James or Lars being hungry or homeless anytime soon.) But the point remains the same, if perhaps less urgent—if there is a duty of loyalty, that duty can be met more or less depending on the sacrifice involved. Personally, I know I'll continue to buy each Metallica studio album; my loyalty can endure that relatively small sacrifice. But I probably won't buy any more European singles, which often cost as much as a domestic full-length CD. Would I be more loyal if I did buy the European singles? Sure, but the sacrifice is too great for me, though it might be acceptable for someone else. With imperfect duties, we expect to see different people making different sacrifices, but nonetheless, each person is fulfilling their imperfect duties, as long as they try to do something, some of the time.

Kant on Metallica and *Load*:
The Final Words (and Fade to Black)

To sum things up, there is no basis in Kantian ethics for a duty that holds bands like Metallica to their original style to please the hardcore fans, but neither is there a strict duty forcing fans to stick by their favorite band if they choose to change styles. In other words, Metallica can record another *Load* if they want, but you don't have to buy it. We let the band off the hook ethically, but we let the fans off the hook in a way also.

We also learned a little about Immanuel Kant and his duty-based system of ethics, though of course we barely scratched the surface.[2] More importantly, we did a little philosophy of our own: we thought about a contemporary ethical dilemma using the writings of somebody who certainly never thought about heavy metal (other than

---

[2] For an excellent introduction to Kant's ethics, read Roger Sullivan's book (appropriately titled) *An Introduction to Kant's Ethics* (Cambridge: Cambridge University Press, 1994).

horseshoes). We'll never know what Kant would have thought about *Load*, or Metallica, or thrash at all, but the great thing about the best philosophers is that we can apply their general ethical principles to new situations and circumstances.[3] So next time you feel betrayed or wronged, after you ask "what would Lemmy do?" you can use the categorical imperative to ask "what would Kant do?"—you might just be surprised with what you come up with.

[3] Thomas E. Hill, a philosopher at the University of North Carolina, is an expert at applying Kantian ethics to modern-day topics like affirmative action and terrorism; see in particular his books *Autonomy and Self-Respect* (Cambridge: Cambridge University Press, 1991), *Dignity and Practical Reason in Kant's Moral Theory* (Ithaca, NY: Cornell University Press, 1992), and *Respect, Pluralism, and Justice: Kantian Perspectives* (Oxford: Oxford University Press, 2000). His book *Human Welfare and Moral Worth: Kantian Perspectives* (Oxford: Oxford University Press, 2002) is more theoretical in nature.

THE UNSOCIAL SOCIABILITY OF HUMANS AND METAL GODS

NIALL SCOTT

The Struggle

Morality is frequently presented as a struggle. A struggle between good and evil; a struggle between right and wrong; a struggle of either competing desires or desire competing with reason. We find ourselves confronted by decisions about things we should do, but do not want to do; and we find ourselves wanting to do things that we think we should not do.

"The Struggle Within" presents us with a character who is beset by such problems, leading ultimately to his self-destruction, sealing his own coffin. We are not told what the struggle involves, apart from dealing with boredom and isolation. But clearly it is one of many Metallica songs that articulates the problem of wanting to do one thing but being drawn to do something else. "So many things you don't want to do / What is it? What have you got to lose?" In the poetry of *Master of Puppets* we find an example of this struggle in the helplessness of trying to rid oneself of the pull of drug addiction, "just a rhyme without a reason." The desire for a fix is so strong it's as if the person is being acted upon from outside, unable to gain rational control to escape the drive for more. This theme is revisited in "Frantic" as Hetfield faces the tension of trying to resist, yet being pulled in by the desire for alcohol: "Do I have the strength / To know how I'll go? / Can I find it inside / To deal with what I shouldn't know?"

Like Metallica, the German philosopher Immanuel Kant (1724–1804) treated human morality very much as a struggle—not just between good and evil, but also between reason and desire. To be more precise, between reason and those desires that are incompatible with reason. Beyond that, Kant thought human beings were engaged in a constant struggle between wanting solitude, but also needing the company of others: "Through the desire for honor, power or property, it drives him to seek status among his fellows whom he cannot bear yet cannot bear to leave."[1] This sounds a lot like Metallica as we meet them in the documentary *Some Kind of Monster*.

Human Nature:
The Struggle Between Good and Evil

Kant held that morality was the *product* of reason, which is reliable and unchanging. By contrast, feelings, desires, and emotions are morally unreliable and constantly changing.[2] The character in "The Struggle Within" is criticized for being content to remain in the struggle, but not resolve it—"Kicking at a dead horse pleases you." Kant sees the struggle between good and evil as similarly unresolved.

In a Diamond Head cover, Metallica answer the question "Am I evil?" with a resounding "Yes I am!" But, of course, the matter is not that simple for Metallica or for Kant. Kant thought that humans had

---

[1] Immanuel Kant, "Idea for a Universal History With Cosmopolitan Purpose," in Hans Reiss (ed.), *Kant, Political Writings* (Cambridge: Cambridge University Press, 1991), p. 44. Further references to this book are given parenthetically in the body of the chapter as references to *I*.

[2] Kant writes in the *Groundwork to the Metaphysics of Morals*: "Empirical principles are wholly incapable of serving as moral laws" and "feelings which can naturally differ in degree cannot furnish a uniform standard of good and evil, nor has anyone a right to form judgments for others by his own feelings." Immanuel Kant, *Groundwork to the Metaphysics of Morals*, 4:442–3, ed. by Laura Denis (Ontario: Broadview, 2005), pp. 99–100. Further references to this book are given parenthetically in the body of the chapter as references to *G* with page numbers.

a predisposition to be good, but this predisposition can just as easily be corrupted into evil. In the book *Religion Within the Boundaries of Mere Reason*, Kant gives us a list of things that can make a person evil.[3] He holds that a human has a propensity to evil in (a) not being able to act morally, because he thinks humans are fragile and weak, that (b) a human can twist moral incentives and turn them into something bad, and (c) a human can act in a depraved way, that is, act according to evil principles.

According to Kant, evil can result from the predisposition to animality, treating the human as a living animal being. This includes "vices grafted on to savagery" in which humans are motivated to act and perform bestial vices: gluttony, lust, and wild lawlessness. To get an idea just listen to Metallica's version of the Anti-Nowhere League track "So What."

Evil can also result from rationality. We can use reason for good or for evil. For example, love of others can lead to generosity and selfless acts. Love of oneself can lead to a healthy self-confidence. But taking love of self too far turns into arrogance, and "Arrogance and ignorance go hand in hand." Self-love leads to a comparison with others and the "inclination to gain worth in the opinion of others" (*R*, 6:27). In addition to this, Kant lists as evil the diabolical "vices of culture: envy, jealousy, rivalry, ingratitude, joy in other's misfortune" (*R*, 6:27). Metallica echoes this: "Holding me back 'cause I'm striving to be / Better than you," as Hetfield sings of unhealthy comparison and competition. What better support for this than the relationship between James Hetfield and Dave Mustaine early on in Metallica's career? Lars Ulrich in *Some Kind of Monster* captures it, saying: "There was an incredible rivalry or competition between you [Mustaine] and James . . . One minute you'd hug and embrace, and the next minute you'd be close to fucking fighting each other. It was quite some energy."[4] And, Lars notes, the product was amazing. Perhaps without this "vice," this evil, there might not have been the living monster of Metallica.

---

[3] Immanuel Kant, *Religion Within the Boundaries of Mere Reason*, 6:29, ed. by Allan Wood and George di Giovanni (Cambridge: Cambridge University Press, 1998), p. 52. Further references to this book are given parenthetically in the body of the chapter as references to *R* with page numbers.

[4] Joe Berlinger with Greg Milner, *Metallica, This Monster Lives* (New York: Robson Books, 2004), p. 128.

Beyond our predispositions to evil through animality and rationality, Kant believed there was a human predisposition to "responsible being" (*R*, 6:26). But can membership in the metal militia ever involve being responsible? For Kant, in "responsible being" the human agent employs reason to motivate him to act, and is thus capable of pure good. But this perfection is not something we're guaranteed to achieve. "Only you can tell in time / If we fall or merely stumble." In a moment, we will turn to overcoming the internal struggle between good and evil. First, let's look at the struggle between seeking out solitude and needing the company of others.

Other People: Can't Live With 'Em, Can't Live Without 'Em

The struggle within between good and evil, right and wrong, is not just a private internal struggle, sealing oneself in one's own coffin, struggling in isolation. It is a struggle in the world of other humans, resulting from our relationships and conflicts with one another. Kant thus speaks of the "unsocial sociability of man," the tension between the human wanting to be in community and also in solitude, that in finding oneself in one place, the other is longed for. As he says:

> This propensity is obviously rooted in Human nature. Man has an inclination to live in society, since he feels in that state more like a man, that is, he feels able to develop his natural capacities. But he also has a great tendency to live as an individual, to isolate himself since he also encounters in himself the unsocial characteristic of wanting to direct everything in accordance with his own ideas. (*I*)

Kant claims this unsociability leads to conflict, even war: "Nature has thus again employed the unsociableness of men, and even of the large societies and states which human beings construct and as a means of arriving at a condition of calm and security through their inevitable antagonism" (*I*). The documentary *Some Kind of Monster* exemplifies this Kantian insight. The tension between the isolated creative Metal God egos and the community of the band (which exists to express creativity) has led to near-break ups, arguments, and personal crises. But the tension has also produced classic albums. It is through antagonism that peace and calm return. A reconciliation of the struggle is made in the music.

The kind of cooperation needed among group members clashes head on with the vices of arrogance, self-love, jealousy, and rivalry that Kant lists as diabolical. But perhaps these need to be experienced before they can be overcome and musical talents can shine. "The secret of group cooperation is very simply the shared knowledge that one has to be bad before being good."[5] Ironically, clashes leading to cooperation may be necessary to fulfil a Kantian moral duty. "For as a rational being, he necessarily wills that all the capacities in him be developed, since they serve him and are given to him for all sorts of possible purposes" (G, 4:423). Purposes, for example, that include Metallica developing their talent for the benefit of their fans. It would be easy for the members of Metallica to disband, deciding the struggle isn't worth it. But, as Kant would see it, they have a duty to themselves and to their fans to develop and express their talents. And if this involves clashes along the way, then so be it.

Overcoming the Struggle

In giving such an important role to reason as the thing that motivates us to perform morally right action, Kant's view of humanity may seem rather strict and overly narrow. Surely there are many features of our emotional responses to situations that bring us to act in a morally praiseworthy way. For example, one might think compassion and feelings of sympathy are the foundation of moral action. Isn't it the feeling of compassion that makes me give money to the homeless? Sure, afterwards I can give reasons for why it is a good thing to do, but what is it that motivates me to perform the act itself? Perhaps we can take something both from what Metallica can offer with their view of humans engaged in a struggle of competing desires, and the insight Kant can give us into resolving such a struggle through reason, to form a more rounded vision of the human moral agent.

---

[5] Stith Bennett quoted in Deena Weinstein, *Heavy Metal: The Music and Its Culture* (Cambridge, MA: Da Capo Press, 2000), p. 73.

Kant's idea of the human as a moral, rational being led him to argue that a principle governing all moral behavior could be uncovered, one that any rational being would agree with once understood; a principle that had universal validity. That principle is known as the *categorical imperative*, a command that dictates how one must act: "Act only in accordance with that maxim through which you can at the same time will that it become a universal law" (G, 4:421). So what does this mean? A maxim is a principle on which a person acts. So the command is stating that I should only act on principles that all can consent to. If another person cannot act according to a maxim that I come up with, then it is not right for me to act that way either.[6] When a person acts according to a maxim that fits with the categorical imperative they act according to duty. For example, it is a moral duty for us to give help to those who need it. Let's turn to Metallica for an example of how this categorical imperative applies in the everyday situation of helping someone. It is in being drawn to help others, in recognizing their need, that we come out of solitude and interact with one another.

In a search for the "Hero of the Day," Hetfield sings: "Don't want your aid / But the fist I've made / For years can't hold or feel / No, I'm not all me / So please excuse me / While I tend to how I feel." Here we have someone rejecting help, wanting to tend to himself instead. The maxim of his action is: "I don't want any help even when I need it. Leave me alone." Would we want this maxim to be a universal law? Would we want everyone to always act that way? No, since much of human society would grind to a halt. It would be possible to live solitary lives, but it would be pretty heavy going. Consistency in such a position would require us to reject help from others and refuse to help others. Any attempt to insist on receiving help but not giving it, or giving help but not wanting any could lead to a charge of hypocrisy. Such hypocrisy is clear in "The Struggle Within" where "Advantages are taken, not handed out."

The Kantian response would be to criticize as irrational this attitude of not wanting aid. Kant doesn't think it's possible for the human to live in solitude without need of assistance from others. So

---

[6] Jonathan Harrisson, "The First Formulation of the Categorical Imperative," *Kant: The Foundations of the Metaphysics of Morals, Text and Critical Essays*, ed. by Robert Paul Wolff (New York: Bobbs-Merrill, 1969), p. 211.

in giving up the need for help from others, and extending this to all situations, we condemn ourselves, probably to death. If we try to, we seal our coffin; our "home it becomes a hell / turning it into your prison cell." Think also of the flip side to the character in "Hero of the Day," a person who doesn't want to give any help to others. Kant asks us to consider someone who is doing quite well, and is satisfied but on noticing others in need thinks: "What is it to me? Let each be as happy as heaven wills or as he can make himself; I shall take nothing from him nor envy him; only I do not care to contribute anything to his welfare or to his assistance in need!" (*G*, 4:424). In other words, "It ain't my fall / It ain't my call / It ain't my bitch / Outta my way / Outta my day." So, Kant argues unless we think that in using reason we can live solitary lives without help from others, we cannot be rationally committed to not receiving or giving help. We have a duty to help others. Do we then have an obligation to help others at all times, sacrificing our own time, effort, and skills for others?

No, a world of self-sacrificing heroes would be irrational. Metallica's disposable hero realizes this: "Bodies fill the fields I see hungry heroes end / No one to play soldier now, no one to pretend / Running blind through killing fields, bred to kill them all / Victim of what said should be, a servant till I fall." If we were all committed to performing heroic acts, it would lead to no one attending to the everyday practical things we need to function and flourish. Recognizing this, Kant does not require us to make extreme acts of self-sacrifice. After all, we have a duty to take care of and perfect ourselves.[7]

Although the categorical imperative may seem extreme, Metallica can help us to see that what Kant intends is pretty reasonable.[8]

---

[7] Niall Scott, "Is Altruism a Moral Duty?" *Imprints, A Journal of Analytical Socialism* 7 (2004), pp. 226–47.

[8] Kant thinks that we have a duty to help others, in the duty of beneficence, but he calls this an imperfect duty. By this he means that there are situations where we cannot possibly help others; for example, I cannot be under obligation to give money to the homeless if I have no money; I cannot be under obligation to save a drowning person by jumping in the water if I cannot swim. He is simply recognizing that as human agents we are limited by our skills and resources. A great discussion on Kant's ethics and saving lives can be found in David Vessey, "Hey-Diddley Ho Neighboreenos: Ned Flanders and Neighborly Love," in Irwin, Conard, and Skoble (eds.), *The Simpsons and Philosophy: The D'Oh of Homer* (Chicago: Open Court, 2001), pp. 202–14.

Despite the irrationality, of *wanting* to not want aid, the desire to be left alone, "Hero of the Day" expresses an emotional state that touches much of human experience. This is a deep desire to be self-sufficient and be left in solitude to our own devices. There is a struggle within between reason pulling us into relationships with others and desire leading to solitude.

But maybe there's a loophole. Kant seems to insist that we have a moral obligation to help others, which does not necessarily commit us to having very much of a relationship with them. If we are indeed to be motivated by reason, rather than desire or inclination, then we can do the right thing yet remain uncaring and cold towards the person we help. The duty to help others does not appear to require anything more. I can live on my own in my way and send the occasional check to a charity. I don't need to get to know those at the receiving end. Kant was criticized on this point by Friedrich Schiller (1759–1805), who satirically suggested that the only way to avoid feelings of love or compassion and still be involved in doing the right thing was to do the right thing but with hatred.[9]

Schiller's suggestion is not far removed from the heroic "My Friend of Misery," doing what seems to be the right thing (saving the world), but doing it in a state of misery: "You're out to save the world / Misery / You insist the weight of the world should be on your shoulders / Misery." Schiller's criticism also connects with a journalist's (I think, wrong) comment on Metallica's relationship with each other in *Some Kind of Monster*, accusing the band of doing their duty to record and perform in order to serve business: "In the end, when Ulrich claims 'the band has proven that it can make aggressive music without negative energy,' one can only laugh, as the film has been a wallow in the negative energy created by big egos that can't get along but must find ways to make their business entity function."[10]

Schiller, of course, was mistaken in assuming that Kant's theory doesn't allow for any emotion to be involved in doing the right thing.

9 Friedrich Schiller, Xenien, "The Philosophers," quoted in Allan Wood, *Kant's Ethical Thought* (Cambridge: Cambridge University Press, 1999), p. 28.
10 Bill White, Seattle Post Special to the Post-Intelligencer *Metallica Doc Strips Down Monsters of Rock to Egomaniacal Pussycats*, Friday July 30, 2004, www.seattlepi.nwsource.com/movies/184138_metallica30q.html.

In truth, Kant thinks showing and developing feelings of love, sympathy, and compassion make it easier for us to do our duty—and that's a good thing.

Do Your Duty

In conclusion, we have a duty to give help to those in need where we can. This duty, though, draws us into a social relationship with others that we can just as quickly be tempted to abandon for solitude. Kant and Metallica both conceive of the human as a being that deserves and demands respect and promotes reason. Kant's argument that we cannot live alone is complemented by Metallica's vision of humans as we are.

CHAPTER 19

BOYS INTERRUPTED

The Drama of Male Bonding in
Some Kind of Monster

JUDITH GRANT

Like any other part of pop culture, rock reflects the ideological currents of its times. But maybe more than any other element of pop culture, rock is also explicitly about sex. And not just sex, but masculine sex. Sure, there are exceptions to this, but the basic elements of rock as well as the artists themselves have most often enacted a male drama about masculinity and sexual prowess. Heavy metal is exemplary of this tendency.

Some Kind of Monster is very crucially about the relationship between Lars Ulrich and James Hetfield. It is about the bond between rock brothers and the erotic nature of that bond. No, I'm not saying Lars and James are gay. This is not about homosexuality, but rather "homosociality." Eve Kosofsky Sedgwick, who developed the term homosocial, explains it as the "social bonds between persons of the same sex."[1] While they are not synonymous, Sedgwick argues that there is a continuum between the homosexual and the homosocial in that they are both linked to desire. Desire, in this sense, does not refer to the sex act, but it does refer to the erotic. Desire as eroticized energy is "the affective or social force, the glue, even when its manifestation is hostility or hatred or something less emotively charged, that shapes an important relationship." In this way, desire

---

[1] Eve Kosofsky Sedgwick, *Between Men: English Literature and Male Homosocial Desire* (New York: Columbia University Press, 1985), p. 1.

(libidinal energy) binds us all to one another whether our relationships are explicitly sexual or not.

As the character Russell says in Cameron Crowe's 1998 film, *Almost Famous*, "Rock and roll is a lifestyle and a way of thinking." Jack Black put it another way in *School of Rock*, telling his students that rock is about "stickin' it to the man." Which is to say that rock bands are as much about their attitude as they are about their sound. The heavy metal pose was lampooned with extraordinary skill in Rob Reiner's 1984 spoof rockumentary, *This is Spinal Tap*. In the film, the hapless metal band Spinal Tap is presented in a loving caricature that includes many of the elements of the quintessential heavy metal band: changing personnel due to deaths and personality conflicts, substance abuse and its resulting problems, and the competitive male bonding among the members. *This is Spinal Tap* was the definitive portrayal of the inner works of a heavy metal band. Until Metallica's *Some Kind of Monster*.

Some Kind of Homo

Directed by Joe Berlinger and Bruce Sinofsky, *Some Kind of Monster* details Metallica's travails as they wrote and recorded the 2003 release, *St. Anger*, the band's first album since 1997. At a creative standstill before getting together to do the album, Metallica members and their management hired a "performance enhancement coach" and therapist Phil Towle. For the sum of $40,000 a month, he was to stay with the band and provide them with group therapy through their three year odyssey. *Some Kind of Monster* is the story of a middle-aged rock band whose members now have wives and children, but who lock themselves in a room to try and recapture the youthful rebelliousness that contributed to their iconic status as the monsters of metal. It is *Spinal Tap* meets *Survivor*.

The film presents a rare opportunity to glimpse a world few of us have seen. In important ways, rock band culture is a trope of masculinity, and seen from a certain angle, homosocial bonding is one of the major conventions of rock. The bond between duos in rock and roll echoes the passion of lovers, as bands become families without women. How else can we explain things like the feud between Jagger and Richards in the 1980s from which the song "Mixed Emotions" is said to have come? Often, a duo figures prominently as the central unifying force in a rock band, the energy between the two fueling an entire libidinal relationship that is key to musical creativity as well as the image of a band. Who could imagine the Beatles without the Lennon and McCartney relationship, the Stones without Jagger and Richards, Aerosmith without Tyler and Perry, Zeppelin without Plant and Paige, or Metallica without Hetfield and Ulrich? On reflection, the energy they create together is unmistakably libidinal. In a real sense, the libidinally charged interplay of the major personalities in the band *is* the band.

From this vantage point, it is predictable that a male-centric band like Metallica would be exemplary of homosociality. We can even say that the more closely a subculture (in this case, a rock band) is contingent on male connection and the exclusion of the feminine, the more it exists on a continuum with sexualized relationships of men loving men. It is a paradox that the more masculine the subculture the more closely it is conceptually related to homosexuality. The more sexualized it is, the more that sexuality is hypermasculine, the more that erotic energy is channeled into the relationships among band members themselves to form the homosocial bond. The homosocial bond is, in that sense, related to the exclusion of the female. Men can be men together because women are excluded.

We can see this with reference to an unrelated example. After the film *Brokeback Mountain* was released in 2006, the Internet was alive with short spoofs of the film. Clever websters took clips from films such as *Goodfellas*, *Back to the Future*, *Lethal Weapon*, and *Top Gun*, gave them the film's music, superimposed a few of the film trailer's key lines (like "It was a friendship that became a secret"), and the films emerged as sometimes hysterically rendered trailers for non-existent gay movies.[2] Why did this work? What made it funny? The concept of the homosocial helps us to explain the joke in that it points to the link between the homosocial and the homosexual, and the fine line between buddy film and gay film. The laugh comes from anxiety related to crossing the line from homosocial into homosexual. The more macho the scenario, the greater the need to

---

[2] See, for examples, www.dailysixer.com/brokeback.shtml.

keep that boundary firmly in place, and the more anxiety (and hence laughter) can be exacted by imagining the line being erased.[3] Sedgwick's work shows that where one draws the line between non-sexual male bonding and homosexual activity is itself a political and ideological process.

What Happens When You *Are* The Man

Seen in terms of masculinity, it is of course completely appropriate that Metallica began work on the album *St. Anger* by renting as their recording space an ex-military barracks, the Presidio in San Francisco. In 2001 the band united in the Presidio with no music, no lyrics, and no permanent bass player. Producer Bob Rock sat in during the sessions and was eventually replaced by new band member Robert Trujillo. At the time of the film, bassist Jason Newsted had recently quit the band when guitarist and front man James Hetfield had told him he couldn't be in Metallica if he continued to pursue his side project, the band Echobrain. Forced to choose, Newsted chose Echobrain. Newsted himself, of course, had been a replacement for the deceased original bassist and songwriter Cliff Burton.

Echobrain aside, tensions between Newsted and the band were already evident around the idea of hiring Phil Towle as a therapist for Metallica. Newsted proclaimed the therapy idea "really fucking lame and weak." For James' part, jealousy seems to have played a significant role in the tensions. Explaining his decision to make Jason choose between his two bands, James said he realized he didn't want Jason to "like Echobrain more than Metallica" and didn't want to feel like "we weren't enough." James' sentiments are consistent with those of a wife who finds her husband cheating. In both cases, jealous energy has its roots in desire; one sexual, the other homosocial.

---

[3]   There is a lot more to be said here. Next time you watch a macho buddy movie, take note of how many times they make jokes about the buddies having sex with each other or being romantically involved. The jokes are there to diffuse the tension. The jokes make explicit what everyone is subconsciously thinking, and the jokes allow the taboo thoughts to be voiced, thus dispensing with them in a manner that is acceptable within the confines of heteronormativity.

As of this writing, Metallica had sold an astonishing 90 million records. Having attained this massive success, they struggled to return to their creative roots as rebel outsiders. The goal was to sound like a "band getting together in a garage for the first time. Only the band's Metallica." The problem Metallica faced was related to masculinity. Their relationships to each other had grown stale and complicated because their homosocial bond had weakened. The intrusion of wives and children and the onset of middle age were transformative. How does one rekindle desire and love in any twenty-five-year marriage? What is left to rebel against once you become "the man" you once opposed? And how can you rebel when many of the usual channels of rebellion (drug use, drunkenness, sexual promiscuity) are foreclosed? Boys will be boys. But boys who become fathers and whose personal lives now include more than one another now look more like adults with responsibilities. Bummer.

This conflict between youthful rebellion and adult membership in the status quo became obvious in the disastrous decision to sue Napster. What better illustration of capitulation to authority and to selling out than the specter of Lars Ulrich testifying before the US Senate that fans were eating into Metallica's profits. Ulrich complained that 350,000 people were downloading their music for free. The Metallica fan backlash was immediate. Some fans destroyed their Metallica collections, and the film shows Lars acknowledging that he was the most hated man in rock and roll. The band was lampooned on the web in a cartoon that portrayed Lars as a whiny sprite and Hetfield as a hulking, knuckle-dragging Frankenstein who stomps around saying "money good, Napster bad."

Under the touchy feely direction of Towle, songwriting became a collaborative process. Hetfield rolled his eyes as the band's new mission statement was read aloud: "We come now to create our album of life. We honor the brilliance of each and the harmony of one . . . We have discovered the true meaning of family. It is both our mission and our destiny to manifest this ideal. As we accomplish the ultimate togetherness we become healers of ourselves and the countless others who embrace us and our message." The sunny mission statement belied the Metallica known to fans. The music has always conjured the rage and angst of a teenage boy seething and alone in his room hiding from a dysfunctional family. Metallica was Columbine just before the shooting.

The arc of the story in *Some Kind of Monster* revolves around James. James is unhappy. James leaves. James returns. Tensions first come to a peak when James goes hunting in Russia and misses his son's first birthday. Returning to the band, he confesses that he's not inspired, complains that Hammett's guitar licks sound stock, and that Lars is picking at him. Hetfield leaves one session slamming the door behind him. From there he vanishes into rehab not telling anyone where he's going, how long he'll be there, or if he'll return. The rest of Metallica is forced to stop working and leave the Presidio.

All in the Family

Hetfield emerges as a narcissistic, controlling, compulsive alpha-male. Though angry and defensive with a perpetual chip on his shoulder and a famously addictive personality, Hetfield also comes across as intelligent, reflective, and charismatic. His pockmarked face tells the story of what his pre-rock star high school years must have been like. The child of an absent father (his parents split when he was twelve), Hetfield lost his mother too when he was sixteen. Aware that wanting to keep everything under control is connected to his abandonment issues, in the film Hetfield confesses that he is afraid to be close because he is not really sure how to do it.

Lars Ulrich, on other hand, had an overbearing all-too present and musically hip father. Watching them together in the film makes it obvious that Lars feels completely overwhelmed by him. Far from James' father who made fun of him for his interest in rock music, Lars' father is almost too knowledgeable on the subject. Looking something like *Rumplestiltskin* meets *ZZ Top*, Torben Ulrich clearly knows a shit load about music. Under the gaze of his father, we watch rock god Lars Ulrich devolve into the intimidated little boy who is never good enough. Speaking to therapist Phil Towle, Lars expresses fearful admiration of his father, saying that if something on the record "sucks" his dad can "see right through that in two seconds flat." Later, in a particularly poignant scene, he plays something from the new record for dad. His father responds: "If you're asking for my advice I would say 'delete that.' For me it doesn't cut it." Lars laughs sardonically, shaking his head: "The only other person who heard that thinks it should open the record." To which dad replies confidently: "I really don't think so."

Mothers are virtually absent from the film. The mothers of the band are never mentioned. The mothers of the band members' children are trotted in and out occasionally. We know they are there, but they are peripheral. The film understands itself to be about the masculine, and the relationship the two men had with their fathers tells much about the dynamic between the two as they come together in Metallica. James' judgmental and controlling nature cannot help but touch off Lars' feelings about his own father's judgments of him. While Lars' need to be loved and appreciated cannot help but make James feel concerned about his inability to share closeness, and consequently to make him feel pestered and smothered by Lars: "The way I learned how to love things was just to choke 'em to death . . . don't go anywhere. Don't leave." The source of their irritation is also the source of their attraction to one another. For each can see in the other the missing component, damaged by their respective upbringings and latent within each of them. Each is attracted to the possibility of resolving a series of Oedipal dramas now made possible by the presence of the other. Thus, Lars projects onto James the sensitive side he longed for in his own father, as James acts out his ambivalence about closeness with Lars on whom he projects his own judgmentalism. In fact, Lars' admiration of James is clearly evident. He says, "I've always felt that James was a softer, more caring, compassionate person than he allowed himself to be to most people."

In the film, we can see how important James is to Lars as a source of approval. Likewise, we can see how James' self-confessed inability to be close creates a cycle in which James' repeated withdrawal from Lars only stokes the fire of Lars' need for James' approval. Lars' need for approval partly explains his jealousy. If James is the master of the temper tantrum, Lars is the master of the sulk. Unable to allow others the spotlight, Lars repeatedly vies for attention with other band members in a flurry of unselfconscious displays of sibling rivalry for the attention of alpha-male James. As illustration, Lars remarks disdainfully on how the posturing of former guitarist Dave Mustaine brought out James' macho side. That style of masculinity is alien to Lars as a mode of connection and competition, and he explains it was anathema to the way he was brought up in Denmark. Reflecting on this, Lars again expresses a desire to offer James closeness, the thing James can neither accept nor reciprocate: "I want to help him. I want to be there for him. I want to help him to be the best person he can be."

As part of therapy, Lars meets guitarist Dave Mustaine in what is apparently one of the few times the two had met since Mustaine left Metallica in 1983. Dave Mustaine's bond with James appears to have been effectuated through alcohol. Only with the band for a brief time, Mustaine was asked to leave because he could not control his temper and drank too much. In the scene between Lars and Mustaine, the two enact the pain of sibling rivalry. Though Mustaine went on to found the successful band Megadeath, he confesses that he feels like a loser, and that it has been "hard to watch everything you guys do turn to gold and everything I do fucking backfire." He continues: "People hate me because of you . . . I walk down the street and I hear some piece of shit yell 'Metallica!' Man, they do that to taunt me . . . Do I wish it was 1983 all over again and you guys woke me up and said, hey, Dave, you need to go to AA? Yeah I'd give anything for that chance."

Sibling jealousy and possibly competition for James' attention is evident on the part of Lars once again when band members go to see Newsted's new band Echobrain play in Los Angeles. Surprised to see that it is a huge, hip event, Lars says candidly, "I expected it to be him playing for 20 drunks downtown . . . I guess that's what I wanted it to be." It gets worse when they go backstage after the show and Newsted has blown them off. The fact that Jason Newsted's band has the kind of fresh, small club, male rebel energy that Metallica has had to pay Towle to try to recapture is not lost on Lars, who re-capitulates Mustaine's bizarre confession by holding his head in his hands and lamenting, "I feel like such a loser. I can't hold my band together. I start records I don't finish . . . Jason is the future, Metallica is the past."

Tellingly, the only person to hear from James during his six-month stay in rehab is the quiet, sensitive guitarist Kirk Hammett. Relaying through Kirk that it is hard to talk to Lars because he is "so controlling," James tells them that his family is the priority before he "reaches out to his other family." Acknowledging the family bond among the men in the band, James' snub of Lars illustrates the special nature of their relationship as particularly passionate and complex.

Perhaps reacting against Kirk's role as James' confidant, Lars acts out against Kirk by going over the top in a self-indulgent melt-down on the occasion of the Hawaiian themed birthday party given for Kirk. The tantrum seems staged or forced, a play for attention with a flimsy excuse. Yet, he succeeds in getting James' attention. Embarrassed that he has not been told that everyone is supposed to wear Hawaiian shirts, Lars shouts: "Nobody ever does anything for fucking me. I don't come in one day and there's a Danish bakery motif or a fucking, you know, 'celebrating H.C. Anderson children's poetry' motif. There's nothing." James appears to take Lars seriously, responding: "How is it that I can come from New York and I know?" Lars turns for support to daddy-figure, therapist Phil: "How do you think it feels showing up here and being the only one who doesn't have a Hawaiian shirt on? And people go 'oh, it's because he's so rebellious' . . . if some fucker would tell me I'm supposed to wear a Hawaiian shirt . . . I'm permanently ambushed with this fucking shit with these shirts." Phil responds in a tone of patronizing chas-tisement: "The moment you got here you could have joined in the festivities, but you chose not to. And then as you distanced yourself from everybody else you felt worse."[4] Thanks, Phil.

The Good Old Days and Kissing Kirk

Male homosocial bonding in rock and roll works on the energy of a family system that is devoid of females. In fact, this is the principal way that all homosocially bonded units function, as can be observed in group dynamics in fraternities, the military, and even the police. A key feature is the absence of women as equals. Indeed, we could go so far as to say that the homosocially bonded male-only family is dis-rupted and unmade by women. Women can be present only as objects around which to bond. When they cease being objects and become real people, love interests, wives, and mothers, the bond of men is broken because the libidinal economy has broken down. This is

---

[4] The scene did not make it into the final cut of the film, but is available on the DVD's special features.

the grain of truth in the notion that Yoko Ono (and Linda Eastman) broke up the Beatles. And, I would argue, this was the key problem Metallica was having when they hired Phil. Married family men Ulrich and Hetfield had difficulty being inspired by one another in the same way that they were earlier in their careers.

The boys have now become productive members of the society against which they once rebelled. To the extent that their music was based on a homosocial bond rooted in youth and counterculture identification and rebelliousness, it was in trouble the more successful they became. Moreover, rock has changed. Indeed, the members of Metallica are now successful and respected in a career that no longer positions itself as Other. Rock is a multi-billion dollar industry. The men themselves are patriarchs in heterosexual family units. No longer positioned as the rebellious Other, they have become The Man.

The problem is that the homosocial bond was largely fueled on adolescent angst and sexual predation. Having removed those things, what unifies the band? What fires the music? The band is no longer a group of boys who are mad at their dads. They have become dads themselves, and can no longer truly assume the rebellious posture of male-centric Other. Thus what the film actually depicts is a homo-social bond interrupted and then rekindled. Phil becomes the dad, and as we shall see, it would appear that it is actually the rejection of Phil that enables the band to reestablish their connection to one another and to move forward. But even before that, hints to the nature of their bond and the path toward their reconciliation appear.

For example, when a recovering James returns from rehab, he is only able to work from noon until 4:00 pm. Now a controlling dry-drunk, James' feeling is that everyone should be on *his* work schedule and no work should be done without him. Making a failed attempt to communicate using therapeutic "I" statements rather than accusa-tions, he says: "When I'm gone things get talked about and the deci-sions are made and I feel I walk into something that something that's already kinda decided, and it's a total uphill battle for me and I don't like that feeling." Not a word is said until the usually silent Kirk offers: "Well, that's like the last 15 years . . . [*pause*] for me." Enacting the very thing Kirk is talking about, everyone ignores him, not even pausing to look his way. Even the therapist does not acknowledge the remark and says instead, "Well, let's talk about it tomorrow." Unsatisfied, James walks out and slams the door.

When they all reunite it is Lars who takes the opportunity to call James on his behavior. "I just think you're so fucking self-absorbed," he charges, pacing. "I think you control on purpose, and I think you control inadvertently, I think you control by the rules you always set . . . by how you always judge people . . . by your absence. You control all this even when you're not here." And then reflectively: "I realize now that I barely knew you before. And all these rules and all this shit, man! This is a fucking rock and roll band! I don't want fucking rules." The speech is wonderful because it allows Lars to remind James (and maybe himself) that rules are in conflict with the rebellious spirit of rock and roll. In that sense the tirade, couched as an attack, can be understood as an important moment in the reestablishment of the homosocial bond between Lars and James, which had been initially forged on their status as rebellious Others.

This emotional climax leads Lars to reflect nostalgically on what his relationship with James was like in the early days of the band. The reflections truly point to the homosocial and its roots in desire. It sounds like someone discussing the early years of a marriage gone bad as Lars expresses his longing for the more sensitive James who comes alive only when the two of them are alone. Lars recalls with sadness: "I can take you back, when me and him were alone in my room in 1981 listening to New Wave of British Heavy Metal singles—as soon as there was somebody else in the room . . . it just had a very different energy to it." He continues, referring again to his rivalry with Dave Mustaine: "The first time I got a real awareness of it was when Mustaine came into the picture. When James was with Mustaine he became like he never really cared about me." And later: "One time during the recording of the *Ride the Lightning* record where me and him went out—42 beers later, 'Oh Dude, I love you,' but it could never have materialized until it got to that 42-beer point and we were alone." Here the relationship almost slips from homosocial into the homoerotic.

Lars has skirted the edges of this boundary between the homosocial and the homosexual before in reportedly French kissing Kirk on several occasions. Discussing this in a 2001 *Playboy* interview, Lars explained that for him, this proved his own security in his masculinity: "Ultimately, why do me and Kirk stick our tongues down each other's throat once in a while in front of the camera? The metal world needs to be fucked with as much as possible. When the band started, everybody would sit around proving their heterosexuality by gay bashing and stuff like that. Like, 'Oh, fucking faggot.' Does that elevate you to some greater he-man status? I never understood that."[5] In fact, Lars' question can be answered easily in terms of the analysis at hand. The homosocial depends on the bonding of men as heterosexuals. Since the female is cast out and disparaged often through sexual objectification, the heterosexuality of the men must be affirmed, and often, by a similar rejection and vilification of homosexuality. The bond is further forged in this ritual which is as if to say, we are men together but we are not gay; we love but we are not in love, we desire but we do not fuck.

Another time that we see the band come together in a vibrant way that evokes the kind of bond that must have brought them together in the first place is when management arranges for them to record a promotion spot for a cash give away on behalf of a major radio chain. Given that they sell records for a living and have sued Napster, it's difficult to understand why this particular commodification feels like a violation to them, but there is no doubt that it does. They joke and deride the spot, and in this scene you can really see them being boys together. Finally, in a telephone call to management, James asks what if they refuse to do the spot. Management responds that the radio station could conceivably retaliate and hurt album sales. What is wonderful is that after twenty-five years in rock and roll, James can still ask incredulously and with alarmed indignation: "They would really do that? You won't help me so I'm gonna hurt you?" When he is told that yes, they would, he mutters under his breath: "Wow. I'm glad I don't live in your world." Of course, he does live in their world. What's more, he is one of their main products. The righteous anger is useful, however, and becomes an inspired song lyric for the song "Sweet Amber," "Wash your back so you don't stab mine / Get in bed with your own kind."[6]

---

[5] *Playboy*, April 2001.

[6] Of course, the song is primarily about drinking, as is discussed in chapter 3 by Bart Engelen, "Alcoholica: When Sweet Amber Becomes the Master of Puppets."

Finally, Fuck Phil

The final example of the reestablishment of the homosocial bond comes in the moment when they fire Phil Towle and come back together as boys. By positioning Phil as disciplinary, patriarchal Other, the band is able to reposition itself as hypermasculine rebellious outsider. Signaling a shift in attitudes toward Phil, James confides to his band mates: "I'm afraid he's under the impression he's like in the band." They all quickly agree that Phil can't come on the road with them and resolve to tell him that their time together is over. Meanwhile Phil, who looks more like a Midwestern accountant than a therapist to a rock band, has been making plans to move to San Francisco from Kansas City, but only "if there's a future with Metallica."

Phil is now feminized. He is the woman who wants to move in and get married and who must be broken up with. Pathetically, he tells them he has "performance coach visions" for each of them and that for him, "the work isn't over." But they are resolved. Phil tells them that he thinks they are firing him because they are not dealing with the trust issues they have with him. Reunited with James at last, Lars chimes in support of James, telling Phil that if the client wants the relationship to end, it ends. As Phil finishes telling them why he thinks he ought to stay on, James cuts in dismissively, nodding to Lars, turning away from Phil and leading the band out of the room with the rock and roll call to arms: "Any-way. Let's jam." Thus the film ends with a return to the music, to excise the disciplinary (and later, the feminizing) force represented by Phil and to reestablish the bond of the band.

Rock on, boys.

JUSTICE FOR ALL?
Metallica's Argument Against Napster and Internet File Sharing

ROBERT A. DELFINO

When somebody fucks with what we do, we go after them.[1]

Lars Ulrich

Thus spoke Lars Ulrich in an interview about Metallica's lawsuit against Napster. This hard-edged, belligerent attitude we love in songs like "Damage, Inc." infuriated many Metallica fans in this case. In fact, other than the complete absence of guitar solos on *St. Anger*, nothing has hurt Metallica more than the Napster fiasco. Was it all really about the money? Were Ulrich's arguments logically sound? Philosophy can help us answer these questions. So hit the lights, and let's jump in the fire that nearly consumed the four horsemen.

Napster: The Thing That Should Not Be

In 1999 Shawn Fanning, a freshman at Northeastern University, stayed awake for sixty hours straight writing the code for a program that would change the music scene forever. Napster, named after its

---

[1] "At Last And At Length: Lars Speaks," posted on May 26, 2000, at www.interviews.slashdot.org/article.pl?sid=00/05/26/1251220; hereafter cited in the text as *Slashdot interview*.

author's nappy hair, allowed people to connect to its centralized file server and share music. The genius of Napster was that its server did not host any songs at all. Instead, it simply provided a listing of songs that were on other people's personal computers and allowed you to download directly from them. Napster turned the Internet into a huge jukebox of free and easily accessible digital music. Word spread and soon millions of people were sharing music over the Internet.

It didn't take long before recording artists, music labels, and the Recording Industry Association of America (RIAA) began to complain. The RIAA sued Napster in December 1999, arguing that it was helping people to pirate copyrighted music "on an unprecedented scale."[2] They requested $100,000 in damages for each time a song was copied.[3] A few months later, in April 2000, Metallica sued. Lars went on record saying that users of Napster were "trafficking in stolen goods" and that this was "morally and legally wrong."[4]

Initially, Napster was defiant. The company refused to remove Metallica's content from its listings unless "Metallica could provide proof of specific violations."[5] That's when things got personal. Metallica hired NetPD, a British company, to monitor Napster. After a forty-eight-hour period they had catalogued 1.4 million violations.[6] A few days later Lars Ulrich personally delivered thirteen boxes of documents that fingered 335,435 Napster usernames who were trading Metallica songs.[7] Within a week Napster had banned most of those users. Angered by Metallica's "Kill 'Em All" approach, some fans decided to fight fire with fire.

One fan, Mark Erickson, helped create the sarcastic website paylars.com, which collected donations to "compensate" Metallica

---

[2] "Recording Industry Sues Napster for Copyright Infringement" posted on December 7, 1999, at www.riaa.com/news/newsletter/press1999/120799.asp.
[3] Joel McIver, *Justice for All: The Truth about Metallica* (New York: Omnibus Press, 2004), p. 296; hereafter cited in the text as McIver.
[4] "Artists, Managers And Industry Leaders Speak Out Against Napster," posted on April 11, 2000, at www.riaa.com/news/newsletter/press2000/041100_2.asp; hereafter cited in the text as *RIAA Newsletter*.
[5] Marilynn Wheeler, "Metallica Drummer: Stop Ripping Us Off!" posted on May 3, 2000 at www.news.zdnet.com/2100-9595_22-520426.html?legacy=zdnn.
[6] Craig Rosen, "Metallica Gives Names To Napster," posted on May 2, 2000, at www.music.yahoo.com/read/news/12044814.
[7] Jessica Litman, *Digital Copyright* (New York: Prometheus Books, 2001), p. 159.

for the money they lost due to Napster.[8] Bob Cesca, another disgruntled fan, produced and released a short but brutal Internet flash movie called "Napster Bad!" It portrayed Ulrich as a greedy, arrogant bastard, and Hetfield as some kind of a dim-witted, giant monster.[9] The movie ends with Ulrich shouting threats at Napster users: "Our team of lawyers and researchers have your names and we're going to hunt you down like the table-scrap-pilfering grab-asses you are."[10] Lars was well on his way to becoming, as he said in the documentary *Some Kind of Monster*, "the most hated man in rock 'n' roll."

The legal battles dragged on until July of 2001, when Metallica finally reached a settlement with Napster. But the damage had been done, and things would never be the same for Metallica or its fans. Sad, but true.

Were the fans right to be angry at Metallica? Or was Metallica right to take action against Napster? The controversy provides us with an excellent opportunity to analyze complex arguments. Our analysis of the controversy will illustrate the importance of Logic, the branch of philosophy concerned with correct argumentation, and Ethics, the branch of philosophy concerned with morality and immorality—good and evil.

Send Me Money, Send Me Green . . .

From the beginning, Lars claimed: "This is not just about money (as some of the more cynical people will think)" (*RIAA Newsletter*). But many fans didn't buy that. One of the reasons Metallica suffered in the public relations part of the Napster controversy was a failure to present one, clear, and consistent argument.

For example, some of Metallica's statements did imply that money was the issue. In an online chat that occurred May 2, 2000, James

[8] Brad King, "Napster Spat Pits Fans vs. Bands," posted on April 21, 2000, at www.wired.com/news/culture/0,1284,35840,00.html.
[9] "Metallica vs Napster," posted on May 15, 2000 at www.guitar.about.com/library/weekly/aa051500a.htm.
[10] Craig Rosen, "Metallica Cartoon Parody All Over Net," posted on May 13, 2000, at www.music.yahoo.com/read/news/12038891.

Hetfield said: "This is a clear case of a middle man [Napster] cutting us out of rewards we should reap for being a band" (McIver, 299). Jason Newsted added that Napster "Didn't ask us to share our music and steal our money."[11] Even Lars himself, in the same chat, said that Napster "is not a service that they're offering for the good of mankind, to spread love and music. They're doing it for potential IPOs [Initial Public Stock Offerings] for alignment with a big company where there will be a major cash transfer to the investors. This is about money."

Lars' initial comment, "This is not just about money," implies that it is *partly* about money. James' comment about "rewards" seems to be only about money. This interpretation is supported by other comments James made during the same online chat: "My question is what is your occupation? What do you do for a living? And would you go do your job five days a week for absolutely nothing, just to do it? . . . essentially, this could kill Metallica and music if we were doing it for free." Lars echoed the same point in an interview on the Charlie Rose Show, saying: "In the United States nobody does anything for free, man."[12] But then, shortly before he was to testify in front of the United States Senate in a hearing on Internet music distribution, Lars said: "It's just got nothing to do with money."[13] Nothing? First, he implied it partly dealt with money. Then James made it seem that it was *all* about money. Now it had "nothing" to do with money. Which was it?

Logic tells us that all three of these views cannot be true. That would be like saying the same baseball team won, lost, and tied the same game! It's impossible. This is called the law of non-contradiction. Aristotle (384–322 BCE), the father of Logic, put it this way: "It is impossible for anything at the same time to be and not to be."[14] Any argument that contains a contradiction is a bad argument.

In fairness to Lars, I believe it is possible to resolve his seemingly contradictory statements. The whole Napster controversy hit him out

---

[11] "Metallica Chat," posted on May 2, 2000, at www.chime.com/about/press/metallica/000503.html.
[12] Charlie Rose Show, May 12, 2000, Transcript #2681.
[13] Craig Rosen, "Metallica Addresses Napster Misconceptions And Greed," posted on June 30, 2000, at www.music.yahoo.com/read/news/12040409.
[14] Aristotle, *Metaphysics* (1006a), trans. by W.D. Ross in *The Basic Works of Aristotle*, ed. Richard McKeon (New York: Random House, 1941), p. 737.

of left field. He was not computer savvy, admitting in the *Slashdot interview* that he could "just barely . . . get onto AOL [America Online]." He wasn't even aware of Napster until his managers told him about it, and even then he had to read daily to educate himself about it. He was angry, and most likely he didn't think through all of the complexities involved before expressing his discontent. Certainly, he did not express himself in the clearest language. Still, I think we can figure out what he meant.

Lars' point appears to be that Metallica was not suing Napster in order to win a sum of money. Metallica already had a lot of money, and any money they were losing to Napster was "pocket change." So in that sense the lawsuit was not about money at all. But the lawsuit was about money in the sense that artists' work should be protected so that they could earn a living. Metallica was simply standing up for arists' rights. This interpretation is supported by Lars' clearest statement of this point:

> Understand one thing: this is not about a lot of money right now, because the money that's being lost right now is really pocket change, OK? It's about the principle of the thing and it's about what could happen if this kind of thing is allowed to exist and run as rampant and out of control for the next five years as it has been for the last six months. Then it can become a money issue. Right now it's not a money issue. I can guarantee you it's costing us tenfold to fight it in lawyers' fees, in lawyers' compensation, than it is for measly little pennies in royalties being lost, that's not what it's about. And also, we're fortunate enough that we sell so many records through the normal channels. Where it can affect people, where it is about money, is for the band that sells 600 copies of their CD, OK? If they all of a sudden go from selling 600 copies of their CD down to 50 copies, because the other 550 copies get downloaded for free, that's where it starts affecting real people with real money. (*Slashdot interview*)

It's My World, You Can't Have It

The focus on artists' rights not only helps explain the quotations about money and earning a living, but it also explains Metallica's talk about "control" and "property." On several occasions Lars argued:

"I want the right to control what is mine . . . I respect the next guy, who wants to put his music on Napster, but I want him to respect the fact that maybe I don't. It's that simple" (*Slashdot interview*).[15] On July 27, 2000, after a District Court ruled in Metallica's favor, the band issued a statement: "We are delighted that the Court has upheld the rights of all artists to protect and control their creative efforts."[16] In the same statement Kirk Hammett added: "We're doing this because we think it's the right thing, the moral thing . . . We're basically standing up for ourselves and other artists in general, and we're standing up for our rights as owners of our own property."

Metallica was making a moral argument that artists, because they create and own their art, have certain rights. These include the right to sell their art, to control how it is sold, and to decide if they wish to give it away for free. What troubled Lars was that people were acting as if "they have a right to any piece of information that comes to them through the Internet" (*Slashdot interview*). Had he been talking about physical property, such as a car, I doubt many would have disagreed with him. After all, no one wants *their* car stolen. Americans take private property rights very seriously.

The topic of property rights, and more generally human rights, is a very interesting one that we will return to later. But what is important about the Napster case is that it involved intellectual property, not physical property. No one was stealing compact discs. In fact Napster's central file server did not even store any songs. It just helped individuals trade digital songs with each other. This seemed so similar to the cassette tape trading of the 1980s that some fans were furious.

How ironic that Metallica was now against music trading when it was the underground tape trading of their demo *No Life 'Til Leather* that led to their success. How could Metallica, a band that encouraged fans to "bootleg" their own shows, be against Napster? Was this hypocrisy? Was there a contradiction within Metallica's argument against file sharing?

Even though I agree with most of Metallica's argument, it has one serious flaw, which a close examination will reveal.

[15] Lars made similar statements on the Charlie Rose Show.
[16] Craig Rosen, "Metallica 'Delighted' By Napster Ruling," posted on July 27, 2000, at www.music.yahoo.com/read/news/12044795.

Same Thing I've Always Heard From You, Do As I Say Not As I Do

Lars, and other members of Metallica, had been arguing that artists have a right to make money from the sale of their art, and to control how it is distributed and sold. It is their property and no one has the right to just take it from them without permission. Because artists own their music they also have the right, if they wish, to give it away for free.

So the fact that Metallica gave away their demo *No Life 'Til Leather* and encouraged others to copy it and spread it worldwide was not a contradiction. It is consistent with Metallica's argument about artists' rights. When Metallica performs live that is also their music. So if Metallica permits fans to "bootleg" their concerts that is their right as artists. But we should note the word "bootleg" means to smuggle in (or steal) something without permission—in earlier times people would literally hide items such as liquor in their tall boots. Metallica was giving their permission to the fans to record the concerts. Thus it is improper to call such activity bootlegging.

The contradiction lies in Lars' position on "home taping," which was popular in the 1980s. For example, my friend owns Iron Maiden's album *Piece of Mind*. I borrow it and I like it—but I don't want to spend the money to buy it—so I just copy it onto cassette tape. That is home taping in a nutshell. Since Iron Maiden has not given me permission to copy their music, and since I have not paid for it, one would expect Lars to argue that this type of activity is wrong. It is wrong because it violates the artist's rights (Iron Maiden's rights in this case). This is what Lars should have said if he wanted to avoid contradiction. But he didn't. Instead, he seemed to say it was OK for several reasons.

His first reason is that the quality of cassette tapes is not that good, and that tapes suffer from generation loss. When you copy a tape there is a loss of sound quality and when you make a copy of a copy there is further loss of quality, and so on for each subsequent generation. On the Charlie Rose Show Lars explained: "We have no particular issues with home taping because you're talking about clear generation losses. But, when it is the original master recording of our song available in a perfect digital format, that is a different story."

His second reason is that the scale (quantity) of tape trading is much smaller than Napster. He explains this most clearly in the *Slashdot interview*:

"How is it [Napster] different from home taping?" I guess is really the question. You know, home taping ten or fifteen years ago really was about, you had vinyl records, and you had the neighbor down the street with you know, his Iron Maiden records, that you wanted to make a tape of so you can play in your car. There is a difference . . . comparing that kind of home taping to basically going on the Internet and getting first generation, perfect digital copies of master recordings from all the world, is just not a fair comparison. We're talking about a network that includes millions and millions of people, and tens and tens of millions of songs that these millions of people have, they can trade. So the old "home taping is killing music," well, OK, so you borrow your neighbor's Iron Maiden record, blah, blah, blah, you know, some guy down at school. There is a long way from that to what's going on right now with perfect first-generation digital copies of music that's available to millions of people all over the world.

Later in this same interview, Lars was asked if he or other members of Metallica had ever copied a tape, record, 8-track, or a CD from a friend. He answered:

Yeah, I mean I think we answered that before. Of course we have, OK? And of course it's a valid point. The bottom line is the size of it. The size of it and the quality of it. When we go in, and check Napster out, we come up with 1.4 million copyright infringements in 48 hours, this is a different thing than trading cassette tapes with your buddy at school. I mean, 48 hours! So it's the quality, the quality and the scale.

Lars just admitted to copyright infringement. This confirms that Lars is being inconsistent. On the one hand he argues for artists' rights, but on the other hand he does not care that home taping violates artists' rights. He cannot have it both ways—that is a contradiction.

He quickly changes the subject, arguing that the lower quality of cassette tapes and the smaller scale are enough to make home taping a different thing from Napster. But I think these arguments fail. To understand why, let's examine them more closely in the order he gave them.

Isn't it true that cassette copies can still have good quality? I remember listening to . . . *And Justice for All* during high school on cassette. (I bought it, in case you were wondering.) I listened to it so many times I wore out the tape—another problem with cassette tapes is that they wear out after a while—so I bought it again! But the second time I bought it I copied it onto a chrome cassette tape and listened to the copy so that I would not have to buy it again. Let me tell you that copy still sounded damn good.

So I think Lars' first argument about tape quality fails. Many people were enjoying second and third generation tape copies during the 1980s. If stealing songs is wrong it should not matter whether you steal them on tape or by mp3. Quality makes no sense. What level of quality is needed for the copying to be OK? And who decides what level of quality is enough? I know some people who listen to music on AM Radio and like it! For the purposes of enjoyment, quality appears to be in the *ear* of the beholder. In philosophy this is known as the problem of relativism: the view that there is no one correct answer, just different but equally valid opinions.

By the way, Lars was mistaken to call the mp3 files of Metallica on Napster "perfect digital copies." While it's true that mp3s don't degrade or wear out, mp3 is a "lossy" format that contains less information than the CD.[17] At high bit rates many people cannot tell the difference between an mp3 and the original CD, but at low bit rates mp3s can sound crappy, especially for heavy metal. "Squishy" cymbals, anyone?

Lars' second argument about scale (quantity) also makes no sense. While he is correct to point out that Napster helped people trade at higher volumes—literally millions of files over a weekend—this would just mean that Napster was far worse than home taping. It does not let home taping off the hook.

Think about it this way. If stealing songs is wrong it does not matter whether you steal two songs or two million. It's all wrong. To be consistent Lars should have condemned home taping. But that would have meant admitting to the fans that he too had sinned. Had he strongly condemned home taping, I am almost certain some fans would have responded: "Well, if you did it why can't we? Do as I say

[17] Bruce Fries and Marty Fries, *The Mp3 and Internet Audio Handbook* (Silver Spring, MD: Teamcom Books, 2000), p. 132.

not as I do? Please." Even though Lars could have rightly replied that "two wrongs don't make a right," the whole thing was already a public relations nightmare.

Aside from the home taping point, Metallica did have a logically consistent argument against Napster and file sharing. But just because something is logically consistent does not make it true. Was Metallica correct to suggest that the act of artistic creation carries with it certain rights? We will address that question in the next section.

All Within My *Hands*

Human rights is one of the most important issues in philosophy. The American way of life we hold dear is based on a philosophy that affirms human rights, including the right to private property. The founding fathers were also aware of the need to protect intellectual property. In Article 1, Section 8, Clause 8 of the Constitution, they granted Congress power to "promote the Progress of Science and useful Arts, by securing for limited Times to Authors and Inventors the exclusive Right to their respective Writings and Discoveries."

The founders used a utilitarian argument to justify the protection of intellectual property. Utilitarianism is an ethical theory that says actions are morally correct to the extent that they maximize utility (usually understood as happiness) for the greatest number of people. Most people would agree that the products of science and art have enriched human life. So the morally correct thing to do, according to utilitarianism, is encourage their production.

For this reason, the Constitution gives Congress the power to reward inventors and artists by granting legal protections (patents and copyrights) to their productions. Patents and copyrights prevent other people from profiting off of the originator's work. What if an author, for example, labored and toiled for years on a novel and soon after publication almost everyone could copy it for free and not pay the author? Certainly, this would discourage many potential artists and inventors.

The utilitarian argument is only one of several arguments philosophers have used to justify intellectual property rights. I do not believe Metallica was using it to defend artists' rights. Instead, Metallica appeared to endorse what is sometimes called the labor theory of property rights. In his statement before the United States Senate, Lars said:

> Just like a carpenter who crafts a table gets to decide whether to keep it, sell, it or give it away, shouldn't we have the same options? My band authored the music which is Napster's lifeblood. We should decide what happens to it, not Napster—a company with no rights in our recordings, which never invested a penny in Metallica's music or had anything to do with its creation . . . When Metallica makes an album we spend many months and many hundreds of thousands of our own dollars writing and recording. We also contribute our inspiration and perspiration.[18]

Lars is arguing that a person has a right to the fruit of his or her own labor. Centuries earlier, the British philosopher John Locke (1632–1704) had argued for the same in *Two Treatises of Government*:

> Though the earth, and all inferior creatures, be common to all men, yet every man has a *property* in his own *person*: this no body has any right to but himself. The *labour* of his body, and the *work* of his hands, we may say, are properly his. Whatsoever then he removes out of the state that nature hath provided, and left it in, he hath mixed his *labour* with, and joined to it something that is his own, and thereby makes it his *property*. It being by him removed from the common state nature hath placed it in, it hath by this *labour* something annexed to it, that excludes the common right of other men: for this *labour* being the unquestionable property of the labourer, no man but he can have a right to what that is once joined to, at least where there is enough, and as good, left in common for others.[19]

Some philosophers have argued that there are serious problems with the labor theory when it is extended to intellectual property. We

---

[18] "Statement of Lars Ulrich Before the Committee on the Judiciary United States Senate," posted on July 11, 2000, at www.riaa.com/news/newsletter/press2000/071100.asp.

[19] John Locke, *Two Treatises of Government*, Book II, Chapter V, Section 27, in *Second Treatise of Government*, ed. C.B. Macpherson (Indianapolis: Hackett, 1980), p. 19; emphasis in original.

cannot cover all of their objections here, but I do want to address an important one raised by Tom G. Palmer.[20]

Palmer points out that Locke's argument for private property is based on a person's right to their own body. Intellectual property, according to Palmer, restricts how people can use their own bodies. Therefore, intellectual property contradicts Locke's initial point that we have a right to our own bodies. For this reason Palmer thinks that Locke's theory cannot be used to defend intellectual property rights. Using music as an example, he explains:

> A copyright over a musical composition means that others cannot use their mouths to blow air in certain sequences and in certain ways into musical instruments they own without obtaining the permission of the copyright holder. Thus the real objects the copyright holder controls are the bodies and instruments of the other musicians. (Palmer, 77)

Is Palmer correct? No. One of the first songs I learned to play on guitar was Metallica's "For Whom the Bell Tolls." According to Palmer, since Metallica owns the copyright to that song I must ask them for permission to use my fingers to play certain power chords in certain sequences on my guitar.

But that is not true! I am allowed to play their songs in my house and with my band in my basement. Why else would stores sell Guitar Tablature books if people were not allowed to play songs? What I cannot do is perform Metallica songs with my band for profit in a club without Metallica's permission. But that is hardly a serious restriction of my rights to my own body.

I can live a very full life without ever performing Metallica songs for profit. This small performance restriction is very similar to the restrictions on my freedom of speech. As everyone knows, you cannot falsely yell "FIRE!" in a crowded theater. For Palmer's argument to work, our right to the use of our bodies would have to be absolute (without any restrictions). But such an extreme view is difficult to defend.

---

[20]   Tom G. Palmer, "Are Patents and Copyrights Morally Justified? The Philosophy of Property Rights and Ideal Objects," in *Copy Fights: The Future of Intellectual Property in the Information Age*, ed. Adam Thierer and Clyde Wayne Crews, Jr. (Washington, DC: Cato Institute, 2002), pp. 43–93; hereafter cited in the text as Palmer.

While focusing on restrictions, Palmer overlooks the indirect benefits people receive when musicians publish their music. In addition to listening pleasure, when I learn to play one of Metallica's songs it helps me to grow as a composer and a musician. It also inspires me to create new music. How many bands would never have existed if some other band didn't inspire them to write music? So the performance restriction on music is at least partially compensated for by these indirect benefits. Palmer might have a stronger point when it comes to patenting mathematical algorithms used in computer programs, but with music his argument fails.

I would need more space than I have available to me in this chapter to defend Metallica's argument for artists' rights using the labor theory, but I think it can be done. What is important is that Metallica had the courage to be the first musical artist in the Internet age to put forth this argument. For that they took a beating. Was it worth it?

All The Shots I Take . . . What Difference Did I Make?

In the song "Shoot Me Again" Lars' lyric refers to the Napster controversy, posing the question: What difference did I make? Let me supply an answer: Metallica did make a difference. They initiated an important debate about the ethics of file sharing while it was in its infancy. They were able to bring millions of fans into the debate in a way the RIAA could never have done. And they advanced a philosophical argument about artists' rights that I think is basically correct.

Sure, they could have done all of this in a clearer and less confrontational way, but hey, they're Metallica, not Britney Spears! The fact that they remained true to their convictions despite heavy backlash only enhances their legacy.[21]

---

[21] I would like to thank William Irwin, Stephen Greeley, Philip Musico, Sean P. Walsh, and my wife, Marialena, for reading this chapter and offering useful comments and suggestions.

WHO'S WHO IN THE METAL MILITIA

Robert Arp is Assistant Professor of Philosophy at Southwest Minnesota State University and author of *Scenario Visualization: An Evolutionary Account of Creative Problem Solving*. Besides being editor of *South Park and Philosophy* (Blackwell), he is also editor (with Francisco Ayala) of *Contemporary Debates in Philosophy of Biology* (Blackwell), and (with George Terzis) *The Ashgate Companion to Contemporary Philosophy of Biology*. *But you'll forget all that when you meet him because Rob has a bad case of motorbreath.*

Kimberly A. Blessing is Assistant Professor of Philosophy at Buffalo State College. She publishes on Descartes' ethics (or lack thereof) and has edited *Movies and The Meaning of Life: Philosophers Take on Hollywood*. *Kim constantly worries that she is praying to the god that failed.*

Manuel Bremer is University Lecturer at the University of Düsseldorf, Germany. His English publications include the books *Information and Information Flow* and *Introduction to Paraconsistent Logics*, as well as papers on analytical philosophy of language and epistemology. Since 1998 he has been a member of the Center for the Study of Logic, Language, and Information at the University of Düsseldorf. *It was Manuel who convinced Lars that "Sabbra Cadabra" has a fucking riff from hell.*

Thom Brooks lectures in political and legal philosophy at the University of Newcastle, UK. He is the author of *Hegel's Political Philosophy* (Edinburgh), *Punishment* (Routledge), and nearly fifty

245

articles; he is the editor of *Locke and Law* (Ashgate), *Rousseau and Law* (Ashgate), *The Global Justice Reader* (Blackwell), (with Fabian Freyenhagen) *The Legacy of John Rawls*, and founding editor of the *Journal of Moral Philosophy* (SAGE). *Here's a little-known fact: Brooks likes to sing "Jump in the Shower" while he lathers up in the morning.*

Scott Calef is Associate Professor and Chair of the Department of Philosophy at Ohio Wesleyan University. He has published in ancient philosophy, applied ethics, metaphysics, and the philosophy of religion. He has also contributed to *The Beatles and Philosophy*. *After final exams Scott's students want him to ride the lightning!*

Brian K. Cameron teaches philosophy and anti-conformism at Saint Louis University, albeit with mixed results. He has authored "A Critique of Marilyn McCord Adams' 'Christian Solution' to the Existential Problem of Evil," in addition to contributions in *Star Wars and Philosophy* and *Star Trek and Philosophy*. *Brian once played a concert with Metallica . . . but they probably wouldn't remember that.*

Daniel Cohnitz is Professor of Theoretical Philosophy at the University of Tartu, Estonia. He is the author of *Information and Information Flow: An Introduction* (with Manuel Bremer), *Nelson Goodman* (with Marcus Rossberg), a book on thought experiments in philosophy (*Gedankenexperimente in der Philosophie*), and a bunch of papers on theoretical philosophy. *Prior to his career in philosophy he gave guitar lessons to Joe Satriani.*

Joanna Corwin started studying philosophy around the same time she started banging her head, back when *Master of Puppets* ruled all. She attended St. John's College (Santa Fe) where contemplation collided with the release of the Black Album. After a few years as a desk jockey she quit and ran off with Metallica's road crew on the Googol Tour. Joanna earned a master's degree in philosophy at the Catholic University of America, where escapes from the classroom included jetting to the west coast for *S&M*. Her love of all things Metallica led her to Virginia Fuel, a local chapter of the Metallica Club, where she served as Social Director and Chapter Head. *Joanna suffers from a perpetual case of Whiplash!*

246

Robert A. Delfino is Assistant Professor of Philosophy at St. John's University, New York. He has published articles on various topics, including metaphysics, human rights, ancient and medieval philosophy, mysticism, and aesthetics. He has edited three books: *Plato's Cratylus*, *Understanding Moral Weakness*, and *What Are We To Understand Gracia To Mean? Realist Challenges to Metaphysical Neutralism*. For Rob, *"Creeping Death" is not just a song, it's how he feels when he wakes up in the morning.*

Justin Donhauser has recently vanished into obscurity, believing that he had corrupted his mind, prostituting his genius to the endeavors of academia. He has been seen teaching janitors and other graveyard shift workers how to find meaning in their absurd lives, gaining their confidences by helping them clean up poo. *Justin is the only contributor to this book who actually has metal in his head and Metallica lyrics tattooed on his body (no kidding).*

Jason T. Eberl is Assistant Professor of Philosophy at Indiana University-Purdue University, Indianapolis. He is the author of *Thomistic Principles and Bioethics* and several articles on medieval philosophy, metaphysics, and bioethics. With Kevin Decker, he has edited *Star Wars and Philosophy* and the forthcoming *Star Trek and Philosophy*. *Jason likes to sing his daughter to sleep with lullabies such as "Twinkle, Twinkle, Little Star" and "Enter Sandman."*

Bart Engelen is a Research Assistant of the Research Foundation— Flanders (FWO-Vlaanderen). He is currently a full-time PhD student at the Centre for Economics and Ethics of the Catholic University, Leuven (Belgium). His research mainly concerns rational choice theory and he has published on public choice theory and the paradox of voting. *Bart is Holier Than Thou (but with good reason).*

Peter S. Fosl is Professor and Chair of Philosophy at Transylvania University in Lexington, Kentucky and is a Contributing Editor to *The Philosophers' Magazine*. Fosl has published on the history of philosophy, skepticism, and the philosophy of religion, including "The Moral Imperative to Rebel Against God" and "The Righteousness of Blasphemy." He is co-author with Julian Baggini of *The Philosopher's Toolkit* (Blackwell) and *The Ethics Toolkit* (Blackwell). *Peter loves the "Left Behind" series because he shares with its author,*

Tim LaHaye, the fantasy that every conservative Christian suddenly disappear from the face of the Earth.

Robert Fudge is Assistant Professor of Philosophy at Weber State University. He has published articles on ethics and aesthetics and is currently completing a book manuscript on the moral significance of empathy. *As a philosophy professor, Bob has always believed that his lifestyle determines his deathstyle.*

Judith Grant is Director of the Women's Studies Program and Professor of Political Science at Ohio University. She is the author of a forthcoming book on the feminist theories of Andrea Dworkin and Catharine MacKinnon, *Fundamental Feminism: Contesting the Core Concepts of Feminist Theory*, and numerous articles on feminist theory and popular culture. *Judith bought Lars Ulrich's art collection for six million dollars.*

William Irwin is Associate Professor of Philosophy at King's College, Pennsylvania. He is the author of *Intentionalist Interpretation: A Philosophical Explanation and Defense* and has published articles on aesthetics in leading journals. He has edited *Seinfeld and Philosophy*, *The Simpsons and Philosophy* (with Conard and Skoble), *The Matrix and Philosophy*, and *More Matrix and Philosophy*. *Bill broke up with Sweet Amber ten years ago and still proudly wears a Metalli-mullet.*

Philip Lindholm is a doctoral student at the University of Oxford. He holds five degrees in the study of philosophy and religion, and has spoken internationally to both academic and popular audiences. He is the author of *The Eleventh Commandment* and published an article in *Poker and Philosophy*. *More importantly, Philip played lead guitar on the No Life 'Til Leather demo.*

Thomas Nys is a postdoctoral researcher at the Catholic University Leuven (Belgium). He is currently attached to the European Centre for Ethics. He has published articles on John Stuart Mill, Isaiah Berlin, assisted suicide, liberalism, the meaning of life, and psychiatry. He is co-editor of *Autonomy and Paternalism*. *Thomas's students swear he was Metallica's inspiration in writing "The Thing That Should Not Be."*

Niall (Tank) Scott is Lecturer in Ethics at the University of Central Lancashire. He is the Secretary for the Association of Legal and

Social Philosophy, a member of the Society for Applied European Thought, and active in the UCLan Rock, Thrash, and Alternative Music Society. He has published on Kantian ethics, altruism, political philosophy, eugenics, and bioethics. *Tank's fist can be seen on the cover of St. Anger.*

Rachael Sotos grew up in the San Francisco Bay Area. In the early 1980s at the famous Stone on Broadway, Cliff Burton would occasionally give her illicit sips of his beverage (true story). After a "rocking" youth, Rachael devoted herself to the philosophical life. She currently studies ancient Greek and Latin at Fordham University and teaches in the Humanities Department at the New School in New York City. Her dissertation, *Arendtian Freedom in Greek Antiquity*, which will soon be published as a book, is a feminist interpretation of Hannah Arendt's view of ancient Greek philosophy and politics. *Rachael now finds her most metallicious fun reading the ancient Greek dictionary (it rules!).*

Mark D. White is Associate Professor in the Department of Political Science, Economics, and Philosophy at the College of Staten Island in New York City, where he teaches courses combining economics, philosophy, and law. He co-edited the book *Economics and the Mind*, and has written many articles and book chapters on economics and philosophy. *He was also the original replacement for Dave Mustaine, but was promptly kicked out of the band for insisting they call the first album "Kiss 'Em All."*

J. Jeremy Wisnewski is Assistant Professor of Philosophy at Hartwick College. Most of his published work is in moral philosophy and recent European philosophy. His neck is impervious to strain, after many years of headbanging. This helped immensely while writing *Wittgenstein and Ethical Inquiry* and articles on everything from anti-realism to cannibalism. He is the editor of *Family Guy and Philosophy* (Blackwell). *And even though Wisnewski is no longer totally thrash, he's still completely metallicious.*

THE PHANTOM LORD'S INDEX

250